Ancient Aliens
and the Lost Islands

Through the Wormhole

Ancient Aliens
and the Lost Islands

Evidence that ancient aliens traveled through a
wormhole to visit Earth and interact with humans

Through the Wormhole

by Sharon Delarose/Lars Bergen

GITYASOME BOOKS - A DIVISION OF GYPSY KING SOFTWARE

Published by Gityasome Books
a division of Gypsy King Software, Inc.
books.gityasome.com

Printed in the United States of America
First Edition

ISBN: 1492812129
EAN-13: 978-1492812128

Dedicated to
everyone who believes
that extraterrestrial life exists
on the other side of a wormhole,
and that ancient alien astronauts
visited us in the past.

Rediscover the lost islands of paradise.

We are not alone.
We have never been alone.

Contents

PROLOGUE

Does Earth have portals to an extraterrestrial world? Do these portals lead to the legendary island paradise where the old grow young again? Our ancestors believed in a physical place that promised health, happiness, and immortality. Today we consider the old legends to be myths, nothing more than sailor's fish stories. Yet some of the most prominent names in history devoted their entire lives to searching for the lost island of paradise — and they found it.

One or more islands were hidden on the other side of a portal, or wormhole, which made the islands accessible to Earth. Extraterrestrials such as the Nordics and giants lived among us on both sides of the wormhole. They traveled from their world to ours and exposed our ancestors to advanced technology that we had no words for, except to call it magic.

We described magic boats, magic mirrors, people with magical powers, and other wonders that seemed beyond belief. The magic was nothing more than motorboats, radios, computers, electricity, voice activated GPS systems, remote controls, prosthetic limbs, advanced medicine, revolving castles, and cloaking technology. We've already achieved most of this magic ourselves. The extraterrestrial visitors had even unlocked the secrets of aging, and for awhile our ancestors had access to it.

On the other side of the wormhole, we saw a sun that was different from our own, and cities or castles suspended in the air. These extraterrestrial cities were described as being "not on Earth." Time flowed differently and you didn't come back to Earth in the same year that you left it. Historic documents all around the world spelled it out for us.

Sometimes the otherworlders took the role of leaders, teaching us and guiding us. Sometimes they took the role of gods who bickered among themselves, or took sides in our battles, sometimes helping us, and other times causing strife. We embraced these beings until humans spread out over the world, and one by one the visitors left. One visitor gave a parting speech, and then ascended up into the air in his vehicle, and disappeared into the clouds.

Apparently we rose up against some of the visitors, and we even targeted them with the witch hunts. We sent the message that they were no longer welcome here, and those we didn't kill retreated back through their wormholes, closing up most of the wormholes behind them. Those who were willing to adapt were embraced, and merged into our society permanently.

A few portals remained, however, even into the 1900s, and humans not only found them, they visited "paradise" and came back to tell the tale. The most compelling clues come from the Native American peacemaker Hiawatha, the Norse gods, and a race of magical people known as the Tuatha dé Danann of Ireland and surrounding regions.

Ancient Aliens and the Lost Islands: Through the Wormhole follows the clues that were left behind, and attempts to piece it all back together. What did the portals look like? What did humans see on the other side? Is there any correlation between these ancient aliens, and the extraterrestrials who are flying the skies today? What unsolved mysteries can we explain with these portals? Has our own science unlocked any of the answers? Do alien portals to paradise still exist?

Island Paradise - Overview

Our ancestors left us with rich descriptions of earthly paradise, which was more often than not on an island. They told stories about the supernatural beings that lived in paradise, or who lived on earth among us. Once you start looking at the details, the descriptions sound suspiciously extraterrestrial.

Today, we have ancient astronaut theorists who've set out to prove that extraterrestrials visited us in the distant past, and overtly interacted with humans, unlike the aliens today who operate in secrecy. These ancient astronaut theorists look for truth hidden in the mysteries of the Nazca lines, Sumerian texts about the Anunnaki deities, petroglyphs and hieroglyphs that appear to depict alien astronauts and their spaceships, and structures built thousands of years ago that couldn't possibly have been built with human technology alone.

However, the island paradise where the extraterrestrials lived is shrouded mostly in myths and legends, lacking even the physical evidence that ancient astronaut theorists can point to. All we have are fragments of stories, many of which were undoubtedly tall tales, and a handful of odd clues hidden in the extraordinary tales.

Paradise went by many names, including Ogygia, Atlantis, Avalon, Otherworld, Yma, Elysium, Land of the Living, Island of the Living, Island of Life, Country of Youth, Land of Youth, Delightful Plain, Land of Virtues, Land of Promise, Earthly Paradise, Terrestrial Paradise, and dozens of others in a multitude of languages. We can't even agree as to whether they pointed to a single location, or multiple locations.

Atlantis would have been wiped out during the great flood by most accounts, the flood being an event told not only in the *Bible*, but also in the legends of the Greeks, East Indians, Native Americans, Mesopotamians, and the Iranian sacred books of Zoroastrianism. Yet this *Otherworld* paradise, as I've chosen to call it from among its various names, survived the flood because those who traveled to the Otherworld and came back to tell the tale lived long after the great flood.

Most descriptions of the Otherworld referred to an island, and through the centuries, maps pinpointed the location of this island in so many different places that the notion of an island that nobody could find became a legend in itself. However, if the island were accessible only through a portal, and portals exist in multiple locations, that could explain how one or more hidden islands could exist in different locations. Even today we have theories about portals in places like the Bermuda Triangle.

By whatever name or location, however, the descriptions were the same. The healing waters rejuvenated you, and as long as you remained there, you never grew old. All of your favorite foods and beverages seemed to be at your beck and call, as if provided by a *Star Trek* food replicator. The sun shined day and night over a land that never got cold, where flowers bloomed year round, and where fruit trees were perpetually laden with fruit. There was no rain, clouds, snow, or hail.

This is the description that most legends agree on, but a few of the legends add details such as a peculiarly bright atmosphere that was amber in color, palaces that floated in midair, revolving castles, nicely trimmed grass, speed boats, computers, cloaking technology, bizarre animals, traveling through a strange mist to get there, and "dark clouds" inside which an entire race of supernatural beings moved to a new location.

One such paradise was the kingdom of Prester John, also known as Presbyter Johannes, whose kingdom bordered Earthly Paradise. Prester John's lost Christian realm was the object of countless expeditions for hundreds of years, with a description straight out of a fairytale book.

Prester John's kingdom boasted streams whose bottoms and banks glistened with precious gemstones so plentiful that John's scepter was made of pure emeralds, and even platters and cups were made of precious gems. Gold was also abundant, and the ants dug it up while tunneling, creating mountains of gold. These little gold diggers actually existed, as exposed in the *Legendary Creatures* chapter.

Prester John's kingdom was the highest place on earth, higher than Noah's flood which saved it from being inundated, so high that it nearly touched the moon. It was surrounded by a moss-covered wall with a single entry which was "closed with burning fire so that no mortal man dared to enter."

Residents lived for hundreds of years by drinking from a rejuvenating spring which reset their bodies back to an age of thirty. Nudiosi pebbles allowed the blind to see again, as well as made the wearer invisible.

John himself was described as having "supernatural longevity" and his kingdom was considered to be both celestial and immortal. Now we have our first clue, as *celestial* can pertain to the sky, the universe beyond earth's atmosphere, celestial bodies such as stars and planets, or an invisible heaven, though even the word *heaven* includes non-spiritual references. Various translations of the word *heaven* include "heights, elevation, sky, clouds," and "whirlwind." Therefore, a celestial kingdom could refer to an orbiting kingdom or one that exists on another planet.

Prester John was a priest as well as a king, and he was allegedly descended from one of the Three Magi who traveled from the east to worship the newborn Jesus. Apparently he wasn't originally a priest, as his story began when he got lost in a forest while hunting. There he met a "celestial being" who promised to guide him back to the road if he embraced the doctrine of Christ. Who was this *celestial* being? And is this linked to his kingdom being described as *celestial*?

"Celestial Empire" was a name given to China, and a Chinaman was sometimes called a *celestial* back when the Prester John legends were prevalent. However, a celestial from China would not likely have had Christian roots. That leaves either a traveler from a distant planet, which would be an *extraterrestrial*, or it could have been an *angel*, which can have extraterrestrial roots according to ancient astronaut theories.

Another clue comes from the bizarre creatures that populated Prester John's kingdom such as Centaurs, Satyrs, Fauns, Cyclops, Gryphons, Phoenix birds, horned men, giants, white lions and white bears. On the surface, this sounds totally far-fetched. Few believe that any of these creatures ever existed. However, in every legend you'll find a grain of truth and for most of these creatures, there exists some basis in fact which I've demonstrated in the *Legendary Creatures* chapter. There you'll find evidence for the existence of Satyrs, Gryphons, Phoenix birds, giants, and gold digging ants.

White lions and white bears are directly linked to extraterrestrial visitation, according to an old African legend that involved an aging, dying queen who was rejuvenated after meeting the occupants of an extraterrestrial craft. Being a story of extraterrestrial visitation, and human rejuvenation, as opposed to an island paradise, this story is told the chapter *Touched By Celestial Beings*. Could Prester John's white lions and bears have been caused by an extraterrestrial visitor as well?

Next to Prester John's kingdom was Earthly Paradise, which was neither in Heaven, nor on Earth, in spite of its name. What does that mean, exactly? If it wasn't on Earth, why was it called

Earthly Paradise? Was it a spirit realm, another dimension, a city or ship orbiting in space, or another planet? Its location was described in conjunction with the biblical flood.

Noah's flood was forty fathoms high, engulfing the tallest mountains on Earth, and Earthly Paradise was forty fathoms higher than that, "hanging" in between Heaven and Earth. *Hanging* or *hangeth* was the word used in the old texts.

This location is given in the 1844 book *St. Patrick's Purgatory; an essay on the legends of purgatory, hell, and paradise* by Thomas Wright. The same description is also given in the 1869 book *Curious Myths of the Middle Ages* by S. Baring-Gould, and both books are quoting from the same source, which is an "unnamed manuscript" in the British Museum.

Earthly Paradise, which is an unfitting name for a place which is obviously not on or of Earth, is described as being perfectly level with no hills or hollows, no frost, snow, hail, rain, heat or hunger. Night never falls, and the sun shines *seven times brighter than Earth's sun*. The Well of Life is found there, along with the Phoenix bird. If the sun shines seven times brighter than Earth's sun, this could indicate a planet orbiting a sun in another galaxy. It could also be describing a climate-controlled city orbiting Earth with very bright, artificial lighting, or sunlight seemingly brighter for its orbiting location.

Prester John's *celestial* kingdom, which was so high that it nearly touched the moon, bordered Earthly Paradise, which "hangs" somewhere between Heaven and Earth. It's no wonder that your average explorer couldn't find them!

Not all paradises had Christian connections. Another paradise was Elysium, which in Celtic depictions was a land of the gods, accessible only to mortals who were related to the gods or invited by the gods. This was not an afterlife, but a place for the living that later got redefined as an afterlife. Humans tend to redefine history to match our current beliefs. An entire discourse was written about Elysium in the *Encyclopedia of Religion and Ethics,*

15

Volume II published in 1910, from different points of view, along with a mention of the Tuatha dé Danann (peoples of the goddess Dana.) The Tuatha were a significant race of supernatural beings who lived among us for hundreds of years, and whose technology far surpassed our own, as subsequent chapters will demonstrate. The encyclopedic entry connected all of the physical paradises together, as if they pointed to a single place with different names, depending on who was giving the description.

Some believed this Otherworld to be an island, while others thought it was underground, or even under the water. In some descriptions, it was a "mysterious land revealing itself suddenly on Earth's surface, and entered through a mist" or where you became enveloped in a mist while journeying into or out of it. Sometimes a supernatural being appeared out of a "magic mist," or the mist hid a "supernatural dwelling."

Ireland was the home of the very real people known as the Tuatha dé Danann, who controlled some of these supernatural mists. In the story of Cormac mac Airt, the king of Ireland in the 3rd century who disappeared for seven months in 248 A.D., Cormac encountered a man from the Land of Promise who described it as a place where nobody had a care in the world. There was no envy, jealousy, sorrow, sin, and nobody grew old.

The mysterious man offered Cormac a glittering silver branch from which dangled several golden apples, that when jangled together produced strange music that made you forget all of your troubles. In exchange for this branch (or wand) with its musical apple chimes, the man wanted his choice of anything in Cormac's kingdom. Cormac accepted the offer not knowing what he'd be trading, and unfortunately what the stranger wanted was Cormac's wife and children, which were whisked away to this Otherworld.

When news spread that the queen and her children were gone, the people raised such an uproar that Cormac jangled the wand that made you forget your troubles, and his people were no

16

longer concerned. Even for Cormac, the wand couldn't permanently replace the loss of his family, and after a year he set out to find his wife and children in the Otherworld.

He set out in the direction that he'd seen the man from the Land of Promise go, and soon a "dark magical mist" surrounded Cormac. When the mist cleared, he was in the Land of Promise. He traveled across flatlands where he saw "strange, foreign-looking" people performing unusual tasks, and eventually he came across a stately palace — one of the homes of Manannán mac Lir, and the very place where his family had been taken. Manannán and his wife appeared to Cormac as a very tall couple wearing clothes of many colors.

Manannán was one of the leaders of the Tuatha dé Danann, and he'd set up this whole trade to lure Cormac to his home so that he could teach Cormac valuable lessons, and so that the two could bond in friendship. That night, Cormac and his family were permanently reunited at Manannán's dinner table, and Manannán reverted to his "true form" though this true form was not described.

Cormac and his family slept at Manannán's house that night, and when they woke the next morning, they were back in their own home, in possession of three magical gifts from their divine host: a goblet that indicated when someone was lying, a tablecloth that produced any food their heart desired, and the wand he'd originally traded for. Cormac was allowed to keep these magical items until the day he died, at which point they'd be taken away, probably back to the Otherworld.

As the wisdom that Manannán shared with Cormac includes incredible links between some of the most sacred sites in the world, I've expanded on the details in a chapter devoted to the teachings and wisdom of these ancient visitors.

Cormac's story has been retold in many old texts including *The Mythology of All Races,* edited by Louis Herbert Gray, Ph.D. in 1918, and *Transactions of the Ossianic Society for the year 1855, Volume*

III in 1857, and *The voyage of Bran, son of Febal, to the land of the living: Volume 1* by Alfred Trübner Nutt in 1895.

Cormac was lucky, because not all who visit the Otherworld come back into their own time. Another Irishman by the name of Bran also visited an Otherworld after receiving a silver branch, though his had white apple blossoms instead of golden apples.

Bran went in search of this Otherworld which was somewhere across the ocean, and along the way Bran and his crew encountered Manannán in a boat, though apparently it was not Manannán's island that they visited. Instead, they traveled to the Island of Joy, and then to the Island of Women, where they lingered. As they ate, the food on their plates seemed to replenish itself, and the food was always what their heart most desired to eat. They stayed for a year, and then attempted to go back home for a visit. They were warned not to disembark from the boat during the visit. They could zip around the ocean on their otherworldly boat, and even talk to people on shore, as long as they remained in the boat.

There's always a rebel who doesn't listen, so of course one man climbed out of the boat and immediately turned into a heap of ashes. Apparently, several hundred years had passed during their absence. Bran stayed in the boat, related his tale of the Otherworld to the people on shore, and then sailed off, presumably to return to the island he'd been living on.

This Otherworld has a time differential where a day passes there, but a year passes on Earth. Those who were able to tell the tale, such as in the Voyage of Bran, did so from a vessel that could travel in between worlds, and as long as they did not leave the vessel, they could communicate with their earthly brethren.

Sometimes the Otherworld is described as being many islands. The Island of Joy, the Island of Women, and Manannán's island are three different islands in the Otherworld. It may be that they visited, literally, some ocean on another world which has many continents and islands, just as we do.

Another reference to paradise which hints at an off-world location falls under the name Terrestrial Paradise. Volumes have been written, including a 750 page treatise by Carlo Giangolino in 1649. Imagine — 750 pages devoted to unlocking the secrets of Terrestrial Paradise. There are as many opinions on its nature and location as there are people pursuing the mystery.

A discussion took place in 1691 that Bishop Pierre Daniel Huet of Avranches, France, summarized as follows: There is no consensus about the location of this paradise as some place it in the Third Heaven, or the Fourth Heaven, or the Lunar Heaven, or on the Moon itself, or on a mountain near the Lunar Heaven, or in the middle region of the air, above the earth, under the earth, in any number of earthly locations, or in a place where men simply cannot reach. They don't even agree on whether this Terrestrial Paradise has animals in it, but some believe that wherever it is, at least three humans are living there as immortals, at least until the end of the world: Enoch, Elias, and St. John the Evangelist.

So the Otherworld of the Tuatha dé Danann may be a series of islands, and the Christian Terrestrial Paradise is a place whose location could be virtually anywhere on the Earth, Moon, some level of Heaven, or anywhere in between.

There is a concept known as *Seven Heavens* which are presumed to be spiritual realms where we go after we die, though some interpretations involve alternate universes or even planets. Several religions have this concept including Islam, Judaism, Hinduism, Hermeticism, and Gnosticism. There are also beliefs in seven levels of an underworld, or seven upper worlds. Even the Ancient Egyptians had a version of Seven Heavens, and Norse mythology spoke of Nine Worlds, one of which was a location that they called Heaven or Asgard, where a physical race of beings lived that traveled to and from Earth across a "bridge" between our worlds.

The word *Heaven* itself means different things including the atmosphere in which birds fly, and the space that holds the Sun,

19

Moon, and stars. It's also the realm where angels travel, and where God resides. Sometimes it's a place of paradise; other times it's a place of hell, as the various "levels" of Heaven are not all paradises. If there's a Christian Rapture, both the living and the dead will be taken where there's a "new" Heaven and Earth. So will the living have to die and become spirits? Or will the dead be brought back to life in physical bodies? We're not given a definitive description of this world except that we are "changed" in order to live there.

The Apostle Paul wrote about a man who went to the Third Heaven, and Paul did not know whether the man went in his physical body or not. In the biblical *2 Corinthians 12:2-4*, the Apostle Paul wrote:

> "I knew a man in Christ above fourteen years ago, (whether in the body, I cannot tell; or whether out of the body, I cannot tell: God knoweth;) such a one caught up to the Third Heaven. And I knew such a man, (whether in the body, or out of the body, I cannot tell: God knoweth;) How that he was caught up into paradise, and heard unspeakable words, which it is not lawful for a man to utter."

So we've got a variety of opinions on the nature and location of Terrestrial Paradise, as well as the various levels of Heaven including their nature. In other words, *it is possible* that Terrestrial Paradise exists on a planetary body, or floating up in the air like a great spaceship city, or hidden somewhere on Earth.

According to the 1855 *Encyclopedia Metropolitana or System of Universal Knowledge*, which reprinted Bishop Huet's summary on the location of Terrestrial Paradise, another aspect was its size, which was sixty times bigger than Earth in its dimensions according to "certain Talmudists" (Huet's quotes, not mine.)

Sixty times bigger than Earth definitely moves it off of Earth, and could indicate another planet if this place were indeed physical as some believe. If this is the same paradise with an amber atmosphere where its sun shines brighter than Earth's sun, and most travelers pass through some sort of strange mist to get there, and then find buildings floating in the air, could the mist be a form of star gate or wormhole across the galaxy?

Some paradise legends have connections beyond the typical description, such as a strange form of wordplay. One involves King Yima in Zoroastrianism, which is an ancient Iranian religion where Yima's kingdom is paradise. Another is about a Christian monk who went in search of, *and found*, the physical paradise island of Yma. Incidentally, the Celts also believed in Yma, a place where the spirits of the departed lived in a happy land called Yma, aka Hy-ma, Flathinnis, Noble Island, Isle of the Just, or Isle of the Good. The Norse gods include the creator god Ymir. So we have both physical and spiritual paradises in the Yima connection.

That's a mighty big coincidence for Zoroastrianism, Nordic and Celtic beliefs, and Christianity to share such similar words, with three of them connected to a land of paradise, and the paradise legends don't end with the Yima connection. They continue with palaces that float in the air, this time, on the island of Ogygia, which some believe was the mythical Atlantis.

Controversy surrounds Ogygia, which is both a place, and a person, and few agree on the details of either one. The person Ogyges or Ogygia was either an aborigine, or the son of a god, or a Titan (giant), or a prince. One historian puts his lifetime at the same time as the biblical *Exodus*, when Moses led the Israelites out of Egypt, while other historians send him much further back in time.

His realm was either a portion of Greece, Ireland, Iceland, America, or the island of Atlantis, or Ogygia. You see how this gets convoluted, with so many different versions floating around, mixing legends with facts, and not all depictions painted a glorified vision of the place known as Ogygia.

Among the paradise legends, however, Ogygia is an island of enchanting beauty, where youths and maidens dance on dewy grass, everything exists in abundance, and a spring flows with waters that bless you with the gift of life. Imagine that… another paradise with a Fountain of Youth.

In the center of the island, *floating in the air*, is a palace of glass with transparent walls, where the souls of the blessed live. The Merddin Emrys visited this house of glass, and here the island intersects with tales of the Merddin Emrys, also known as the legendary wizard Merlin who was gifted with supernatural powers.

The next paradise is the island of Avalon, also called the Vale of Apples, which also boasts a *glass palace where time passes differently*, which is ruled by the Lady of the Lake, or in some accounts, the fairy Morgana, who is linked to both Merlin, as well as the Tuatha dé Danann.

A curious phrase comes to us from the Avalon tales, which suggests that Avalon is *not of this Earth* but either exists in another dimension or on another planet. This reference comes from the 1869 book *Curious Myths of the Middle Ages* by S. Baring-Gould in which a man visited paradise and met Morgana.

Ogier the Dane traveled on horseback to a valley where he rested by a sparkling fountain surrounded by fragrant shrubs. There he encountered a beautiful maiden who gave him a golden crown wreathed in blossoms. The minute he put the crown on, he completely forgot his past, his battles, and everything that had ever happened in his life. All of his memories were replaced with desire for this beautiful maiden — Morgana.

One day the crown fell off and he remembered his old life, and grew homesick for his family and friends. He begged Morgana to permit him to "return to Earth" and she consented. He'd spent no more than a few hours in Avalon, but back "on Earth" a full two hundred years had passed. Everyone and everything he knew was gone, so he went back to Avalon and remained there with Morgana.

This legend differs from stories where the traveler turns to dust as soon as they set foot on their home turf. Ogier simply traveled through time, found the world changed, and then went back to Avalon. The key phrase is that he asked permission *to return to Earth*. So where was he, if not on Earth? And what sort of place would have such a time differential?

Morgana was also known as Morgan le Fay, or Morgan the Fairy, who was a powerful sorceress connected to Merlin and the Arthurian legends, as well as Avalon, which was also known as the Isle of Apples.

A description of Avalon was echoed almost word for word in a description of Ogygia, both being islands of enchanting beauty where youths and maidens danced in dewy grass among green trees laden with apples. In Avalon, everything existed in abundance, and a *glass palace with transparent walls floated in the air*, visited by the Merddin Emrys! Here we have one island, with many names, where each story provides another clue, and all of the clues point to a place of extraterrestrial origin or construct, accessible to Earth, *but not existing on Earth*.

Avalon is a legendary island, and is also known as one of the Fortunate Isles, which is another name for Yma — the name of the island(s) that the monks were searching for *and found* in the year 512 A.D. This island was seen as recently as 1958.

Avalon produced such an abundance of food that no one needed to plough or work for food. Apple trees, grain, and grapes grew naturally, and the green grass was always clipped close. Keep that little factoid in mind about the trimmed grass, as it becomes important in the *Legendary Creatures* chapter.

Avalon had no thieves, no robbers, no enemies, no violence, no sickness, no death, no sorrow, no old age, no winter, and no summer, which mirrors all of the other paradises. It was forever springtime, and the apple trees produced both fruit and flowers on the same branch.

This legend differs by telling us who was in charge — nine sisters (including Morgana) who ruled over Avalon with a pleasing set of laws. Morgana was a fairy, and Merlin was a shape shifter, which brings us to the legends surrounding the Isle of Man which is a real island situated off the coast of Ireland.

Dating events in ancient history is difficult, because we aren't always given a clear set of dates for events, but so much revolves around Manannán mac Lir that we can at least attempt to narrow it down. The first king of the Tuatha dé Danann was Nuada, who ruled Ireland sometime around 1500 B.C., which gives us a starting date.

We have two people whose lives intersect with Manannán — Cormac mac Airt, and Manannán's run in with none other than the legendary St. Patrick. Cormac existed somewhere between the 2nd and 4th centuries A.D., and St. Patrick's time would have been in the 5th century, which situates Manannán somewhere between 100 A.D. and 500 A.D., or even spanning that entire range considering the Tuatha dé Danann lifespan. So the next reference to *ancient times*, and the later references to motor boats and revolving castles, should put the timeline into perspective as far as what you'd expect to find technologically.

In ancient times, the Isle of Man was ruled by Manannán mac Lir, who gave the island his name, and whose nickname was *king of the mists*. He was a sea god who "drew his misty cloak around the island" to hide it from invaders. The Isle of Man was home to several shape shifters, including a giant, a hairy ogre known as a Buggane, and a hairy water goblin or horse called a Glashtyn. With all the shape shifting going on, I'm not sure how they knew that the beings were different. You can't help but wonder with shape shifters — what is their true form? It's interesting that the Buggane was actually intelligent enough to talk to humans, and he was magical.

Fairies also inhabited the island, though they weren't called fairies, they were called *the little folk* or *themselves*, and wouldn't you know it? Fairies were also shape shifters. Coincidentally, so were the Tuatha dé Danann. About the only creature on the Isle of Man who was NOT a shape shifter was the Fenodyree — a busy little being who was stuck with his small, hairy form. Along with magical creatures, this island had a revolving castle, a magic cauldron, and a speed boat called Wave Sweeper, all of which were hidden behind Manannán's otherworldly mist.

Today's Isle of Man is not a hidden land of supernatural beings who live in revolving castles. There are several possible explanations. Ancient history was interlaced with highly imaginative fiction; or the advanced visitors simply up and moved elsewhere taking all of their extraordinary paraphernalia with them; or Manannán's island was through a portal *near* the Isle of Man; or the island itself had a portal to their world — a portal which is now closed.

Consider our concept of space travel. We don't envision ourselves moving into the housing of the locals, nor do we envision ourselves building houses like the ones we live in on Earth. We envision our space travelers landing on a planet in their ship, and *living in* that ship, until such time that we decide to fire up the engines and fly away. The television series *Stargate Atlantis* was based on this premise, which could explain not only rotating castles, but "islands" which were surrounded by a shining mirrored wall.

As for evidence, which they surely would have left behind — what happens to evidence today? The government *immediately* surrounds the area, gathers up every last shred of evidence, and hides it away. For example, in Texas a segment of roadway was replaced *twice* after the Cash-Landrum UFO incident. Once wasn't good enough to remove the evidence — they dug it up and hauled it away *twice*. Governments gather up the pieces like hamsters hoarding away food, and they don't show the rest of us what they've gathered. So is there physical evidence beyond the descriptions? Probably, but until the government throws open the doors of information, we'll never see it.

So who were these Tuatha dé Danann? They were depicted as tall humans with blond hair, and blue or gray eyes, created of flesh and bone which could be injured, just like us. They had a succession of high kings that ruled Ireland including one named Eochaidh Ollathair who carried a special title of *Dagda Mór* or *the Dagda*, which meant either "shining divinity" or "the good god" while *ollathair* meant "all father." The Dagda was not the father of the Tuatha race, but he was one of the most important among them as evidenced by his titles.

The Dagda was immortal, and forever young, which were traits shared by all of the Tuatha dé Danann. At one point, the Tuatha lived in some undefined "northern islands" of the world, but later moved "in dark clouds" to Ireland, drawing an invisible wall around them which hid them from the eyes of men, and which was impassable, which is a reference to Manannán mac Lir's cloaking technology.

This is further expanded in *The Book of the Taking of Ireland* which is also known as *The Book of Invasions* — a controversial early history of Ireland from which many of the Tuatha dé Danann legends come. Trouble arises because an accurate, unbiased, pre-Christian history simply doesn't exist. Early writers did everything in their power to erase all vestiges of blasphemous worship, and this was sometimes done by burning the existing texts and then rewriting history in a way that was more favorable to a new set of beliefs.

The arrival of the Tuatha dé Danann to Ireland brought darkness over the sun for three days and three nights, and "the truth was not known beneath the sky of stars, *whether they were of Heaven or of Earth*." Almost 4,000 years have passed since these extraterrestrials made Irish history, and humans still haven't duplicated some of the technologies they possessed such as the cloaking device, though it isn't for lack of trying.

Scientists yearn to create cloaking technology that renders our ships invisible, and if there's any truth to the *Philadelphia Experiment* stories, we've actually made progress though at great cost. This cloaking experiment caused us to "move through time" as well as to a different location. Fact or fiction? I don't know, but you can bet they're working hard on turning it into fact.

The Tuatha dé Danann often retreated to a hidden island which went by many names including Land of the Young, Land of Promise, Earthly Paradise, Land of the Ever Living, Mag Mell, and even within a single story you might see this island given three different names. That's what makes the whole concept of an island paradise confusing — all of the different names — so we don't know if they were talking about one island, or ten islands.

Another clue that their hidey hole was not located on Earth was the amber-colored, "peculiarly bright atmosphere." Sometimes glittering city domes and pinnacles make up the skyline, and other times you see fortresses which appear to be built of gold, silver or white marble. If these cities or fortresses existed on Earth, even the government couldn't have erased all traces of them. Time flowed differently there and one hundred years was as a single day, or several hundred years passed in the span of one of our years.

Other names for this place included Theirna-na-Oge, Tír-na-m Beo, Oilean-na-m Beo, Tír-na-m Buadha, Hy-na-Beatha, Tír-na-nóg, and Tír-Tairngire. All of these translate into variations of "land" or "island" of the living, of life, of the young, of promise, of virtues, or delightful plain. Sometimes it's described as an island, and other times it's an underwater city.

Sometimes the island appeared as if out of nowhere, and when you attempted to travel to it, with your eyes looking straight at it, the island suddenly disappeared right in front of you (which sounds suspiciously like a cloaking device.)

Something else that figures in not only the Tuatha dé Danann legends, but also the Norse and Native American legends, are the self-propelled boats made of crystal, glass, stone, or copper. These boats are identical to motorboats, and they figure into many of the legends, along with a magical mist that

27

descends on a man and seemingly transports him to an unusual place. In other words, this mist doesn't always stay in one place to hide an island — it can move around, envelope a person wherever they are standing, and suddenly that person is somewhere else.

Were all of these legends flat out myths created in the imaginations of ancient man? Or was it simply a case of misinterpretation of advanced extraterrestrial technology?

If you plucked an ordinary man from a thousand years ago and brought him into our world today, he'd probably be bowing at our feet, kissing the ground and calling us gods. A thousand years ago they were dying by the millions from plagues, while we're reattaching severed limbs and replacing worn out hearts.

Our ancestors fought battles hand-to-hand with swords, or at a distance with crossbows. Imagine their reaction to witnessing a bomb dropped from an airplane, or shots fired from a war plane which could take out an entire troop with a single blow.

How would they interpret the simple act of putting dirty dishes into a box, pushing a button, and later opening the box to find clean dishes? We put dirty clothes in a machine, and magically the clothes come out clean, and then dry. We hit a button and our homes are heated, with no visible source of fire anywhere. Hot air without a fire? Cold air in the middle of summer? This would surely have been called magic.

We see incredible visions on a screen in our living room, which can be beautiful, magical, or terrifying. We carry telephones which show us the living image of our friends and family who are thousands of miles away. We send messages which they receive instantly, a feat that in centuries past would have taken *months* via letter carried on horseback. What would our ancestors have called us, if they could see us now? Wizards? Genies? Witches? Gods?

How many ancient stories referred to voices of the gods coming out of nowhere? Would a cell phone or radio projecting a voice be interpreted the same way? We travel in an enclosed vehicle on wheels with temperature control, music, lights, electric windows, electric seats, heated seats, and a gas pedal which propels us forward at "magic speeds." Even the power of electricity, prior to its invention, would have been called magic. When the camera was first invented, some people believed it would steal your very soul to have a photo taken.

We fly through the air in planes. Food is at our fingertips in grocery stores. We dine in revolving restaurants at the top of tall towers. Wouldn't all of this be described as some mystical, magical, godlike paradise to someone who lived four thousand years ago? If a simple camera had a terrifying effect, how would they have perceived our current technology?

What technologies have we not yet mastered, that an extraterrestrial civilization might bring? Human transporters that would beam you from here to there? Such a transporter would seemingly make a person "disappear" like a genie. Would they have brought cloaking devices to hide humans, vehicles, or entire cities, as in islands "hidden in the mists" that appeared and disappeared? What about flying cities that could move from one location to another, float on the water, or hover in the air? Aren't we now building space stations that people can live on?

If you believe that we will master these technologies, then you have to consider the possibility that an extraterrestrial race already mastered it, and visited us in the distant past, leaving behind legends so fantastic that we don't believe them today, but our ancestors believed them enough to chase after these earthly paradises that seemingly just vanished from the maps.

One of the oldest paradise legends comes from a text dated approximately 3000 B.C., which Sumerian clay tablets referred to as *Dilmun* or *Telmun*. Unlike paradise where everyone seems to be permanently at leisure, Dilmun had an active trade route with surrounding regions. Dilmun was also known as the Land of the Living, as well as being the place where Ziusudra — the hero of

29

the Sumerian flood epic — was taken by the gods to live forever. His very name means "found long life" or "life of long days."

Dilmun is described as a faraway place, an island by some accounts, where there is no sickness, death, or strife, and where the wolf doesn't snatch the lamb, and neither do any of the other animals kill one another. It was a pure, clean, bright, prosperous land, dotted with "great dwellings." Archeologists are still trying to locate Dilmun.

LEGENDARY CREATURES

It's easy to dismiss the wild stories of our ancestors, especially when they believed in fantastic creatures which we *know* couldn't possibly have existed. However, some of the legends have their feet planted in fact. Some can be explained with fossil bones, scientific facts and technology, while others are corroborated by multiple historical texts and not just fairy tales.

The legends begin on Manannán's Isle of Man, where the Manx people originated and still live to this day, and where the Fenodyree legends came into being. *Fenodyree*, which has several spellings, is an alternate name for a Satyr. In the biblical passage *Isaiah 34:14* where the *King James Bible* uses *Satyr*, and modern bibles have changed it to *wild goat*, the 1819 *Manx Bible* called it a *Fynnoderee*.

Nobody really knows exactly what this creature referred to, and biblical translations came up with several possibilities: Satyr, Fenodyree, wild goat, hairy one, and demon. I'm not sure how you can confuse a goat with a demon unless it eats your underwear, but those are some of the translations. Whatever Satyrs were, they were alive and well in the biblical days and could easily have existed in Prester John's kingdom.

Let's analyze the possibilities. Prester John's kingdom was a place that boasted nothing but the most incredible, outrageous, magical, and mystical legends. The Satyr/Fenodyree has been changed from its original wording into *wild goat, hairy one* and *demon* depending on which version of the *Bible* you have. A *wild goat* would have been too ordinary to rate a mention in John's marvelous kingdom, and while a *hairy one* sounds interesting, it's simply too vague for John. No, his kingdom boasted about its inhabitants, leaving little to the imagination. Being a Christian kingdom, I cannot imagine John harboring a demon. That leaves the original translations of *Satyr* and *Fenodyree*, and the detailed descriptions of the latter are a slam-dunk winner as a mythical marvel worthy of John's kingdom.

Now this is where it gets interesting. The Fenodyree humanoids could transport huge blocks of stone that were much too heavy for humans to lift. Manx legends tell us that in the course of a single night, one Fenodyree transported an entire quarry of rocks — more than one hundred cart loads — including an enormous block of white stone that "all the men in the parish" *united*, could not move. This is not the action of a wild goat.

In another narrative, a Fenodyree took hold of the iron sock of a plough and with one hand, squeezed the iron sock as if it were a piece of clay. You'd think this would come from a big, powerful giant but no, the Fenodyree were usually described as small, hairy humanoids, whose legs were especially hairy, and who refused to wear clothes even if they were offered, though they would occasionally accept food. They also spoke, and understood, human language. Fenodyrees were more than a beast, but less than a human, and in scientific circles were believed to represent an anthropoid ape or pithecoid man — which is a sort of primitive ape-man.

In the *Return of the Gods* chapter, you'll meet Flores Man, a genuine humanoid whose bones we've discovered, and which could account for the Fenodyree description. In the book *Phonetic Transcription of Indian Languages* published by the Smithsonian Institution in 1916, as reported by the American Anthropological

Association, there's a theory that *Satyr* was synonymous with wild man, ape, Kobold, and Elf.

Was the Fenodyree a creature of myth that lived only in the imaginations of our ancestors? Was it a primitive ape-man? Was this powerful stone mover the creature that helped to build some of the ancient stone structures that we're still puzzling over today?

In addition to superhuman strength, the Fenodyree could also clip the grass at a tremendous speed. Yessirree, this was another of his claims to fame — clipping the grass to help his human neighbors. He was so good at cutting the grass that his nickname was "the nimble mower." So the biblical Satyr was a creature who clipped the grass? As in all the paradise stories with nice, neatly trimmed grass as if clipped by a lawn mower, which didn't exist back then? What manner of creature was this Fenodyree that could lift huge blocks of stone that no man could move, and who clipped the grass in paradise? Was it a living creature with superhuman strength? Or was this biblical creature just a tall tale?

Beings such as the Fenodyree could solve one of the greatest mysteries of the old world — how did our ancestors transport stones that weighed more than a thousand pounds when they built ancient structures such as the *Stone of the Pregnant Woman* in Heliopolis? One legend claims that pregnant *Jinn* were given the task to cut and move the stone, possibly under the orders of King Solomon who was one of the few humans who held power over the magical Jinn. As the legend goes, the structures that the Jinn were building were abandoned on King Solomon's death, when the power he wielded over the Jinn died along with him.

Solomon himself was surrounded in legend, having the ability to *fly* his entire army around the world on the winds, in addition to controlling the Jinn — a species of magical being. His legends appear in the *Koran*, the Christian and Jewish *Old Testament*, as well as extra-biblical texts. He could communicate with birds and ants, and in one passage of the *Koran* where

Solomon was traveling with men, birds, and Jinn, it says, "At length, when they came to a valley of ants, one of the ants said: 'O ye ants, get into your habitations, lest Solomon and his hosts crush you (under foot) without knowing it.' So he (Solomon) smiled, amused at her speech…" I wonder if these were the gold digging ants associated with Prester John's kingdom?

The Jinn were a supernatural race of beings mentioned in the *Koran*, which existed in addition to humans and angels. They were magical beings that could travel vast distances at great speeds. They had the power of invisibility, and were made of a smokeless, scorching fire. Their description does not match the Fenodyree, however, except to share a legend about moving giant stones, so the two would be distinctly different entities; and there were others "gifted" with the ability to move large stones, as well.

Another ancient site with large stones is in the region of Tiahuanacu, Bolivia called *Pumapunku*. This stone complex is cited by ancient astronaut theorists as proof that our ancestors had extraterrestrial helpers. Portions of Pumapunku date back to 536 A.D., and yet the blocks that make up the walls were cut so precisely that they appeared to be prefabricated or mass produced. In addition, the joints fit together so tightly that you can't even slide a razor blade in between the stones.

Tiahuanacu is 13,000 feet above sea level. Even with our current technology, we'd be struggling to haul gargantuan blocks up such a mountain. In addition, Tiahuanacu could not have supported the sheer number of humans it would have taken to haul the blocks and build the sprawling temple. The climate is so bitter that it's difficult to grow crops. The only grain that grows at all is barley, and even the barley rarely matures. Bitter potatoes and quinoa grow in small quantities — barely enough to feed the "pinched and impoverished inhabitants" according to archeologist Ephraim George Squier in *Peru Incidents of Travel and Exploration in the Land of the Incas* published in 1877. Tiahuanacu could not have produced enough food to feed an entire work force.

However, like the Fenodyree who moved stones on the Isle of Man, and the Jinn who moved stones in Heliopolis, superhuman helpers existed in Tiahuanacu as well. According to the legends of the Aymara people, as told to a Spanish traveler not long after the Spanish conquest, supernatural beings built Pumapunku during the age of Chamak-pacha or *First Creation*. These beings could levitate stones up off the ground and into the air, and then move the stones *through the air* to the sound of a trumpet. An alternate legend states that Pumapunku was built by *huaris*, or giants, prior to the First Creation.

Three different regions of the world: the Isle of Man which is located in between Great Britain and Ireland, Heliopolis which is now Lebanon situated north of Israel, and Bolivia in South America — all with legends of supernatural stone movers.

Another stone mover hailed from the United States. There's a Cherokee legend about an ogress called Spear-finger who also possessed this stone moving magic. Spear-finger was a shape shifter who could take on the appearance of your best friend, which was a bad thing as she allegedly ate human livers. By pretending to be someone you knew, she could get close enough to jab you with her spear-like finger and get at your liver.

Underneath the fake, friendly exterior, her body was as hard as rock and impenetrable to all weapons. In addition, she could lift heavy stones as if they weighed no more than a feather. Spear-finger's prowess as a stone mover went a step further. She could also *cement stones together by striking them*, and she single-handedly built a stone bridge across a deep river. The legend itself claims that this could only have been done by building the bridge while flying through the air!

No doubt there are other magical creatures gifted with the ability to move 1,500 pound stones up a mountain or build stone bridges across deep rivers. The point is that all around the world, our legends speak of these stone movers, and our ancient monuments can't always be explained by humans wielding sleds and ropes, which lends credence to the Fenodyree/Satyr of Prester John's kingdom.

Giants were another resident of his magic kingdom, and you can't read an ancient text without finding stories of giants. In the *Bible* they were called *Nephilim*, and these Nephilim were the offspring of the "sons of the gods" and the "daughters of men." The terminology varies depending on the passage itself, and which translation of the *Bible* you've got. The existence of these Nephilim so angered God that he sent Noah's flood to wipe them all out. However, it didn't work, as giants still existed after the flood, such as Goliath in the well-known biblical story of David and Goliath.

In Greek mythology, giants were the children of the goddess Gaia and they were called *Titans*. The island of Atlantis was named after a second-generation Titan known as Atlas.

A giant named *Bran the Blessed* was the king of Britain according to a Welch legend, and Bran was so big that he couldn't fit into any dwelling. He owned a magic cauldron that could bring the dead back to life. Coincidentally, Bran was also the name of the fellow in the Voyage of Bran who met Manannán, though the story of Manannán's Bran differs from Bran the Blessed and doesn't involve the cauldron.

The Norse had their giants as well, called the *Jötnar*, which were the children of the giant Ymir. The Hindus had the *Daityas*, the Native American Paiutes believed in a red-haired giant known as *Si-te-cah*, and the list goes on. In mythologies that depict Earth as having several "ages" prior to the age of Adamic man, there was usually an age of giants.

Bones substantiate these legends, such as the *Giant of Castelnau* bones found in France in 1890. These human bones came from a man who was eleven and a half feet tall. Four years later, more giant bones were discovered in Montpelier, France, which indicate that a race of men existed who were between ten and fifteen feet tall.

So Prester John's collection of the unusual is becoming less mythical, as one by one we see that these beings could actually have existed. If John's paradise existed, then all of the other paradises could have existed with their speed boats, revolving castles, cloaking mists, and otherworldly creatures such as the Gryphon, which also lived in John's kingdom.

The Egyptians, Greeks, and Europeans who described Prester John's kingdom, all believed in a creature known as a *Gryphon*. It had the body of a lion, and the head and wings of an eagle. Sometimes it was represented with the forelegs of a lion, and other times with the talons of an eagle. As lions were the king of beasts and eagles were the king of birds, the Gryphon was an especially powerful creature, and it was associated with gold and treasure.

Legends often have a basis in fact, and the Gryphon demonstrates this to perfection. His fossilized remains have been found in the gold mines of the Altai Mountains that border China, Russia, Mongolia, and other countries, thus the Gryphon legends originated from a genuine prehistoric creature.

The Gryphon bones were actually a protoceratops, which means "first horned face" in Greek. These dinosaur bones could have been mistaken for a lion's body with a frightening, beaked head that would cause any human to go weak in the knees. The head and neck frill of the protoceratops looks like a gigantic, ferocious bird with a beak full of teeth that could chomp a man's leg off in a single snap, not that this creature would, but ancient man finding his skeleton would surely have believed so. The neck frill was probably mistaken for a lion's mane, giving birth to the lion-bird legends. The Gryphon wouldn't have been alive in Prester John's day, but if protoceratops' bones had been found there, then folks would have expected to find Gryphons nearby.

The *Phoenix* bird also lived in Prester John's kingdom. The seeds of truth that spawned the Phoenix bird legends didn't come from bones, but something far more bizarre, but we'll digress a moment before bringing you the most amazing true story that surely spawned this legend.

The Greeks believed that the Phoenix bird could live for a thousand years but when it grew old, it built a nest for its resurrection, and then both the Phoenix bird and its nest burst into flames until nothing was left but ashes. From these ashes, a new Phoenix arose, though no one knew whether it was the original bird reborn, or its offspring.

A Persian creature called the *Simurgh* combined the Phoenix and Gryphon into a single legend of a winged creature so large that it could pluck an elephant off the ground and carry it away through the air. The Simurgh had the head of a dog, claws of a lion, and feathers of a peacock, and was sometimes called a dog-bird. Though the Simurgh could fly like a bird, it was actually a mammal which gave birth to live young rather than eggs. Like the Phoenix, it plunged itself into flames.

This benevolent creature possessed the knowledge of the ages, having witnessed the destruction of the world three times over, and made its home in the Tree of Life, which was the *gaokerena* tree. The Tree of Life promised health and immortality, and its fruit had the ability to resurrect the dead. It was also known as the "haoma/hauma/hom" plant, and there is a *Homa/Huma* bird legend which intersects the Phoenix/Simurgh legends. By whatever name you call it — Simurgh, Phoenix, or Huma — this bird crosses paths with the Gryphon.

The Simurgh legend may have risen from prehistoric bones as well, being a bird so big and powerful that it could pluck an elephant up into the air and carry it off with ease. Colonel Henry Yule, a scholar-historian-traveler-author in the 1800s, was awarded a gold medal by the Royal Geographical Society for his *Book of Marco Polo*. He translated several books from Latin, and compiled an Anglo-Indian dictionary called *Hobson-Jobson*. In other words, his opinion carried a lot of weight, and he believed that Marco Polo's *Gryphon*, the Hindu *Garuda* bird, the Jewish *Bar*

Yachre, and the Persian *Simurgh* were one in the same creature, which in various descriptions was: an eagle-like bird big enough to block out the sun, whose wings created hurricane winds that could blow down a house, and who was strong enough to carry three elephants at one time. This giant bird-creature was seen in the region of the China seas, as well as Madagascar and Northern Siberia.

Native Americans believed in a *Thunderbird* whose wings created great windstorms, and who could lift whales right out of the ocean. In some descriptions the Thunderbird was a multi-colored bird with two horns and teeth in its beak. The Gryphon also had teeth.

Several genuine giant birds existed in the Old World alongside humans, one being the *Elephant Bird* of Madagascar who lived up into the 17th century. Elephant Birds were ten feet tall and weighed up to 880 pounds. They may have been named for Marco Polo's giant bird that could fly off carrying an elephant, except that Elephant Bird's can't actually fly.

Another species of big bird who lived alongside humans was the *Teratorns*, and though they were not big enough to pick up an elephant, they were big enough to instill terror in humans. *Teratornis merriami* had a 12 foot wingspan and was big enough to eat human infants as a tasty little snack, not that humans were on the menu. *Teratornis woodburnensis* had a 14 foot wingspan, and *Teratornis incredibilis* had an 18 foot wingspan. The scientific name of the latter was changed to *Aiolornis incredibilis*, which means "incredible god of the winds," and this gigantic bird lived alongside humans.

Sit in your exposed back yard where a bird can fly over whatever fence you erect, and imagine a bird with an 18 foot wingspan flying overhead. There was an even bigger flying creature with a 30 foot wingspan known as *Quetzalcoatlus*. His bones were discovered in Texas. He is a pterosaur, which is a species of giant flying reptile, some of which had needle-like teeth. Pterosaurs were known for their elaborate head crests, and a few were covered in hair which would have made them resemble mammals. Even though it could fly, Quetzalcoatlus walked on four "feet" like a mammal when it walked.

As far as we know, pterosaurs did not exist at the same time as humans, but our ancestors would have found their bones just as we have, and speculated about the creature behind the bones, perhaps studying the activities of smaller teratorns and superimposing those activities onto the giant, bird-like bones of the pterosaurs.

Even today, we have rumors of a pterosaur-like creature flying the skies called *Kongamato*, which means "breaker of boats." As with Bigfoot and the Loch Ness monster, sightings abound but we can't find solid evidence. Still, the bones of giant flying creatures with 36 foot wingspans, and Elephant Birds who lived in Madagascar as recently as the 17th century which towered over humans, is enough to spark a few giant bird legends, which brings us to the most interesting legend of all — that of the Phoenix rising from the ashes.

The Phoenix and Simurgh legends, as impossible as they sound with a bird bursting into flames and being born anew, may have been spawned by the bizarre behavior of some birds. Over 250 species of birds engage in a behavior known as "anting" where they rub ants on their feathers.

The chemicals secreted by certain ants protect the birds from fungus, bacteria, feather mites, and louse flies, so the theory is that they are engaging in personal pest control. Studies have shown that anting kills the pesky mites that plague the birds, as well as treating fungal and bacterial infections. Another theory is that the birds are rubbing off the distasteful chemicals before eating the ants. Though this activity is called *anting*, birds do it with other chemical-bearing entities as well, including millipedes, garlic snails, and the puss moth caterpillar which is loaded with nasty defense chemicals.

Anting birds also rub plants on their feathers that humans use as insecticides, fueling the insecticide theory, but some of the other objects that they ant with border on the bizarre. Birds have used citrus peels, mothballs, burning embers, burning coals, and smoldering cigarette butts. These birds become highly excited, dancing and prancing while they are anting. Sometimes they spread their wings wide, open their beaks, and flop around in the grass like a dog rolling on a dead bug.

Other birds engage in passive anting, where they lie prostrate on top of an anthill, letting ants crawl all over them. Or they'll dust themselves with anthill dirt which is full of ant chemicals. A related activity is called *smoking* where they perch near a smoking chimney or fire and take a "smoke bath."

Birds who rub themselves with burning embers or cigarette butts have actually set houses and trees on fire, as well as their own nests. Traveling even deeper into the *Twilight Zone* are the birds who figure out how to light a match, and then proceed to light matches to ant with. I kid you not, this is a known bird activity. One bird by the name of Corbie even figured out how to turn on an electric fireplace to feed his need to ant with burning materials.

This bizarre bird activity has been recorded for centuries, weaving its way through myth and legend, with tales of birds setting houses on fire. Richard Fitter wrote about the great London fires in his book *London's Natural History*:

> "In 1203, it was said that birds were seen flying in the air with burning coals in their bills, which set light to many houses in London."

So here we have birds who delight in rubbing themselves with burning embers, accidentally setting their own nests on fire, fanning the flames with their anting antics, and possibly perishing in these fires of their own making — just like the Phoenix and Simurgh who burst into flames. Then we have birds who actively seek out burning embers in the ashes of a recent fire.

Our ancestors, seeing a bird prancing around in the center of a pile of smoldering ashes, and being familiar with the Phoenix legend, could have easily assumed that the bird was a Phoenix rising from the ashes. This is the stuff legends are made of, and it shows that the Phoenix legends have a basis in fact, which brings us to the next bizarre resident of Prester John's kingdom — gold digging ants.

Allegedly these ants left mountains of gold in their wake. On the surface, the concept of ants digging to create mountains of gold is one of the sticky points of Prester John's legend, until you refer to another meaning for the word "ants."

In a 1915 book published by the *Brooklyn Entomological Society*, there's an entry that discussed the ancient kingdom of Turan, which also figures in the *Magic Mirrors* and *Enchanted Castles* chapters. This tidbit has to do with the Turan people, the Myrmidon people, and dissecting words which relate to ants:

> "It is hardly the word for the Persian *maka*, or *myci*, which fathers the word for ants. The confusion of the Turan tribes of *maka*, or *myci*, or various spellings arises from the vague translations of Sir Henry Rawlinson. The *mike* appears again as the Myrmidons, and are the ants. They were a tribe of the Turan. The word *myrmex* is merely *muria* plus *mike*, i.e., the ants occurring in 10,000 colonies."

This peaked my interest, wondering if somehow they were going to start referring to people as *ants*. The narration went on about a bunch of human wars, and then came back to another ant reference:

> "The Myrmidons, ancestors of the Macedonian race, came, it was claimed, from the island of Aegina, hard by Athens. The island having become depopulated, the gods gave permission to an ancestor of Achilles to repopulate by converting the ants into human beings. These migrated to Macedonia, and always boasted of being descended from ants."

Okay, that was a little weird, converting ants into human beings, unless this was a reference to freeing slaves which is what these people sound like they were being treated as, and this next paragraph clinches the link between ants and humans. I've omitted the ancient debate on whether ants could become humans, and skipped to the closing statement:

> "It was finally officially declared that the Myrmidons were freeborn Greeks, descended from the ants of Aegina. More probably the truth is that the Myrmidons were descendants of the Turanic tribe (or tribes) known as *ants*, and formed the exception to the rule of Iran versus Turan."

In short, the Myrmidon's were known as the *ant people,* so the reference to ants digging up mountains of gold, rather than referring to insects, was actually referring to people!

Five creatures that usually get dismissed as fairy tales — the Satyr/Fenodyree, giants, Gryphons, Phoenix birds, and ants who create mountains of gold — each with a basis in fact, so what else contributed to the paradise legends?

TOUCHED BY CELESTIAL BEINGS

In a class by itself are the white animals, which on the surface do not appear to have an otherworldly link. After all, it's not unheard to encounter a rare birth of a white animal in a species that doesn't normally produce them. However, white animals appearing in conjunction with a celestial visitor, added to their link with paradise, is significant.

Prester John's *celestial kingdom* boasted white lions and white bears, and there's a captivating legend that surrounds the white Kruger lions of Africa. There is a rare color mutation caused by a recessive gene known as the *color inhibitor gene*. This anomaly specifically affects the Kruger lions, aka *Panthera leo krugeri*, and it has been perpetuated by selective breeding. Their ancestry, however, has more otherworldly roots.

White lions are found naturally in only one place — Kruger National Park in Africa — where they are considered sacred creatures. Legend has it that several hundred years ago, Queen Numbi reigned over an area now known as Timbavati, which is a region at the western edge of Kruger National Park in the Limpopo province of South Africa. In ancient times it was called *Timba-vaati* or *Tsimba-vaati* which means "to come down (like a bird) to the ground." Another possible translation is "the place where star lions came down from the heavens."

The elderly Queen Numbi was very ill, and her legs and stomach were grossly swollen. One moonless night as the bedridden queen waited for death, a bright star fell slowly from the sky, lighting up the village in an eerie blue light as if it were daytime. The star circled and landed in a nearby valley.

As soon as the queen was told about this star coming down from the sky, she ordered two of her servants to help her get to the valley to investigate, where they found a huge sphere of light sitting on the ground. This light was "brighter than the sun" and yet the sphere produced very little heat. In addition, the sphere made a humming noise.

Afraid of angering the gods, who were surely responsible for sending this object, the queen and her servants started back toward the village, but they were stopped by a human-shaped entity that emerged from the sphere. The celestial visitor seemed to be made of yellow fire or light, though they could make out a body, limbs, and a featureless face. The light-being approached them and lifted its glowing hand, which did not appear to have fingers. The queen raised her own hand in answer. Their hands touched, and then the light-being vanished.

Queen Numbi's eyes were now glowing with celestial light. She told the servants that the gods wanted her, and that she must go with them. Then she walked into the blue light that surrounded the sphere, where the light-beings surrounded her. They looked like yellow, humanoid ghosts in the blue light. Her servants watched in amazement as their queen disappeared.

The servants stood frozen as if spellbound, but eventually the spell broke and they returned to the village. From the safety of the village, they watched the sphere rise up from the valley, lighting up the village as if the sun were high in the sky. Then it shot off like a lightning bolt into the distant skies.

Soon after, animals in the vicinity started giving birth to snow-white babies with blue eyes. Lions, leopards, baboons, elephants, and entire herds of antelope, eland, and impala were born as white as snow. Deformities also afflicted these snow-white animals which were sometimes born with deformed hooves and horns, such as one horn instead of two, or having two heads.

This was clearly a UFO encounter — a close encounter of the fourth kind which indicates an actual abduction — although not all abductions are against the wishes of the human. The word "abduction" doesn't apply if the human wanted to go, and in some cases, extraterrestrial contact is actually beneficial to the human, as was the case with the dying Queen Numbi.

Our ancestors often used words such as "transfixed" or "spellbound" and we gloss right over it, not seeing the significance of that single word. For Numbi's servants, it meant that they were temporarily paralyzed, unable to move as they watched their queen interact with, and enter the ship of, these extraterrestrial beings.

When it comes to alien-human contact, we mostly hear about little gray aliens, or tall, blond, humanoids, but there have been stories of light-beings throughout history, often with a positive outcome. As unexpectedly as the queen had disappeared with the light-beings, she reappeared young and healthy, and went on to rule her people for a long time. Not only had the celestial visitors restored her health and rejuvenated her, Queen Numbi came back gifted with special powers, and she performed extraordinary deeds during her reign.

This is a genuine story of someone who was rejuvenated, but rather than drinking from a Fountain of Youth, the rejuvenation came through extraterrestrial contact. Let's play *what if*. What if Queen Numbi's rejuvenation came from drinking a substance, and alien astronauts poured that substance into a water well? Wouldn't it be like "blessing" that well with healing powers? Could they create an actual Fountain of Youth, whose powers would run out once the water was used up?

Look at the other clues that surround Queen Numbi's experience — the white animals, and animals born with birth defects. Both can occur with radiation exposure, as might come from a spacecraft. Queen Numbi's story intersects with the beliefs of the Zulus and the origin of their people. Timbavati came to be known as a sacred place not only for the legend of Numbi, but for the sacred snow-white animals as well, which were gifted by the gods.

Queen Numbi eventually passed away, and many kings came after her including King Npepo I, who banned all hunting in the region to protect the sacred white animals. The only way to acquire a sacred white animal skin was to get it after the animal passed away of natural causes.

One of these sacred white lion skins was given to King Dinizulu and soon after, Dinizulu began to dream prophecies about his people, and all of Earth, which often happens to people who've had extraterrestrial contact. King Dinizulu and his father, King Malandela, may have been ancestors of the Zulu people.

There was a King Malandela kaLuzumana who lived in the early 17th century, that some believe was the son of the founder of the royal Zulu line, or perhaps even the founder himself. His great-great grandfather was Mnguni, and his grandson was Zulu kaNtombela, though by another account he had a son named Zulu kaMalandela.

There was also a clan leader Malandela of the Nguni tribe in the 16th or early 17th century whose son was named Zulu, which meant *heaven* or *sky*, and who established a place called KwaZulu which meant *Place of Heaven*, located south of the Mkhumbane River basin. The various Malandela's may have all referred to the same person.

In another account of Zulu history, there was a Nguni named Malandela who settled in the uMhlathuze Valley around 1670, where he begat Ntombela, who was the father of the Zulu people. Eleven generations after him came one named Dinizulu.

While some of the details in these varied accounts differ due to history being passed down verbally from generation to generation, enough of the stories match to connect the origin of the Zulus to King Dinizulu who received the sacred white lion skin and the gift of prophecy, as a result of the beings of light who came down from the sky during the reign of Queen Numbi.

Both the Mkhumbane River and the Mhlathuze River are located in the KwaZulu-Natal province of South Africa, and the uMhlathuze Municipality is named after the Mhlathuze River, matching up the various Malandela Zulu stories as being one in the same.

Zulu means "people of the sky" or "people of heaven" and the Zulus believed that their god was a sky god — *Lord of the Sky* or *Lord of Heaven*. They also believed that this sky god was their direct physical ancestor, creating yet another link to the otherworldly white lions and extraterrestrial beings, who descended in a spaceship, and whose presence forever altered the genes of the Kruger lions and restored the youth of Queen Numbi.

If it's possible that the Kruger lions' genetic mutation was originally caused by an otherworldly visitation, then we may have another, similar proof in the tailless Manx cats. This missing tail is a genetic mutation, and along with the missing tail, Manx cats are often born with bigger hind legs and a distinctive way of walking, which caused our ancestors to believe that they were cat/rabbit hybrids.

Manx cats originated on the Isle of Man, the very island which is associated with the Tuatha dé Danann and Manannán mac Lir. Remember how the Tuatha came to Ireland in dark clouds, and the truth was not known whether they were of Heaven or of Earth?

Another genetic mutation is also associated with the Isle of Man, in the form of a breed of sheep called the *Manx Loaghtan*. These sheep are sometimes born with four, five, or six horns, just like the animals in Queen Numbi's story. There's an interesting legend about the Manx Loaghtan that connects it to the Fenodyree who often helped with chores while humans were sleeping.

A farmer near Glenmaye on the Isle of Man made a comment one night, just before going to sleep, that he needed to go up into the mountains the next day and gather his sheep. The Fenodyree must have been listening because when the farmer woke up, all of his sheep were in the farmyard, and the Fenodyree was up in the loft of the barn.

The Fenodyree called down to the farmer, telling him that there was one sheep that he hadn't been able to bring home, but that a hare had sprung up amongst the sheep, so he brought the hare along with the others. The "hare" was actually a Loaghtan sheep, and the farmer was amused that the Fenodyree did not know the difference between a hare and a sheep. In a different version, it really was a hare which the Fenodyree had confused with a Loaghtan sheep.

It's difficult to get a good description of the original Manx Loaghtan sheep because breeders have taken over these sheep and molded them into a different version. In their primitive state, Loaghtan's are smaller than other sheep. They have high, narrow backs, narrow ribs, long legs, are "deficient in the shoulder" and have tails that resemble a goat's tail. They almost went extinct on the island during the 1800s.

It's interesting that two very different animals, the Manx cat and the Manx sheep, are both associated with the Isle of Man and whose legends link them to, or confuse them with, rabbits and hares. Both have genetic mutations, and the Isle of Man is linked to the celestial Tuatha dé Danann, just like the Kruger lions and Queen Numbi's extraterrestrial visitors. Are these animals living proof that somewhere in the distant past, extraterrestrials paid us a visit?

THE YIMA CONNECTION

Another oddity connects several paradise stories — a word connection involving the similar words of Yima, Yma, Hy-ma, Ymir, and Hy-mir.

- King Yima — the Zoroastrian who ruled over a paradise that had a white haoma tree, or Tree of Life, whose healing juice was so powerful it could raise the dead. He also had a magic mirror in which he could keep an eye on worldly events.
- Yma or Hy-ma afterlife — a Celtic belief that after death, our spirits live in a happy land called Yma or Hy-ma, which is sometimes described as an island.
- Yma or Hy-ma island — the paradise island of Yma or Hy-ma which several monks found after traveling through a dense, otherworldly mist, and came back to tell the story.
- Ymir god — the creator god of the Norse, connected to Odin and Thor, disappearing palaces, the ability to see everything going on in the world, and magic boats.
- Hymir giant — a Norse giant with a magic cauldron similar to the cauldron of plenty of the Tuatha dé Danann.

King Yima ruled over a land called Airyana Vaego which was similar to the Garden of Eden, though he ruled under the god Ahura Mazda. Like the Garden of Eden, Yima's kingdom had a Tree of Knowledge, and a Tree of Life sometimes referred to as the *white haoma*, the latter being the "source of life" around which all healing plants grew, and whose juice could resurrect the dead. The haoma plant is linked to other legends such as the Simurgh, who lives in the gaokerena Tree of Life which promises health and immortality with its fruit that can resurrect the dead. The gaokerena is also known as a haoma.

King Yima ruled for several hundred years over this land of happiness where no one got sick, or lied, or cried. But one day he had a meeting with Ahura Mazda and the celestial gods, who warned Yima of their intent to punish the sins of mankind with a great flood.

Like the story of Noah's Ark, Yima was instructed to build a *vara* and load it up with two of every animal, along with plant seeds to repopulate the world. This vara was lighted with "created lights" and "uncreated lights" which translates as "material lights" which shine from below, and "heavenly lights" which shine from above. Yima's paradise would thus have been wiped off the face of the Earth, except that not all of the ancient flood stories agree that the entire Earth was inundated.

An interesting book entitled *Atlantis: The Antediluvian World* by Ignatius Donnelly, published in 1882, compares a number of flood stories in a quest to not only prove the existence of Atlantis, but to depict it as an island paradise known by many names. Donnelly demonstrated a possibility that the great flood wiped out this island, but did not cover every continent on Earth, which means that unless all of the paradise legends were indeed Atlantis, any of them could still have existed after the great flood, even ones that predated the flood.

Along with ruling over paradise with its Tree of Life, another marvel existed in Yima's kingdom — a mirror in which he could see all of the events in the world. Coincidentally, Prester John also owned such a mirror.

We don't know the exact location of Prester John's kingdom, or Yima's kingdom, or the gaokerena Tree of Life. Nor do we know the location of the island of Yma or Hy-ma.

The Celts believed that after death, our spirits went to a happy place to live a new, and never-ending life. This place was called Yma or Hy-ma (Isle of the Just, or Isle of the Good) and they believed that it was a physical island. They called it other names as well including Flathinnis (Noble Island), Tír-na-m Beo (Land of the Living), Tír-na-nóg (Land of Youth), and Hy-Breasail (Isle of the Blest.)

This is where you have to wonder whether history got rewritten, because not only was this island the very same place that the Christian St. Brendan set out to find, but "Land of the Living" was also one of the islands associated with the Tuatha dé Danann. It was also another name for Dilmun — a paradise that archeologists look for believing that it's physical, and can't find. If all of the other Lands of the Living were allegedly places that a physical person could go, and which St. Brendan and his monks searched for, then you've got to wonder whether Celtic history was rewritten to match Christianity regarding our spirits after death.

Such rewrites were not unheard of, as the book, *A Dictionary of Miracles* by Reverend Ebenezer Cobham Brewer in 1894, states in its introduction:

> "It was customary in religious houses for someone to read aloud during meal time, and a favorite amusement was to adapt some heathen tale and spiritualize it. Popular adaptations would be remembered, and handed down, and in time these traditions would be lifted into the national hagiography."

Unfortunately, this was done not only with "heathen tales" but the lives of saints as well, so it's possible that not all miracles attributed to saints actually occurred. Even the travels of St. Brendan are called into question for truthfulness.

In the year 512 A.D., several Christian monks — including St. Brendan and St. Machatus — sailed off in search of the Fortunate Islands where men led angelic lives. Another variation said that they were searching for the paradise island of Yma, which was believed to be surrounded by a wall of shining gold, as shiny as a mirror and with no visible entrance, inhabited by heavenly angels — and *the monks found it*. Other explorers found it as well, all of whose stories are told in the *Paradise Found* chapter.

It's just odd that we have so many similar words, from totally unrelated legends and regions of the world, all pointing to a paradise which is now hidden from us. There's another strange "disappearing city" story, with a more distant Yima connection, this one relating to the Norse gods.

One of the most prominent of the Norse gods was the Aesir god Odin, who was an "all father" god (like the Dagda) as well as being the ruler of Asgard, which was one of the Nine Worlds of Norse mythology. Asgard was the home world of the Aesir race of gods.

Each of the Nine Worlds of Norse mythology is the home world of a particular race of beings. Giants live on one, the Aesir gods on another, the Vanir gods on another, and so forth. Earth is one of these Nine Worlds and is called Midgard. Earth is connected to Asgard by way of *bifröst*, which is a bridge that links our two worlds.

Humans are left trying to figure out exactly what these other worlds are, whether physical, spiritual, or other-dimensional, as well as the nature of the bifröst bridge. Possible interpretations include: shimmering path, rainbow bridge, swaying road to Heaven, or even the Milky Way itself.

The Aesir were at war with a race of giants known as the Jötnar, which were descended from the creator god Ymir, who Odin and his brothers eventually killed. As Odin's grandfather was Jötnar, then Ymir was likely Odin's direct ancestor, which would have made Odin both Jötnar and Aesir. While the god

Ymir doesn't seem to have any direct connection to paradise or technology, I found the name similarity interesting, and his descendant Odin does have interesting connections.

From his throne, Odin could see everything that was happening in the world. He could survey all the lands, and witness every man's acts. While it's not clear whether he had a "magic mirror" as some of the others, Odin and his brethren did possess several technological marvels which included a magic boat, and Asgard itself was linked to a disappearing city.

A king named Gylfi got the notion to travel to Asgard (presumably by way of the bifröst bridge) and have a little chit chat with the Aesir gods. One of their goddesses had tricked him, and he was irritable over her deception. He set out for Asgard disguised as an old man, apparently believing that he needed to sneak in, but the Aesir could not be deceived and they knew of his arrival in advance.

He came to a city with a building so high that he couldn't see the top of it. The walls were thatched with golden shields similar to a shingled roof. In the doorway stood a juggler, who led him inside where he saw a huge room full of people who were gaming, drinking, or fighting with weapons.

Three men sat on high seats, one above the other, and they riddled him with questions to test his knowledge of the gods, mankind, the creation of Earth, and of the apocalypse that will end the world. This questioning went on and on and the Aesir were impressed with King Gylfi's knowledge.

After an exhaustive line of questioning, which was preserved for future humans (like us) to read, King Gylfi heard thunderous noises all around him and suddenly found himself outdoors, with no castle or city anywhere to be seen. His exit from the Aesir city sounds like a transporter or wormhole. He made his way back home and told everyone what he had experienced.

What if the *bifröst bridge* was actually a wormhole to a physical planet that was populated by an extraterrestrial race who called themselves the Aesir? What if Gylfi's journey represented a trip to this planet? What if the "disappearing castle" was instead, Gylfi's transport back through a wormhole where one minute, he was inside a room in Asgard, and the next, he was back on Earth?

The next link in the Yima connection is Hymir, who also comes from Norse legends. Hymir was a giant who possessed a cauldron that was coveted by the Aesir gods. Presumably being a giant makes him one of the Jötnar who had their own world, and these Jötnar were the bane of both the Aesir and humans.

Hymir is an interesting name. It's similar to Hy-ma, which was another name for the Celtic island of Yma; and if you remove the "H" you end up with Ymir, the name of the Norse creator god, which all ties in with the strange Yima connection.

Hymir's cauldron was similar to the Tuatha dé Danann cauldron which never went empty no matter how many people it was supposed to feed. The Norse god Aegir was hosting a feast, and the liquor ran out just as Thor was looking for a refill. Aegir made the comment that there wasn't a cauldron big enough to hold the amount of liquor needed to satisfy Thor. Then they remembered Hymir's "mile-deep" cauldron which would surely do the trick.

So what does this Yima connection mean? Is it just a series of coincidences with similar words, which link to similar legends? Four different religions are involved in the coincidence: Christianity, Celtic, Zoroastrianism, and Norse.

The paradise island of Yma, which was hidden behind an otherworldly mist, is associated with Christian monks. The spiritual (or physical?) island paradise of Yma that offered never-ending life was a Celtic belief. King Yima ruled over a physical paradise which boasted a Tree of Life whose properties were the same as the Fountain of Youth, and he had a magic mirror. Then come all the Norse legends with the creator god Ymir, bridges that link our world to another, magic boats, and a giant named Ymir with his cauldron of plenty, which is similar to other magical cauldrons.

MAGIC MIRRORS

Today we have computers linked up to spy cams that allow us to see everything that's going on in the world, while we sit in a chair in our "castle" looking at a thin, flat screen. Between the traffic cameras on every street corner, and the satellite cameras pointing down from above, our leaders can zoom in on a country, a single city block, a house, and even pull the numbers off of a license plate passing through an intersection. We can also watch ships in the middle of the ocean. This is not magic — it's technology, and it appears that the leaders of our ancient ancestors possessed similar technology, only back then they told the peons that they owned a "magic mirror."

The Christian king Prester John had a magic mirror in which he could see everything that was happening "in the length and breadth of his dominions."

The Norse god Odin could see everything that was happening in the world as he sat on his throne. He could survey all the lands, and witness every man's acts. We don't know if a magic mirror was involved, but considering his other technology, it would be implied.

Alexander the Great, who was also called Iskander/Sikander, owned a magic mirror that allowed him to see all of the people that he hadn't yet conquered. He could see unknown regions, or deep inside an enemy camp, and even watch ships at sea. Allegedly, Alexander never lost a battle even when he was outnumbered. That's what a good spy cam will do for you.

Along with the desire to conquer, Alexander had a personal quest to find the Fountain of Youth and its secret of immortality, so apparently he came into possession of the magic mirror, but did not have access to those who created the mirror with their Tree of Life and its fruit of immortality.

Alexander believed himself to be semi-divine, possibly the son of Zeus — a god who fathered countless children through both goddesses, and mortal women. The era of Zeus was associated with giants, multiple gods, and immortality, though not for Alexander. Zeus was a sky god, but many Greek cities honored a Zeus who lived underground, similar to when the Tuatha dé Danann went underground toward the end of their reign.

Unfortunately, like the history of the Tuatha dé Danann, much of what was written down about Alexander was destroyed. This allowed the truth to get diluted with legends, and rewritten to better align with the beliefs of those who came later, which is what happened with the Tuatha dé Danann histories as well as the Norse legends. Perhaps the Egyptians were wise beyond their years to inscribe their history and beliefs in stone, where it could not so easily be altered.

For all whose histories were written on paper, or not written at all, our current knowledge is not as pure as for civilizations whose legends were inscribed in stone. Physical planets and islands were redefined as being spiritual, such as the Nine Worlds of the Norse which had its own version of Heaven and Hel (one L), and the Celtic island of Yma which was once believed to be a physical place.

Even the nature of the people involved was redefined, to erase all vestiges of extraterrestrial visitors and turn them into fairy tales, literally. The official history of these people discounts every legend that we can't explain.

Alexander lived from 356-323 B.C., and at various times ruled over Macedonia, Egypt, Persia, and Asia, so he is connected to Persia where King Yima reigned. Allegedly, Alexander inherited his magic mirror from pre-Adamite times, referring to an era that pre-dated Adam and Eve, and the mirror was described as being identical to the magic mirror of King Yima, or possibly even Yima's mirror itself. As Alexander ruled over Persia, he would have had access to artifacts that existed there.

If Alexander's mirror was King Yima's mirror, and King Yima predates Zoroastrianism, then we're deep into the B.C. era. If this same mirror came from pre-Adamite times, it could date back before 5500 B.C., which is one of the more prominent dates calculated for Adam and Eve.

Persian history takes us much farther back in time than Adam and Eve, by way of a race of giants who predated modern man. These giants had 72 successive kings whose names, or titles, were *Suleiman*, which is the Islamic spelling of Solomon. King Solomon of both the *Old Testament* and the *Koran* held power over the Jinn — a rare ability that few humans have ever been able to claim, and which may have come from a ring he wore.

These 72 Suleiman kings, three of which ruled for a thousand years each, also held power over the Jinn by way of a ring. Some believe that King Solomon himself was the last of the mighty Suleiman rulers, which would fit perfectly with the mirror's timeline of ownership.

King Yima also held power over magical beings, and his mirror was described as a "world reflecting mirror" in which he could see all of the events in the world. Yima's mirror was referred to as "Solomon's Mirror" and "Alexander's Mirror," so whatever this magic mirror was, three powerful rulers were linked to it, or identical versions of it, before the time of Christ. If Solomon was the last of the 72 Suleiman kings, and Alexander's pre-Adamite magic mirror came from Solomon, then Solomon would have inherited it from an earlier, pre-Adamite Suleiman.

Another magic mirror belonged to the immortal Emperor Afrāsīāb, the King of Turan who did have access to the secret of immortality, which is expanded in the *Forever Young* chapter. Both Alexander and Afrāsīāb were enemies of the Zoroastrians. Afrāsīāb's magic mirror showed him the universe, and he acquired this mirror from King Yima, though how the mirror came into Afrāsīāb's possession is unclear. So the magic mirror that had been owned by King Solomon and King Yima, also came into the possession of King Afrāsīāb, and later Alexander the Great.

Afrāsīāb may have been one of the giants, as you'll see in the *Enchanted Castles* chapter. By some calculations, Solomon's reign goes back to 950 B.C., and if he was a Suleiman king, he was of the race of giants. King Yima was linked to a great flood just as Noah was, and if it was the same flood, it would have come after Adam and Eve but before Christ. Alexander's reign goes back to 325 B.C.

This gives us six powerful rulers who owned a magic mirror: Prester John; the Norse god Odin; King Solomon who ruled Israel, and Judah; Alexander the Great who ruled Macedonia, Egypt, Persia, and Asia; King Yima and the Zoroastrians in Persia; and King Afrāsīāb who was their rival in Persia.

That's a lot of different people talking about an amazing piece of technology, whose histories spanned several regions of the world and multiple religions. Were all of these legends fictional? Every single one of them? Or is this evidence that magic mirrors, in the form of computers that showed news and maps of the world, existed?

Magic mirrors are explained away as being nothing more than crystal balls or divining goblets, both of which also existed in the Old World, though usually in more recent times. Were crystal balls our ancestor's attempts at mimicking the true magic mirrors brought down by extraterrestrial visitors? Odin was assuredly from another world — Asgard — on the other side of the bifröst wormhole. Alexander believed himself to be fathered by a deity. Prester John's kingdom was located somewhere off-world. As for the others whose origins I'm not familiar with, we know that for awhile the gods walked among men, and shared their technology, so any great king could have had access to the technology of the gods, whether or not he was from their world.

SPEED BOATS

Magic boats which needed no oars and yet zoomed across the water, taking the rider wherever he wanted to go simply by being told to go there — these were more amazements witnessed by our ancestors. One of the boats even traveled up into the air.

Imagine the awe that our ancestors must have felt, watching self-propelled boats in an era where boats were powered with muscles, oars and sails. They described speed boats with built-in navigational computers, but they lacked the terminology that we use today such as *motor* and *GPS system*.

The self-navigating boats driven by the extraterrestrials were so advanced that even today, we haven't achieved their level of technology. GPS systems in cars tell us which direction to turn to get somewhere, but they don't actually take us there yet. However, we do have weapons that lock onto a target and navigate themselves toward it. We've achieved the technology behind the magic mirror, but we're still chasing after the self-navigating speed boats, some of which could also fly. Some even boasted voice recognition and cloaking technology, yet these magic boats existed almost 4,000 years ago!

Several "magic" boats were own by the Tuatha dé Danann — that race of beings whose name pops up with almost every piece advanced technology, and who lived on the hidden island paradise as well as on Earth, traveling back and forth between the two. Their arrival dates back as early as 1500 B.C. and continues to about 400 A.D., after which they went into hiding. The reign of the Tuatha dé Danann was so legendary that we still talked about them centuries after they went on their merry way, or went underground, or were killed off, depending on which version of history you believe.

One of their boats was called Wave Sweeper or Ocean Sweeper, and was owned by Lugh. It was sometimes depicted as just a narrow canoe, or with a narrow stern of copper, but according to *A Textbook of Irish Literature* by Eleanor Hull in 1906, it was a "magic copper boat ... which needed no oar or rudder, but went directly to whatever place its master desired." Even as a canoe it responded to verbal commands.

Another of the Tuatha dé Danann had a magic canoe, this one belonging to Manannán mac Lir as described in *The Gaelic Journal, Volume II* dated 1884.

> "'Accordingly we demand of thee, thou canoe of Manannán, which art under us, to sail with us to the garden of the Hesperides.' And this command was not neglected by the canoe, as was its custom, for it sailed forward in its career upon the tops of the green-sided waves, straight across all abysses, until it reached the harbour and shoreport in the lands of the Hesperides."

In other words, they told it where to go, and under its own power, it went there. The reference to traveling "across all abysses" is interesting. *Abyss* can refer to a vast chasm or gorge, a subterranean (underground or hidden) ocean, the bottom of the sea, a bottomless pit, or anything so vast that it's hard to measure.

Another Tuatha boat reference comes from *Proceedings of the Royal Irish Academy, Irish MSS Series, Volume 1, Part 1*, dated 1870. On page 38, it tells the story of the Irish king known as *Conn of the Hundred Battles*, who reigned toward the end of the 2nd century A.D. Conn was sitting on a hill gazing out over the ocean, grieving over the death of his wife Eithné. Then "he beheld a boat approaching with rapidity, without the agency of any rowers."

When the self-propelled boat landed, its only occupant was a beautiful woman dressed in splendid garments. She came and sat beside Conn as if she knew him. Her name was Bécuma Cneisgel, and she was one of the Tuatha dé Danann. She'd been married to a man named Labraid, but got caught having an adulterous affair with the son of Manannán mac Lir.

After a great assembly, which presumably means a trial, they banished Bécuma from the Land of Promise. They sentenced her "to be sent adrift upon the sea in a self-moving boat" into the human world of their enemies — the Milesians in Ireland.

The Tuatha dé Danann would not have given up this magic boat to an adulterous woman who was being banished, unless they had several such boats. The self-propelled boats of Bécuma, Lugh, and Manannán must have been a standard piece of technology for the Tuatha.

Several accounts of Bécuma's banishment described the boat as a "gleaming, straight-gliding, strong, crystal canoe." This indicates that it was not built of wood, as you'd expect from a canoe. Glass or crystal boats appear in other legends as well, though not in the story of Hiawatha, whose canoe was described as "dazzling white stone" which shined with a supernatural luster.

Hiawatha was a Native American peacemaker who brought several warring tribes together to become the great nation of the Iroquois, possibly as early as 1142 A.D., though like the Tuatha dé Danann, we don't have definitive dates that historians agree on. Hiawatha was known by several names including Tarenyawagon, whose legends give us some of the best descriptions of the boat.

One Tarenyawagon legend is told in *A Critical History of the Doctrine of a Future Life* by William Rounseville Alger, published in 1864. Alger spoke of the Iroquois leader Tarenyawagon who sprang across vast chasms between cliffs, and shot over lakes with incredible speed in a spotless white canoe. Tarenyawagon also possessed supernatural knowledge and power, and was last seen ascending up into the sky in his speedy white canoe, which sounds suspiciously extraterrestrial. Tarenyawagon was called "holder of the heavens" and allegedly *descended from the heavens* to become the demigod or divinity Chief Hiawatha.

His canoe was a "light and magic canoe which shone with a supernatural luster" inside which he performed many extraordinary feats, though details of those feats was a bit sketchy, except for a reference to Hiawatha himself being both a giant and a shape shifter.

The special powers that the dazzling, white, stone canoe possessed included the ability to move without paddles. All Hiawatha had to do was utter a single word, which consisted of one syllable, and the boat would instantly set off toward a destination. This word did not belong to any known language, and it had no definable meaning. He simply willed the canoe to go, with this one word, and off the canoe went. In modern day lingo, he used voice recognition technology.

The magic canoe rushed toward its goal with a speed that would "outstrip the wind." Hundreds of miles were covered in as many minutes, which would translate as a mile a minute, or sixty miles an hour. In addition, he could "leap over extensive regions of the country like an *ignis fatuus*."

The phrase *ignis fatuus* has several meanings including: "something that misleads, an illusion, foolish fire, or a phosphorescent light that hovers or flits over swampy ground at night." In addition to traveling vast distances, speeding across the water, and leaping across the country, his boat either flew, or was lifted, up into the sky.

Hiawatha united several tribes including the Onondaga, Oneida, Seneca, Cayuga, and Mohawk nations into a single Iroquois confederacy. Then he gave a speech explaining that he'd fulfilled his mission, and that he'd been allowed by the Great

Spirit to communicate with them and teach them, but now it was time for him to leave.

As Hiawatha said his final farewell, sweet music filled the air. The entire sky seemed to be filled with celestial music, and everyone's eyes raised upward hoping to catch a glimpse of the source. Hiawatha was seated in his snow white canoe, rising into the air, rising higher with every choral chant that burst out. The higher the canoe rose, the softer the music became, until he vanished into the summer clouds. Thus ended the labors and cares of the long-cherished Hiawatha/Tarenyawagon.

This version was told in the book *Legends, Traditions and Laws of the Iroquois, or Six Nations, and History of the Tuscarora Indians* by Elias Johnson, a Native Tuscarora Chief, published in 1881. Being told by a Tuscarora Chief brings the story closer to the original version, as opposed to a version spun by those who had subjected the Native Americans and didn't understand their beliefs.

Think about how this event unfolded. If the music was loud while Hiawatha's vehicle was on the ground, and then faded as it rose up toward the clouds, that suggests that the music came from the magic canoe itself, like a radio. Hearing music all around you without seeing who is making the music, in itself, was a wonder.

Another odd tale sounds suspiciously like a radio as well, this one from the Norse god Odin, who several earthly kings had honored by making a gold-plated statue in his likeness. Odin was overjoyed by the notoriety that the statue represented, but his queen, Frigga, wanted the gold for her own purposes so she ordered blacksmiths strip the gold from the statue.

Odin was angered at having his statue tampered with, and he had the blacksmiths killed for their part in it. He then mounted the statue on a pedestal, and by the "marvelous skill of his art," Odin made the statue speak when a mortal touched it.

Today we have lamps that turn on and off with a touch, or a clap of the hands, and we have kid's toys that talk when touched or squeezed. We manufacture radios and speakers in all sorts of shapes including cars, boats, cows, dogs, rocks, beer cans, and even Elvis Presley. The only reason that Odin's talking statue was amazing is because humans had not yet invented the technology, but the Tuatha dé Danann, Hiawatha, and Odin had all sorts of technology, including an even more amazing boat.

This magic boat existed in the Norse legends of a ship named *Skidbladnir*, which was owned at various times by the gods Odin and Frey. The attributes of Skidbladnir were so amazing that those who witnessed this marvel believed that incredible skill, cunning, and a "very great magic" must have been used to build her.

Skidbladnir was a huge ship — big enough to carry an entire army across the ocean with all of their weapons and armament. As soon as her sails were set, no matter what the weather or wind, a "favorable breeze would arise and carry her to the place of destination." They never had to worry about the wind, the weather, or the waves — Skidbladnir went wherever they wanted her to go — because "she supplied her own breezes." In addition, she could sail through the air as easily as she could sail on water. That sounds similar to what we call an *Unidentified Submersible Object* or USO, which is a UFO that can travel underwater like a submarine, as well as fly through the air, and which is big enough to hold a fully equipped garrison.

If a vehicle that could travel by water or air wasn't amazing enough, Skidbladnir had an even more incredible attribute. She was made of so many pieces, and with so much skill, that she could be folded together like a napkin and stored in your pocket, which on the surface sounds too far-fetched to believe, but if you look at it like a magician's trick, it becomes fully possible.

Odin and Frey were gods who in themselves were very powerful. Odin was a shape shifter with the ability to travel to faraway lands "in the twinkle of an eye." Just by saying a word, he could put out a fire, calm the sea, or turn the winds in any direction he wished. He was a father god, known as *all father, father of all*, and *father of men*, and he was borne of a giantess.

If you consider the possibility that the magic boats used by Lugh, Manannán, Hiawatha, and Odin were powered with technology from an extraterrestrial race, during an era where we hadn't even coined the word *technology* yet, then take it one step further and add cloaking technology, which we already know that the Tuatha dé Danann possessed. Manannán mac Lir used cloaking technology to hide their island from humans, and that's one of the most prominent legends surrounding this race.

We haven't mastered cloaking technology yet, but obviously the extraterrestrials had it. We do, however, have remote controls for just about everything including vehicles. If you were to combine the concept of a remote control device *that fits in your pocket*, with a cloaking device that could make an object disappear, then you've got the seeds of truth to explain a fantastic tale.

Imagine all eyes on the boat in question, fully expecting the boat to perform this fold-up miracle. Like a magician's trick, all eyes are on the boat, and nobody is looking at the remote control in the magician's hand.

Suddenly, the boat disappears. Then the magician brings your attention to the remote control which he slips into his pocket. Perhaps, just to toy with the disbelief of the natives, meaning our ancestors with their piddly wooden canoes, the magician pulls the remote control back out of his pocket, clicks a button, palms the remote so that it is no longer visible, and the "magic boat" reveals itself by uncloaking. This could easily be interpreted as a boat which folds up small enough to carry in your pocket.

Our kids play with remote control planes and cars, and we have unmanned drones that fly around and perform all sorts of tasks, sometimes directed by a built-in computer, and sometimes through a remote control device. The only missing link is that we haven't yet mastered the cloaking technology.

ENCHANTED CASTLES

Our technological visitors didn't do anything halfway. Along with self-navigating, self-propelled speed boats that could also fly, radios, remote controls, voice recognition, and cloaking technology, they had the ability to see everything that was going on in their kingdom. They watched worldly events unfold on a screen like a modern-day computer from the comfort of a chair, and they lived in amazing palaces and castles.

Some castles rotated as if powered with electricity; other castles hung suspended in the air like a spacecraft; while others were located underwater. Virtually all of them were artificially lighted. These castles or palaces were linked variously to King Afrāsīab, the island of Ogygia, the island of Avalon, Prince Eirek of Drontheim, the Norse god Aegir, and the Tuatha dé Danann.

Afrāsīab, the immortal King of Turan, had several strongholds, including a "metal-encircled" subterranean fortress called Hankana that was immune to mortal attack. Its iron walls were one thousand times the height of a man, and they were supported by a hundred columns. Presumably, Afrāsīab and his family were giants, because in an epic poem his son was described as being so big that ninety fur cloaks of skin could not cover his legs, which would explain the immense size of the fortress and the height of its walls.

The fortress was brilliantly lit by its own sun, moon, and stars, all fashioned by the magic of King Afrāsīab himself. It had no "frost of winter" or "heat of summer." In addition, four rivers ran through Hankana: of water, wine, milk, and beaten sour milk.

King Afrāsīab was linked to King Yima's magic mirror. He either came into possession of the mirror, or one just like it, and there's also a strange link to Prester John's kingdom. Remember the gold digging ants under *Legendary Creatures*, who were actually humans from a tribe in Turan that were now living in Prester John's kingdom? Here we are talking about an actual King of Turan — Afrāsīab. It seems that wherever you find a paradise legend, or a description of advanced technology, the same historical names seem to pop up. Like Prester John's kingdom and all of the other physical paradises, the location of Afrāsīab's Hankana fortress remains a mystery.

This underground fortress was fully lit by its own sun, moon, and stars, which gives us a clue. Skeptics attempt to explain it by comparing Afrāsīab's fortress to the astral dome in the Palace of Ḵosrow Parvēz in Azerbaijan, where they fabricated the sun, moon and stars to imitate heaven. However, this would not explain how an underground fortress was "brilliantly lit" by Afrāsīab's magic, or why it had several rivers flowing through it. Obviously the lighting wasn't something our ancestors recognized, such as torches.

Is it possible that the entrance to Hankana was a portal, and that the fortress itself was located off-world? That would explain the sun, moon, stars, and rivers. Afrāsīab's fortress is reminiscent of the off-world city that King Gylfi traveled to in his quest to talk to the Aesir gods in Asgard — a world which was accessible to ours only by way of a special bridge between worlds. Like Hankana, the walls that Gylfi saw were so high that he could barely see the top, and they were thatched with golden shingles.

Enchanted castles really come into their own when you get to the islands of Ogygia and Avalon. Both were legendary physical paradises that were also inaccessible by standard travel routes, and the two names may have referred to the same island.

Ogygia boasted a palace of glass with transparent walls which floated in the air. Whether the island named Ogygia was connected to the person named Ogygia is another mystery, but the person may have been a prince, a giant, or a god (or perhaps even all three.) If he was a giant, he had something in common with King Afrāsīab.

Avalon also had a glass palace with transparent walls that floated in the air, and the island was ruled by the Lady of the Lake, or possibly the fairy Morgana, who was linked to the Tuatha dé Danann.

Pliny the Elder, who wrote one of the first encyclopedias which we still reference today, died in 79 A.D. He wrote about the world, in which he himself traveled extensively as a military officer. He covered botany, zoology, astronomy, geology, mineralogy, archeology, as well as political and world history.

He also wrote about palaces with glass walls which he called "glassy chambers." In Pliny's day, the Roman Emperor Nero built portions of the Temple of Fortune with a transparent stone called *phengites*, which was semi-transparent and as hard as marble. Even with the doors closed, the temple was as light as if it were daytime, so the concept of ancient glass palaces is possible, and Ogygia and Avalon may well indeed have had them. Today's office buildings with their solid outer walls of glass might have been called "glass palaces" in the days of yore.

The story of Ogier the Dane, whose father reigned as king from 804-810 A.D., clearly stated that the island of Avalon was *not located on Earth*. His trip to Avalon is told in the chapter *Paradise Found*, and it dates one sighting of Avalon and its floating glass castle to the early 800s.

Time flowed differently in Avalon, with two hundred years passing on Earth while just a few hours passed on Avalon, and the fairy Morgana had the ability to make you forget your life on

Earth. It just doesn't get more enchanting than transparent glass castles suspended in the air, located on another world, but still accessible from Earth.

We end up with another confusing link here though, because Ogygia/Avalon is also considered to be one of the Fortunate Isles, aka Celtic Terrestrial Paradise, Isle of the Blessed, Land of the Living, and Yma — the island which St. Brendan and his fellow monks were searching for. We can't be sure that it was the exact same island, because all of the island legends had so many different names for the same place.

The monks could only find the island with the help of a guide, after traveling through a very dark cloud, which is described more fully in the *Paradise Found* chapter. They saw a shiny golden wall of great height with no visible entrance, which shares a trait with both Hankana and the city that King Gylfi visited — all three had walls of great height.

Apparently the monks gained entry, because a magnificent castle was inside the wall, which was lighted with self-luminous stones and adorned with precious jewels. When they left the island, they discovered that an entire year had passed in just fifteen days. This is yet another place whose entrance remains hidden most of the time.

Another reference to "Land of the Living Folk" comes from a Norwegian named Prince Eirek, who traveled to an immortal region, though his was called *Deathless Land* or *Deathless Acre* "by the heathens," and *Land of Living Folk* or *Paradise* "by the Christians." Residents of Deathless Acre remained forever young and healthy, and never died. It's no wonder that so many kings and explorers spent their lifetimes searching for these places. If you lucked into finding it, you were promised rejuvenation and immortality as long as you stayed there.

Like the others who came back to tell us what they saw, Eirek visited but did not stay, nor did he mention giants, though in some legends Deathless Acre was the home of a giant. We don't know where this mystical place was located (fancy that!) but the emperor who gave Eirek directions thought it was important to tell him the distance between Heaven and Earth, which turned out to be less than halfway to the Moon.

Whether this was relevant to the location of Deathless Acre is another mystery, but Eirek did have to enter into what was no less than a portal to get there, and his journey is given in more detail in the *Paradise Found* chapter. Through the portal, he found a region where night never fell, Earth was as bright as the Sun, and half a year slipped by in just a few moments.

Deathless Acre had a tower or steeple suspended in the air, without any support to hold it up. The only entry was a slender ladder leading up into it. Eirek didn't mention whether this floating tower was of transparent glass like in Ogygia and Avalon, but it does demonstrate three different occurrences of castles floating in the air. We can only guess at the science behind these floating buildings, whether it's gravity, technology, or a spacecraft of some sort. In all three stories, however, the clues suggest that they traveled off-world to these enchanted castles.

Not all enchanted castles are floating in the air, or hidden behind walls so tall that you can barely see the top. The Norse giant Aegir, who hosted the party that ran out of liquor and irritated Thor, had an underwater dwelling in addition to living on an island. His home world was Jötunheim, which was one of the Nine Worlds, though no mention is made of a bridge between Earth and Jötunheim like the one to Asgard.

Aegir's underwater palace, rather than being lighted with torches, was lit by the glitter of gold according to Friedrich Kauffmann in *Northern Mythology* published in 1903. Another source claims that "light was shed from shining gold," and yet another stated that "bright gold was brought in and set on the floor, where it illuminated the hall and served as lights at the banquet.

Aegir had many aliases including *Hler*, which translates as *the concealer*, or *the wave which hides many things*. An interesting coincidence is that Manannán mac Lir was also a sea god, sometimes spelled *Ler*, who had quite a reputation as a concealer, hiding entire islands inside his cloaking mist.

Manannán mac Lir and his brethren bring us two revolving castle stories. The first was the stronghold of Midir who was one of the Tuatha dé Danann. His castle was located on the island of Falga. This island is another of those mythical islands that nobody is quite sure where it was, but it's now believed to be the Isle of Man which had been home to, hidden by, and named after Manannán mac Lir.

There's an interesting story regarding the birth of the Tuatha dé Danann who attacked Midir's revolving castle. A group of nobles were hunting a flock of magical birds when it began to snow. They were given shelter at a house, and the hostess went into labor that night and produced a baby boy. At the same time, a horse went into labor and gave birth to two colts.

When the nobles woke up the next morning, the entire house and its occupants had completely vanished, and all that remained were the two colts and the baby boy, who later came to be known as Cúchulainn, though at birth he was named Sétanta.

As a young man, Cúchulainn attacked Midir's revolving castle and stole several items, including a cauldron of plenty, which some believe was the Holy Grail. This cauldron was bottomless — it left no man unsatisfied — and it originally belonged to the Land Beneath the Waves. That gives us another odd coincidence, as the Norse giant Aegir lived beneath the waves and coveted a mile-deep cauldron.

Cúchulainn's era is linked to his foster-son, Lugaid Riab nDerg, who ruled as high king of Ireland somewhere between 33 B.C. and 54 A.D., which dates the rotating castle to 1,000 years before the existing Peel Castle was built on the Isle of Man. So if the revolving castle was located on the Isle of Man as some believe, it is now long gone and a more human castle has been erected in its place.

Cúchulainn caused quite a bit of trouble along the way. He had an affair with Manannán mac Lir's wife Fand, and he coveted Midir's daughter. He attacked Midir's castle with the help of his friend Cúroí, who had been promised his choice of the spoils. Unfortunately for Cúchulainn, his so-called friend chose Midir's daughter Blathnát as part of the spoils, even though she was in love with Cúchulainn.

The attack on Midir's castle only tells us that it was a revolving castle, but Cúroí's castle story gives us more detail, and if he's involved with Midir's daughter, it's possible that the two castles were one in the same. Cúroí lived in a revolving castle according to *The Mythology of All Races* edited by Louis Herbert Gray, Ph.D., and published in 1918.

> "In whatever part of the world Cúroí was, he sang a spell over the castle at night, and it revolved as swiftly as a millstone, so that the entrance could not be found." A different book adds that the entrance could never be found after sunset.

Midir and Manannán were cousins, and Manannán was the first ruler of the Isle of Man. If the island of Falga really was the Isle of Man as some historians believe, then Midir's castle may well have been Manannán's previously. If so, then Midir's rotating castle may have been the same as the "mysterious palace" that Manannán lived in, on an island out of reach of ordinary navigators, which indicates another off-world location. These legends get all mixed up together, and no name ever stands alone, because Falga is another name for both the Otherworld, and the Land of Promise, according to several texts including *Irish Texts Society, Volume II*, edited by George Henderson in 1899, as transcribed from an earlier source.

In the 1891 book, *The Folk-Lore of the Isle of Man*, by A.W. Moore, Falga was "variously supposed to have been the Isle of Man, or *Insi Gall, i.e.*, the Western Isles." Insi Gall usually refers to the Outer Hebrides islands, though it can also translate as "islands of the foreigners" or "strangers."

Logic would dictate that Cúroí was living in Midir's revolving castle, if he were dallying with Midir's daughter. However, on the opposite side of Ireland from the Isle of Man is the Dingle Peninsula, and local legends claim this to be the location of Cúroí's revolving castle, where he brought Midir's kidnapped daughter. If the latter is true, that gives us two revolving castles during the same era — which is roughly around the time of Christ.

OTHER WONDERS

It's easy to look at the more prominent wonders such as speed boats, computers, cloaking technology, castles in the air, or revolving castles, but sometimes the details are in the little things. Trees which produced every manner of fruit existed, with both winter and summer fruits on the same tree, or with fruit and flowers on the same branch.

There's a scientific explanation and it's called *grafting*, which allows you to grow a single tree in your suburban back yard that produces several types of fruit.

Multi-fruit trees go by names such as *fruit salad tree* or *stone fruit tree*. The citrus version produces lemons, limes, oranges, mandarins, tangelos, grapefruit, and lemonade fruit. The stone fruit tree gives you peaches, apricots, nectarines, peachcots, and plums. A master gardener could add almonds to a stone fruit tree, as almonds are compatible with peaches and plums and can be grafted together. A *stop light* or *traffic light tree* offers red, yellow, and green apples on the same tree, so named for matching the colors of a traffic light.

The science of grafting is how they make dwarf varieties of trees for smaller back yards. Arborists graft a dwarf tree onto the root stock of a local tree, which gives it hardy local roots without growing as big as the original tree.

If our technological visitors were limited to a single island, city, ship, or whatever it was they lived on, they would undoubtedly have grown grafted trees for themselves to best utilize the limited space. There wasn't anything mystical, mythical, or magical about it — this is common science for us today. Our distant ancestors were awed to encounter advanced technology and trees that grew different kinds of fruit. If you could go back in time and pluck a handful of people from the ancient world, and allow them to visit a common household today, and then send them back to tell the story, you'd end up with the same mythology.

If we loaded our technology onto an intergalactic spaceship, and happened to land on a world whose people were in the early stages of development, their mythology would sound just like ours. If we were to set up an outpost there, and attempt to limit how many natives had access to the outpost, the end result would be the same. There'd always be a few who'd "see" our magical outpost and spread the story. Word travels fast — especially news of the fantastic.

In the *Forever Young* chapter, you'll read about one of the Tuatha dé Danann receiving a fully-functional, life-like, prosthetic arm — 3,000 years before we developed this technology. Humans invented the radio in the late 1800s, and yet both Hiawatha and Odin had access to radio-like devices — Hiawatha in the 1100s and Odin prior to 369 A.D.

FOREVER YOUNG

Magic boats and fantastic creatures were more of a sideshow in the paradise legends. One of the biggest draws was the hope of finding eternal youth and immortality in the rejuvenating waters. Our ancestors believed in the existence of a Fountain of Youth, and it wasn't just some backwoods peasant chasing after this legend — great kings and some of our most renowned explorers searched for it, even in the centuries before Christ, such as Alexander III of Macedon — aka "the Great."

The stories that surrounded Alexander the Great, which are now collectively called the Alexander Romance, spoke about mystical waters of rejuvenation which Alexander referred to as the *Water of Life*. Alexander lived from 356-323 B.C. and he searched extensively for this water of life. Along the way he became King of Macedonia, King of Persia, King of Asia, as well as Pharaoh of Egypt — an amazing accomplishment for a man who lived only 33 years, which indicates that he did not find the water of life.

Almost 2,000 years later, and halfway around the world, we were still searching for this mystical fountain, especially after the Spanish conquests of the New World. Ponce de León had sailed under Christopher Columbus all around the Caribbean Sea, which led to his becoming governor of Puerto Rico.

Unfortunately for Ponce, the son of Columbus waged a legal battle over the rights to inherit the titles and privileges which had been granted to his father, and Puerto Rico was taken away from Ponce and handed over to Diego Colón in 1511.

In the meantime, Ponce had gotten fired up over stories told by the Arawaks in Hispaniola, Cuba, and Puerto Rico, who spoke of an island that was variously written down as Beimeni, Beniny, Mimini, or Bimini. This island was rich in gold, and it supplied healing waters which restored the youth, and renewed the vigor of any aged person who drank from, or bathed in it. Apparently the Arawaks had been searching for it, too, and they referred to it as the *Fountain of Life* or *River of Life*.

These stories fueled a massive search for the Fountain of Youth throughout the Caribbean and Florida. According to *Records of the American Catholic Historical Society of Philadelphia, Volume XXIII* published in 1912, Juan Ponce de León (who was a Roman Catholic) was issued "royal patents" to discover and colonize the Islands of Beniny. His explorations stayed north of Cuba.

In 1508, a similar search existed for an island called Boyuca, Boinca, or Aganeo, which was celebrated for a spring whose waters made old men young again. Boyuca was somewhere in the Gulf of Honduras — a portion of the Caribbean Sea southwest of Cuba — far from where Ponce had sailed. This expedition was also funded by the Spanish crown.

Juan Díaz de Solís searched for Boyuca, which was located "beyond Veragua" where the coast bends northward, opposite the *Pillars of Hercules* natural rock formation on the island of Antigua. Veragua encompassed portions of what is now Nicaragua, Costa Rica, and Panama.

Their explorations continued down the east coast of South America until they came to a major estuary. Solís and his crew sailed into this gulf where rivers come together and meet the ocean, and it sparkled with mica crystals floating on the water. For this it was named *Rio de la Plata*, or River of Silver.

Crowded along the riverbanks were the Charruas natives greeting them with signs of joy and friendship, holding up offers of meat, fruit and vegetables in welcome. Solís was suspicious and did not immediately disembark. The Charruas left the gifts of friendship on the beach and retired out of sight. Bolstered by the signs of goodwill, Solís and a few of his men left the ship.

He should have listened to his inner voice because suddenly, from a small grove of trees, there erupted a frenzy of natives in an unexpected attack. The carnage was described in horrifying detail: "... de Solís and several of his crew were slain by the natives, who, in sight of the ships, cut their bodies in pieces, roasted, and devoured them." Terrified by the shocking spectacle, the survivors who'd remained on board quickly sailed to the Cape of St. Augustine, loaded up with Brazil wood, and made a beeline for Europe without exploring any further.

Unfortunately, Solís and his crew had not found the long life that they were searching for. The survivors arrived in Spain to tell the sordid tale but it did not hinder further exploration, and other stories filtered out of the region that "a man had to have a strong stomach to hear." Perhaps the natives were reacting to tales of European takeovers and hoped to repel the invasion by way of these atrocities.

The last journey of Solís was chronicled in several books including *American Annals: Or, A Chronological History of America, Volume 1*, by Abiel Holmes in 1813; *A voyage to South America, Volume 2*, by Antonio de Ulloa and Jorge Juan in 1758; and *The Paraná: With Incidents of the Paraguayan War, and South American Recollections, from 1861 to 68*, by Thomas J. Hutchinson in 1868.

Stories of cannibalistic tribes and trickery did not stem the flow of European explorers who were determined to find gold, silver, and the Fountain of Youth. Peter Chieza in his *History of Peru* mentioned a *Miracle Fountain* at Lucaya in America, which washed away all the marks of old age. The Lucayans were the original inhabitants of the Bahamas, which set off another round of legends marking possible locations. Allegedly, a Lucayan man who was "broken by age" was rejuvenated when he bathed in, and drank from this miracle water, after which he appeared young and fresh, went on to marry and have children.

These legends spread when the explorers pulled into the Spanish ports and gave detailed accounts of what they'd seen and heard to chroniclers such as Peter Martyr d'Anghiera, who wrote it all down. Martyr published the sailors' reports in a series of dispatches called *Decades of the New World*.

Miracle water was being reported all around the world, sometimes by esteemed members of society such as the physician of Cardinal Ascanio Colonna who later became Pope Sixtus V. Coming from the upper echelons of the church gave the story credibility. Colonna's physician, Andreas Baccius, spoke of the Greek island Euboea where you could find a fountain that changed old age into youth.

Any miracle of rejuvenation fueled the human spirit to find these fountains, even if fountains weren't given credit. The Abbess at Morvedre in Spain was granted such a miracle. She had been a wrinkled, decrepit, withered old woman whose back was bowed with age. The change was so amazing that they stopped calling her Reverend Mother, and instead referred to her as *Dear Sister* for transforming into the body of a young novice.

Her wrinkles became dimples, yellowed teeth now gleamed brilliantly white, and her hair grew back full and without a strand of gray. Her previously bent body stood up straight and strong, and even her breasts took on the shape and lift of youth, being described as "budding breasts." The story of this miracle was shared by Valasco Tarentazzio.

Another Fountain of Youth called *Canathus* was located in Morea in southern Greece, near the ruins of Nauplion. Once a year, the goddess Juno bathed in Canathus to restore the ravages that time had left on her. A later reference to this fountain, which referred to it as the *Fountain of Canathe*, claimed that the water had lost all of its virtues, "if it ever had any." This is one of the few fountains whose location was known, and apparently the miracle water could get used up. Juno's yearly rejuvenation bath demonstrates that the effects were not permanent. It simply set your clock back to an earlier time, but it did not stop the clock from ticking.

Prester John had "supernatural longevity" and the residents of his kingdom lived for hundreds of years, by regularly drinking from a spring that reset their bodies back to an age of thirty. John's kingdom was considered both celestial and immortal.

All of these stories, such as Juno's fountain losing its potency, in addition to the advanced technology demonstrated by the extraterrestrials, combine to formulate a Fountain of Youth theory that fits everything that we know, especially with the following description where the water is "different."

The Greek historian Herodotus, known as the *Father of History*, lived from 484-425 B.C., and he believed that the Fountain of Youth was located in Macrobia (which means Land of Longevity) in the Horn of Africa. The Macrobians were the tallest and handsomest of men, standing a full head taller than the Persians, and their lifespans were counted in centuries rather than decades. They lived exceptionally long lives in a state of blissful tranquility, and when they died, they mummified their dead and encapsulated the bodies in hollow crystal pillars.

Herodotus described their magic fountain, further supporting the theory that I'm going to put forth. After you bathed in the fountain, your skin became shiny as if anointed with oil, and your whole body smelled of violets. The water in this fountain was so "insubstantial in nature" that nothing would float on its surface, not even a piece of light wood, which would immediately sink to the bottom. The historian Pliny stated that the *shortest* Macrobian lifespan was 130 years, barring accident or injury.

Of all the quests that humans have undertaken, none were more sought after than the elusive Fountain of Youth and the paradises that surrounded it. Combine the notion of miracle water with the belief that supernatural, immortal beings once lived among us, and you've solved the centuries old mystery.

Speed boats, radios, electricity, computers, and prosthetic limbs are pretty easy to decipher, but how do you explain youth and immortality in a way that satisfies all of the facts and legends? The first clue is that it was provided through both water and food — particularly fruit.

One such fruit came from the *gaokerena* tree, and eating this fruit promised health, immortality, and could even resurrect the dead. A similar tree grew in Yima's kingdom called the *haoma* tree, which was described as the "source of life" around which all healing plants grew, and whose juice would resurrect the dead. King Yima ruled happily for nine hundred years, demonstrating the power of the tree. Under the alternate spelling of *homa*, there was an ancient dynasty of Pishdadian kings who lived on pure homa, or *Water of Life*. The Pishdadian kings were men of law and justice, and Yima was one of these esteemed rulers under his alternate name of Jamshid.

In an article written by Dieter Taillieu entitled *Haoma Plant*, the Avestan haoma is linked to the Vedic sauma/soma, which is a beverage mentioned in the sacred *Rigveda* text of the Hindus: "We have drunk soma and become immortal." Like the Fountain of Youth, the actual location of soma has become lost to us, and today's soma plants are substitutes for the legendary original. The original soma of immortality came from a plant which grew on the banks of a body of water called Sharyanavat, whose location was a mystery like the Fountain of Youth, and which was described as "bright shining" and "green tinted."

Fruit was another life-giving substance. The youth and longevity of the Norse Aesir gods was linked to eating the apples of immortality that were kept safe by the goddess Idunn. At one point, Idunn was kidnapped by giants, who were the archenemies of the Aesir, and Idunn's absence caused the Aesir gods to grow old and gray. They carried out a rescue mission, and their youth was once again restored by eating Idunn's apples. Losing their apples of youth was a dangerous moment in human history, as it could have upset the balance of power on the Nine Worlds. The Aesir gods protect Earth from destructive giants, and if the Aesir fall, so do humans.

Food and drink also gave immortality to the Tuatha dé Danann, through drinking Goibniu's immortal beer or eating from his banquet. The secret ingredients that went into the victuals that he cooked up protected the Tuatha from sickness, pain, and old age.

Juno's fountain, Prester John's fountain, Idunn's apples, and Goibniu's secret ingredient that could be added to food or drink, all demonstrate that the immortal gods weren't actually immortal, but only seemed that way by a process of rejuvenation that wasn't permanent. In addition, they were not immune to injury, and their rejuvenation apparently had limits, which brings us to the amazing story of the prosthetic arm.

The first of the Tuatha dé Danann to rule over Ireland was Nuada, whose rule ended in either 1897 B.C. or 1477 B.C. depending on the source, and for the sake of comparison we'll round it to 1500 B.C. The Tuatha's reign in Ireland did not begin peacefully, as they displaced an existing group of people known as the Fir Bolg in a series of battles.

In the heat of battle, Nuada's right forearm was completely severed, and because of this he lost his kingship. Apparently the Tuatha dé Danann had a law that a king must be physically perfect, so Nuada was forced to step down. Kingship was handed over to Bres, who was half-Tuatha and half-Fomorian, which was another race of gods in the region.

The Tuatha physician Dian Cecht crafted a custom-made silver prosthetic, complete with movable joints which were as flexible and dexterous as a real forearm. This wasn't some old wooden peg leg or pirate hook — this was a fully functional prosthetic arm. You'd expect Nuada to be delighted with the replacement, but he wasn't. The prosthetic irritated him at the point of attachment, which led to an even more miraculous repair. Dian's son Miach converted the prosthesis into a flesh-and-blood arm, though the details are a bit fuzzy. Either he caused flesh to grow over the silver prosthesis, or he reattached the original severed forearm, depending on which version of history you are reading. By whatever means this deed was accomplished, functional prosthetic arms did not come into existence for humans until 1500 A.D. — a full 3,000 years after Nuada's reign!

This wasn't some form of hocus pocus magic — it was advanced medical technology being put to use by a race of beings that flew into Ireland from the sky, according to eyewitness accounts of their arrival, and who demonstrated medical technology 3,000 years more advanced than our own.

Once these Otherworlders were settled in, Dian "blessed" a particular well, and gave it such healing powers that it would cure any wound except decapitation. In addition, the Tuatha dé Danann possessed a drink that would heal almost any wound or cure any disease. Their good health, youthfulness, and immortality were attributed to these foods and drinks.

The Norse gods and the Tuatha dé Danann were not alone in these legends of health and longevity that were linked to foods, beverages, and modern medicine. Remember the immortal Afrāsīab, the king of Turan, and his underground fortress Hankana with its own sun, moon, and stars?

Various histories put Afrāsīab's longevity at either 400 years or 2,000 years, showing that he wasn't actually immortal but simply long-lived. In spite of the strength of his kingdom, the sheer height of his iron walls, and his own magical abilities, he was captured by a priest named Haoma (like the tree) and *stripped of his immortality* by the god Ahura Mazda. Once Afrāsīab's immortality was taken away, he was killed. This priest Haoma also played a part in the birth of King Yima, further connecting the various entities of ancient Earth.

Afrāsīab being stripped of his immortality is one of the most telling clues of all, indicating that immortality could be taken away. If you had to ingest specific foods or water in order to rejuvenate, and you were prevented from partaking of these substances, it would explain every single story and lay the foundation for what happened to the various Fountains of Youth.

A more recent, and very human mystery would also find a perfect comparison to Afrāsīab. Thomas Parr was born in Shropshire, England in 1483, and married his first wife Jane Taylor when he was 82 years old. Twenty years later, he had an illegitimate affair with Catharine Milton which produced a child. Then, at the age of 120, he married Jane Lloyd.

He became known as *Old Parr* or *Old Tom Parr* and as the legend of his age spread, the Earl of Arundel decided to pay him a visit. Old Tom Parr had become a national celebrity for his advanced age, and the earl wanted to present Tom to King Charles I. By this time, Old Tom Parr was 152 years old, and the visit from the Earl of Arundel led to his unexpected demise. They traveled to London to meet the king, where Old Tom died a few weeks later in the year 1635, without ever making it back home.

An autopsy was done and all of his internal organs were in perfect condition, with no apparent cause of death. The only explanation that the coroner could offer was that the change in diet, along with pollution from the city, did him in.

Today's physicians who've studied the autopsy report have a different theory, demonstrating their disbelief that he really was 152 years old. They believe that Tom Parr's age, along with all of the other historical accounts of extreme longevity, are just plain false, especially considering the pristine state that his internal organs were found in. The skeptical explanation is that he had a grandfather named Thomas born in 1483, and that their histories just got mixed up. There's a flaw in the skeptical theory, however.

This other Parr — Sir Thomas Parr whose daughter married King Henry VIII, and whose family tree boasted several barons and earls — doesn't appear to link to Old Tom Parr.

Old Tom's father is listed as John Parr of Winnington, in the Parish of Alberbury. His alleged grandfather, Sir Thomas Parr, lived a charmed life, with his mother and grandmother being ladies-in-waiting. Sir Thomas was brought up in the English court. Theirs was a titled family of landowners and knights who rubbed elbows with kings and queens.

Sir Thomas Parr had three children who made it to adulthood — Anne, William, and Catherine. Anne had three children, none of which were named John, so Old Tom's father couldn't have been one of hers.

William must have been infertile, because he married three times without producing kids. He did have an affair, however, and his mistress had children, though not by him. Even if they'd been his, none were named John.

Sir Thomas' daughter Catherine became the queen of England through her marriage to Henry VIII. She boasted four husbands but only one child, a girl. She did have a stepson John through her marriage to John Nevill, the 3rd Baron of Latimer. This John had a rocky road all through his life, and was excluded from his father's will. He took up a sword and went into battle, and was knighted in Scotland, and fought in France. He later landed himself in Fleet Prison for assaulting a servant. He was also arrested for rape and assault, and separately for murder. This John's children were all daughters.

Thus there is no link between Sir Thomas Parr, and Old Tom Parr, for one to be the other's grandfather. They did not hail from the same region of England, and even their lifestyles were so radically different that it's obvious they were not of the same family. Every family member connected to Sir Thomas lived in luxury, and if they didn't personally hold a title, they rubbed elbows with people who did. They were the upper echelon of society, so if Sir Thomas had been Old Parr's grandfather, then Old Parr's aunt would have been the queen of England.

Does this sound like the family of a man who lived on rancid cheese, sour whey, milk in every form, and coarse, hard bread? Old Tom's lifestyle was poor, and he lived on "sorry fare." His age was not a case of mistaken identity.

So what if his age was true? What if Old Tom Parr really did live to be 152 years old as everyone in his time believed, and then suddenly dropped dead for no reason when he traveled to London? Is it possible that something on his home turf, something that he was eating or drinking or coming into contact with, kept his body young inside? Like the story of Afrāsīāb who was stripped of his immortality and then killed, and the Tuatha dé Danann and Norse gods whose longevity was linked to food or drink, did Old Tom require something to stay alive that got left behind during that fateful trip?

If there was a fountain, water well, or fruit that kept him young, you'd have to wonder why his family and neighbors weren't also living long, healthy lives. Along with Old Tom's pitiful diet of milk, stale bread, and rancid cheese, he drank *metheglin*, which is a variety of honey mead made with herbs and spices.

Remember King Yima's tree around which all healing plants grew, and whose juice could resurrect the dead? And the Hindu soma of immortality which may have come from a plant that grew along the banks of a body of water? Is it possible that Old Tom's spiced honey mead was made with an herb that was nourished by water leftover from a bygone era of immortality?

It's easy to question one account of longevity, or even two or three, but what about dozens? In olden times, humans were reputed to live for hundreds of years. According to the *Bible*, one man lived to be 969 years old and perished one week before Noah's great flood. His name was Methuselah and he was Noah's grandfather. Other notable lifespans were Noah at 950, Adam at 930, Eve at 940, and more recently three women.

In New Jersey, Anne Feinseth was listed in the Social Security death index at 195 years old in 2004; in California, Elizabeth M. Mahony's death certificate listed her at 191 years old; and in France, Jeanne Calmet was listed as the longest confirmed lifespan at 122. Were all of these "mistakes" like Old Tom Parr?

Prior to Noah's flood, people were commonly listed in the *Bible* as living for hundreds of years such as Jared at 962, Seth at 912, Mahalaleel at 895, and Lamech at 777. Then came the flood, and our lifespans started to dwindle: Shem-600, Salah-433, Peleg-239, Serug-230, Terah-205, Isaac-180, Jacob-147, and even Moses only made it to 120 years old.

Longevity was not limited to biblical figures, however, and a number of other names were also blessed with extraordinarily long lives. King Arganthonius of Tartessus, Spain lived either 120 years according to Pliny, 150 per Anacreon, or 300 years per Italicus. Emperor Zhong Ding of China ruled for 300 years, and Emperor Xinung for 140.

Thomas Carn, according to the parish register of St. Leonard in Shoreditch, died in 1588 at the age of 207. Don John Taveira de Lima died in Portugal in 1738 at the age of 198. Gillour Maccraine is listed in the Code of Health for the Isle of Jura at 190 years old at the time of his death.

Petratsch Zortan died in 1724 at 185, and is listed in a Dutch dictionary, though he was Hungarian. Petratsch was nearly blind, had lost most of his teeth, and his hair and beard had taken on a greenish tinge like moldy bread. Like Old Tom Parr, he ate little more than milk and cakes with an occasional brandy.

John Baldeck, the Abbot of Kilchberg in Switzerland, died at 185. In his old age, his gray hair turned black again, his teeth fell out and he grew new teeth.

Janos Roven and his wife Sarah, both of Stradova, Hungary were married 147 years. He died at 172 and she at 164. Johannes de Temporibus, who served under King Charlemagne as a warrior, lived to be 361 years old.

Epimenides, a Cretan born in 659 B.C., had a supernatural longevity. While tending his father's sheep, he fell asleep in a cave and slept for 57 years. He'd fallen asleep as a young man, but woke up an old man with long, gray hair, and a flowing beard, and of course, the sheep were long gone.

He immediately went home but his father was long dead, the house belonged to someone else, and his brother, who'd been a child, was now an adult man. His younger brother recognized him and filled him in on the last 57 years.

Everything was so changed. The town was full of houses and people he'd never seen before. More astonishing than his supernatural sleep, was what he'd learned while sleeping.

Epimenides woke up with a head full of knowledge of medicine and natural history "which appeared more than human." He'd also been gifted with the art of prophecy, and could send his soul out of his body at will.

Of course there was a lot of skepticism about his wild story, though one person noted that "the average commentator was unable to conceive of a prophet not of the Hebrews." His point was that what is acceptable under the umbrella of a religion — any religion — is otherwise beyond belief, though it shouldn't be. Either we believe in the incredible (such as extraterrestrials riding around in motorboats,) or we don't.

If you think about Epimenides falling asleep in a cave for 57 years, and then waking up in good health except for the part about getting old, this is no different than visiting paradise for a day while a hundred years pass, except that he woke up with no memory of where he'd been.

The next piece of his story, however, gives a strong indication that he'd been to the Otherworld, because not only did he become friendly with the gods, *the only food he ate* thereafter was provided by the nymphs, though we don't know which species. An odd coincidence is that there is a class of nymph called Epimelides, which is very similar to his own name, who are the protectors of apple trees, talk about shades of the Norse goddess Idunn! The ancient Greek word for "apple" also means *sheep*, which is another coincidence since that's what he was doing just before he fell asleep — tending his father's sheep. Thus these Epimelides nymphs that may have provided him with their special food after he emerged from the cave, would have been the protectors of both apple trees, and sheep.

As for the wise Epimenides who emerged from the cave, he became a prolific author with his newfound wisdom, and was quoted in the biblical *New Testament*, as well as by Aristotle and Plutarch. Various accounts of his age at death include 154, 157, 175, 197, 199, or 299. These are the discrepancies you get when you don't have an official death certificate.

So are all of the stories of longevity simply tall tales? Ordinary men, biblical patriarchs, kings and emperors, abbots, philosophers, and other notables? One or two legends might be boasting, but a whole history full of lifespans far in excess of our own demonstrates that we had it, and we lost it.

We have stories of humans, and supernatural beings, whose youth and immortality were linked to something that could be taken away — such as food or water. Then we have trees of rejuvenation, where even the plants that grow around the trees have special healing qualities. Finally, there's the water well that the Tuatha dé Danann physician Dian "blessed" so that it would cure any wound except decapitation. This last clue exposes the secret of health and immortality. We had all the clues, we just weren't putting them together.

What if extraterrestrial visitors came, and brought some sort of healing/rejuvenating medicine with them, which they treated the water with? Because these visitors walked among us, lived among us, and interacted with us, the treated water was everywhere. They probably didn't treat it for our benefit, but their own. If the medicinal water also nourished plants and trees, wouldn't those plants and trees take on healing properties as well, giving us gaokerena, haoma, and soma? It's a well known fact that plants can make us sick if they absorb toxic chemicals, so why wouldn't the reverse be true?

Treated water would eventually get used up, and if not "re-blessed" with more of this extraterrestrial elixir, then one by one all of the healing waters would lose their potency, just like the Fountain of Canathe. This would explain how the Fountain of Youth stayed just out of reach, and why we lived for 900 years, and then 800, and 700, and on down the line to our current, rather short lifespans. The medicinal water got used up.

These visitors did not leave all at once. They disappeared from our world gradually, just as the length of our lives diminished gradually. It sounds pretty dismal, losing hope that somewhere there exists a magical body of water that restores youth. However, there is scientific evidence that the Fountain of Youth was simply modern medicine, and we're on track to unlock the secrets.

We know that our bodies should rejuvenate without any miracle water. When we're young, our bodies replace worn out cells, but then they stop. We've figured out that our chromosomes have what's called a *telomere*, and this telomere is linked to aging.

Telomeres are a fixed length when we're born, and every time their cells divide, the telomeres get a little bit shorter. When they get too short, the cell stops dividing. This process has been described more simply as a time bomb with a fuse, with our lives starting with a full fuse, and shortening as the fuse gets smaller until we go BOOM and die.

An enzyme called *telomerase* can lengthen the fuse, and in theory, if we could figure out how to "immortalize" human cells with telomerase, we could cure all sorts of diseases and extend our lives. Geneticist Richard Cawthon suggests that if we could halt the process of aging and repair the oxidative damage, we could conceivably live to be 1,000 years old again.

Another medical breakthrough involves stem cell therapy, which theoretically can be used to repair damaged organs. If we could lengthen our telomeres, and repair existing damage with stem cell therapy, the result sounds a lot like the "blessed" water of the Tuatha dé Danann that could cure almost anything.

In 2003, Korean researchers treated a woman with a severe spinal cord injury who hadn't been able to stand up for 19 years, even with a walker. After stem cell treatments and physical therapy, she was able to walk with a walker. An MRI showed that the spinal cord had regenerated at the injury site.

Corneal stem cells have been used to restore vision, and all around the world we're either studying, or utilizing, stem cell therapy on everything from diabetes to Parkinson's disease to arthritis. We're even working on technology that will allow us to regrow missing teeth, by coaxing stem cells into a tooth bud that can be implanted into the gums, which grows into a new tooth. We're farther along with stem cells than with telomeres, and we're still a long way from the magical rejuvenation that the Otherworlders brought with them.

Sooner or later we will unlock the secrets, and perhaps we, too, will someday manufacture a substance that you simply pour into water that will heal and rejuvenate anyone who comes into contact with it.

Magic Marvels

Science and technology can explain speed boats, rotating castles, spy screens, disembodied voices or music, prosthetic limbs, and rejuvenation, but how do you explain the other magic?

These beings could control the weather, raise the dead, move objects through the air, become invisible, and shape shift. They had unusual cloth or skins that could stretch to gigantic dimensions when needed, and food that never diminished. Surely these marvels are beyond belief, right? Would you believe it if I told you that humans have been credited with the same marvels?

We actually have a word that denotes these magic marvels — *thaumaturgy* — and it is defined as "miracle work, marvels, the capability of a magician or saint to work magic or miracles, or wonderworker."

While there are examples all through history, you don't find many that aren't attributed to Christian saints or other religious figures, and there's an explanation for the oversight. If a miracle is performed by a member of a church, it's accepted. If the same miracle comes from someone outside the church, it's called the work of the devil. The latter gets all mixed up with allegations of witchcraft, and it calls up shades of the Salem witch trials. The witch hunts opened the door for people to accuse anyone they didn't like of nefarious magic. Once a finger pointed at you, that was it, you were toast, literally. Even a medical problem such as lazy eye (evil eye) or Turret's Syndrome (demonic possession) made you a target. Because of the high volume of false accusations, examples won't be taken from the Salem witch stories. Most of what follows is limited to Christian saints who lived centuries after the Apostles. As the saints were humans who performed amazing works that we don't generally hear about, they make excellent human examples to demonstrate that the powers of the supernatural visitors were not only possible, but could be achieved by humans as well.

Healing, and raising the dead:

Through special water, fruit, or trees, several of the supernatural races could bring someone back from the dead, or heal almost any injury. The Norse gods, the Tuatha dé Danann, King Yima, Prester John, and Afrāsīāb all had access to substances that would rejuvenate and even resurrect them. Beyond the science of stem cells and lengthening our telomeres, what about the human factor of healing sickness and injury, or raising the dead?

To name just a few of the many saints who also performed such miracles — St. Brigid, St. Columba, St. Gerard Majella, St. Patrick, and a host of others restored sight to the blind and *raised the dead* — and you can't explain it away by saying that maybe the dead weren't really all the way dead.

These stories are going to sound pretty incredible, as in "you really expect me to believe *this*?" If you don't believe it, you might as well call all the saints liars, as well as the Popes who canonized them. What you really need to look at, is what they had to do in order to earn the title of *saint* in the first place, and liars didn't qualify. What's more, the body of a saint was incredibly valuable, and you don't fight over the ownership of just any old dead body.

The lives of the saints were full of marvels, but their relics were also powerful. Holy relics from the body of a deceased saint who had performed miracles was a powerful draw. Their bodies were so valuable that great lengths were taken to protect the bodies from theft. At the Cistercian Abbey of Fossanova, they removed the head of St. Thomas Aquinas, so that if his body were later stolen, they'd still have his head.

The skull of St. Ivo of Kermartin is displayed at Tréguier's cathedral in France. The body of Buddha was divided up and divvied out, and his tooth is in a temple in Sri Lanka which is appropriately known as *The Temple of the Tooth*. Your life had to be pretty miraculous for your body to be treated as a holy relic. So what stories surrounded the saints?

St. Patrick raised countless people from the dead, including someone who'd been dead for 27 years. On one occasion, St. Patrick performed 33 resurrections at one time. St. Columba resurrected several people who'd been dead, including Conla, an artisan who'd been burned to ashes many years earlier. Considering that some of these people had been dead for years and even cremated, a resurrection really was a resurrection, and not just someone who appeared to be dead but wasn't quite there yet. How is this even possible? It goes way beyond an easy technological answer. Allegedly our ancient alien visitors had the power, and so did our holy men and saints.

Healings were another miracle. Several monks were chopping wood in a forest, and a priest named Winnoc was watching with amazement at the ease in which their tools sliced into the trunk of an oak tree. Suddenly, a chunk of wood came flying out at him and sliced his forehead down to the bone. Waves of blood gushed out of his veins. St. Columban, who was standing nearby, fell to the ground and prayed. Then Columban got up, and *healed the wound with his saliva*, closing it up leaving barely a scar. One minute Winnoc had a gaping wound with exposed bone gushing blood, and the next minute the wound was completely healed over with hardly a mark of evidence. We attribute such miracles to Jesus and his Apostles, but we never hear the thousands of stories that came down through the centuries of the saints who also performed these miracles. St. Columban may have been the same person as St. Columbanus of the beer keg stories.

Food that never runs out:

You wouldn't think that raising the dead could be outdone, as far as miracles go, but you'd be wrong. The Tuatha dé Danann had seven white cows which could provide milk for the entire world, and a cauldron which never went empty until every man had eaten his fill. This cauldron held exactly what was needed to satisfy every guest — no more, and no less — no matter what food or beverage you put into it. They could also feed the entire world with seven pigs. They could put the bones of a pig back into the sty, and in the morning it would be a live pig again. The Norse gods also had a regenerating boar called Saehrímnir. So what human stories could match these marvels?

As unbelievable as the renewable pig stories are, they are not without precedent. The Roman Catholic St. Francis of Paola, born in 1416 A.D., performed such a feat. St. Francis brought his pet lamb, Martinello, back from the dead after it had been eaten by workmen. The hungry workmen didn't have anything else to eat, so they roasted the lamb and sat down to dinner. St. Francis came looking for his pet lamb just as they were eating, and they confessed what they'd done.

He went to the flaming furnace where they'd discarded the fleece and bones, and called out to the lamb, "Martinello, come out!" To the great surprise of the workmen, the little lamb jumped out of the fire as if nothing had happened, bleating happily upon seeing his master. St. Francis was canonized in 1519 by Pope Leo X for his exemplary life, holy acts, and many miracles. If you can raise people from the dead, there's no reason that you can't also raise animals from the dead.

Regenerating food almost pales in comparison, but it was a common enough miracle in the days of yore that if you look up the miracles of almost any saint, you'll find stories where a little bit of food fed a lot of people. St. Columbanus, born in 543 A.D., fed sixty monks with two loaves of bread, with bread left over.

On the flip side, he became angry when a gathering of Swabians (an ancient race of Germans) were about to offer up a giant keg of beer to Odin. Honoring the heathen god Odin was totally unacceptable, and the saint was determined to obliterate every vestige of this Odin from their lives, so he "breathed on the cask" and it crashed, breaking into pieces. Apparently the act of smashing the beer keg using only his breath succeeded in converting a few heathen Swabians to Christianity.

St. Columbanus had his own keg of beer, so the Swabian story wasn't about the beer, it was about their devotion to Odin. Columbanus' keg of beer was in the cellar, and instead of diminishing when you drank it, the keg would instead refill itself.

St. Mocheus, a disciple of St. Patrick who was born in 420 A.D., possessed the rare secret of making one pound of butter last four full years, while under constant consumption, and without diminution.

St. Gerard Majella was born in Italy in 1726 A.D., and one of his miracles involved multiplying the wheat for a poor family who wouldn't have made it through the winter. He increased their scant supply of wheat enough to last until the next harvest.

This concept of food replenishing itself wasn't just a miracle of saints. The fairy mythology of Ireland was full of stories of peasants who'd done some kind deed for a fairy, and the fairy repaid them by "blessing" a bin of grain so that it never ran out.

Other food miracles involved turning a random object into food. St. Patrick turned water into honey, stones into milk, and snow balls into butter and cheese. Conjuring food where it doesn't exist sounds like something straight out of a futuristic science fiction show. Everything in the world can be broken down into its most basic subatomic particles, and in theory, matter can be reorganized to become something else. This recycling technology would fulfill our wildest dreams, and it's common technology in science fiction, such as the *Star Trek Replicator.* Beyond the miracles of extraterrestrials, saints, and fairies, is there any basis in fact to hope that we could actually develop this technology? Well... yes.

NASA just approved a grant to a Texas company called *Systems and Materials Research Corp.* to develop a 3-D printer that creates "nutritious and flavorful" food for astronauts at the touch of a button. The machine follows a digital recipe to combine various powders to produce food with the same structure, texture, and smell of actual food, and it all began when a man named Anjan Contractor experimented with the idea and "printed" chocolate for his wife.

Anjan's vision is to revolutionize the concept of feeding humans, by using machines in our kitchens that synthesize food one layer at a time from cartridges of powder and oils that you buy at the grocery store. The powders would include sugars, complex carbohydrates, proteins, and other building blocks in a form that wouldn't spoil for at least 30 years.

We've also coined two phrases — *molecular assembler* and *matter compiler* — to describe a device that can rearrange molecules with atomic precision. The *Engineering and Physical Sciences Research Council*, which is a government agency in the UK, is pursuing this technology, as are other agencies around the world. The point is that our scientists believe that it's possible, and governments believe that it's possible or they wouldn't be handing out research money. It's just a matter of time before this science fiction becomes science fact.

Moving objects through the air:

Miracles and magic took many forms, and four different races of supernatural beings could float gigantic stones through the air: the Fenodyree, Jinn, an unnamed being from an Aymara legend, and the Spear-finger witch. How did our saints stack up?

There's an interesting story about St. Colman of Kilmacduagh, Ireland, born in 550 A.D., whose miracles started before he was even born. It had been prophesied that his mother would bear a son who would surpass all others of the existing king's lineage in greatness, so when she became pregnant, the reigning king ordered her death fearing that her son would replace him.

She attempted to flee the kingdom, but was caught. A rock was tied to her neck and she was thrown into the deepest part of the Kiltartan River to drown. By some miracle, the rock floated to the surface, allowing her to swim to shore and save herself. The bigger miracle came later, when St. Colman was an adult, and this bizarre miracle is called "road of the dishes."

St. Colman and several disciples were in the Burren limestone desert, destitute and without food. King Aidus the 2nd was thinking about Colman as he sat down in his palace to a sumptuous dinner, and the king made a wish out loud, never expecting the wish to come true. He said, "Would that these dishes before me, were rather before Colman, the man of God, in the wilderness, who by his manifold mortifications and his prolonged fasts, much better deserves his dinner this day."

Suddenly, all the food and dishes took flight from the royal table, and went flying off through the air. The king and his court jumped up in amazement, grabbed their horses and galloped off after the flying dishes. No hunting expedition could have matched the chase that followed. They chased platters of steaming meat and stew, and rattling spoons and knives, as their own mouths watered at the feast which had been plucked out from under their noses.

Finally the royal party arrived in Burren, galloping over the white, slippery stones toward St. Colman and his disciples who were gathered on a bare limestone hill. The food "landed" and spread itself out as if on a table. You'd have thought they could all sit down to a communal dinner, but this was not the case. Whatever magic had granted the king's wish to send the food flying to the monks, also caused the king and his cronies to become rooted to the spot, unable to move forward to join in the feast. They were relegated to watching the monks eat their dinner. Perhaps some invisible being, whether magical or angelic, decided to humorously grant the king's wish. Or maybe it was the king himself — unwittingly.

We have names for this — telekinesis and psychokinesis — the ability to move solid matter through the air with the power of the mind, psyche, spirit, soul, or whatever power of unseen nature lives within us.

The government must believe in the possibility that objects can be transported from one place to another, because they sponsored the *Teleportation Physics Study* at the Air Force Research Laboratory at Edwards Air Force Base. Several methods of teleportation were discussed, including psychic teleportation, along with other quantum physics and space-time methods.

Invisibility:

Speaking of invisible entities, this ability seemed to be a given, especially for the Jinn and the Tuatha dé Danann. In one Tuatha legend, the Dagda was invisible and his son Midir said, "We behold, and are not beheld." In other words, you can't see us, but we can see you.

On a few occasions, our human saints became invisible as well. King Ferdinand I so hated St. Francis of Paola (of the resurrected lamb story) that he sent a company of soldiers to arrest the saint in Naples. This would have been in the latter half of the 1400s. The king had been at odds with two different Popes during his reign, one of which supported a rebellion to have him removed as king for his oppressive government. Whether this came into play during the St. Francis incident, one could only guess, but it does set the stage for the king's enmity against church leaders.

St. Francis had entered the cathedral and knelt in front of the altar, but when the soldiers entered, they didn't see him because he'd become invisible. As they stood looking around, St.

Francis suddenly appeared out of thin air right in front of their eyes. The captain immediately fell at his feet, begging forgiveness for having undertaken a mission against the holy saint. St. Francis gave the captain a warning to take back to the king, after which the king decided to back off and leave St. Francis alone.

The Reverend Father Paul of Moll, born in 1824, also had the gift of invisibility. In the church at Thielt, a woman witnessed him vanishing on two occasions as he prayed. The saints may not have had the power to turn it on and off at will, or remain invisible for any length of time, but it does demonstrate that humans have the power to become invisible, just like the magical beings of legend.

Invisibility wasn't limited to Christian saints. The Yamabushi monks of Japan were noted for their ability to walk on fire or swords, immerse themselves in boiling water, exorcise demons, cure disease, foretell the future, channel the gods as oracles, fly through the air, and cloak themselves with invisibility.

They followed a strict form of Shugendō Buddhism, which loosely translated means "the path of training and testing to achieve spiritual power through discipline," and the supernatural abilities took decades to achieve. At one point the practice of Shugendō was banned, and like the witch-hunts, its followers were accused of witchcraft. This caused the sect to go underground with their beliefs, rather than practicing out in the open. Thus, you'll only see a hint of the abilities today.

The ability to fly:

Not only could both the Jinn and the Tuatha dé Danann become invisible at will, they could also fly. These beings were not limited by gravity. They could travel through the air, or appear above men's heads.

As with fleeting moments of invisibility, humans occasionally float up into the air in a process called *levitation*. An 1899 article about *Gerardo Majolla*, which probably referred to St. Gerard Majella, said that Gerardo had been beatified by the

Pope, and mentioned his many miracles including levitation. On one occasion he balanced himself in mid-air for a full three hours while praying.

On another occasion, St. Gerard and two peasants were walking down the road when they came to a church dedicated to the Blessed Virgin. Gerard became so exuberant in his joy, that he appeared transformed. He wrote a few words on a piece of paper and threw it up into the air, as if attempting to send a letter to Heaven, and then he leaped into the air himself.

To the great astonishment of his companions, instead of immediately coming back down, he walked a half a mile while up in the air before whatever power had raised him up, abated. If traveling a half a mile through the air doesn't qualify as flying, I don't know what does. This incident was recorded on page 115 of *Life of Blessed Gerard Majella* translated from German by Father Charles Dilgskron in 1896.

Numerous accounts of levitation come from all corners of the globe. For example, Yogi Subbayah Pullavar levitated for four minutes in front of 150 people, and Yogi Bhaduri Mahasaya was so adept at levitation, that he earned the title of *The Levitating Saint*. In Japan, the Yamabushi monks could "fly through the air" in the days of yore.

St. Joseph of Cupertino in Italy was so prone to levitate that he became the *Patron Saint of Air Travelers, Aviators and Astronauts*. Unfortunately, he lived during the heat of the witch hunts, and his levitation caused him to be denounced to the Inquisition, but apparently he did not suffer the horrific fate of an accused witch due to his connection with the church. However, his levitations disrupted Mass so often that he was banned from celebrating Mass in public for the last 35 years of his life.

Walking on water:

Hand in hand with flying and levitating is the act of walking on top of the water, or something similar. St. Francis of Paola needed to cross the Straits of Messina, but he didn't have the money to pay the ferryman, whose name was Peter Colossus. This was a treacherous stretch of water near the Gulf of Charybdis which had taken many a seasoned navigator down.

Undaunted by the ferryman who stood laughing on shore, St. Francis tossed his cloak on top of the water, jumped onto it, and bade his six disciples to join him. Seven men sailed across the strait on a cloak, to the amazement of the ferryman. The waves and the sea obeyed St. Francis, and by the time his little group reached the other side, a large crowd had gathered to welcome him as if he were an angel from Heaven.

Passing through a solid door:

The Tuatha dé Danann could appear inside of a castle that had been locked up tight. If they wanted in, no barrier could deter them. Whether this was done by teleportation, or whether they walked through the walls, the end result was the same, and humans have accomplished this same feat.

St. Francis Hieronimus, who was canonized in 1839, passed through a solid closed door several times to give comfort to a dying man named Cataldo.

St. Paul of the Cross was born in 1694, as Paolo Francesco Danei. In Perugia, Italy, he was mistaken for a vagabond and locked up in a "safe room" by a parish priest. He was secured in a locked room with iron bars on the windows. The next morning, he was gone, and the only way out was to walk straight through a wall or door.

St. Martin de Porres often passed through doors to comfort sick people. On one occasion, Brother Francisco was sick with a fever and chills so severe, that priests performed the Last Sacraments over him believing that he was close to death, and then locked his door for the night. The doctors wanted the door locked to prevent anyone from giving him water, which would make him worse.

St. Martin, unfettered by the locked door, appeared at his bedside, sponged him, freshened his bed, changed his fever-soaked garments, and left him with a sprig of rosemary. Francisco asked St. Martin if he were going to die, and Martin replied, "Do you want to die?"

Francisco answered, "No."

St. Martin replied, "Then you will not."

The next day, Brother Francisco was fully recovered. On another occasion during an epidemic in Lima, sixty friars had taken ill and were locked in a remote section of a convent. St. Martin did not have a key, but that didn't stop him from passing through the door to take care of them.

Perhaps this was related to his ability to bilocate. It's not uncommon for saints to appear in two places at once, and St. Martin de Porres did exactly that. He never left Lima, Peru, and yet he appeared to people in China, Japan, Algeria, Africa, and even on ships at sea. St. Martin died in 1639, was buried, and 25 years later they exhumed his body. It was "incorrupt" and exhaled a fine fragrance.

One of the most amazing accounts of bilocation comes from the Quechan people of the Southwestern United States, and it was documented by either Father Eusibio Kino, a Jesuit missionary who traveled to the region in 1698, or by the army officer he was traveling with, Lt. Juan Mateo Manje.

They were told the story of a white woman wearing a veil, along with white, gray and blue clothing, who decades earlier had come to the Quechan people in Arizona holding a cross in her hand. She spoke in a language they didn't understand, and became angry and started to shout when she couldn't get her message across. Someone shot her with an arrow and she fell to the ground, and they left, believing her to be dead.

The next day she was back again, unsuccessfully attempting to communicate, and they shot her again. She should have been dead, but two days later she was back again as if nothing had happened. No evidence existed to substantiate the claim that nuns had ever visited Arizona in the early 1600s, let alone survived being shot by an arrow twice. Yet a seemingly unrelated story took place in Texas which is nearly identical.

In 1629, a delegation of Native American Jumanos visited a Spanish mission asking to be baptized, and for missionaries to teach their tribe. Of course the good friar Alonso de Benavides who ran the mission was delighted, but also curious how they even knew about Christianity, especially to desire it with such fervor.

They explained that a woman had visited them. She spoke their language, preached to them, and ordered them to go to the mission to be baptized. Baffled as to this woman's identity, the friar showed them a painting of a nun. They said that yes, this woman wore the same clothing, but that it was not the same woman, and that the woman who'd visited them was much younger.

Meanwhile, in 1699, a similar event occurred in Texas, where the Native Americans were requesting blue cloth to use as burial shrouds. They'd adopted this custom after a beautiful woman dressed in blue had visited them years earlier. This strange white woman dressed in blue had also appeared to the people of Sonoita, Arizona.

She turned out to be Sister Maria de Jesus, the abbess of a Spanish convent, who had *never* physically traveled to the United States. She was 29 years old, and wore brown sack cloth covered by a blue cloak over white. She had made the claim in 1630 that while in a trance, she was miraculously transported to a faraway land where she taught Christianity to the native people.

On hearing the claims made by Sister Maria, friar Benavides went to Spain to visit her in person in 1631. She told him that she'd been visiting these people in her trances since 1620, and that she'd specifically told the Jumanos to be baptized at the mission. How she'd been able to communicate with the Jumanos but not the Quechans is just as much of a mystery as her ability to bilocate — or be in two places at once.

Did the Tuatha dé Danann actually walk through walls or teleport into locked up castles, or was this ability related to bilocation where some nonphysical aspect of a person travels somewhere, as with Sister Maria?

Shape shifting:

The ability to appear in another place could be related to the concept of appearing in a different form. If this bilocated self is some aspect of our spirit body, perhaps it isn't limited in what form it can take when it manifests. However, bilocation doesn't explain the Curse of St. Natalis.

Several shape shifters lived in our legends — Odin, the Tuatha dé Danann, and Spear-finger could appear as any animal or human, and could take the form of someone you knew and trusted. The Tuatha had the power to turn other people into animals, which brings us to the legend of St. Natalis — a Christian born in 470 A.D. in the middle of an ancient feud. St. Natalis was intricately linked to Ossory, Ireland. He founded the *Chapel of the Monks* in Ossory, and was its first abbot.

Aengus Osrithe was the first king of Ossory, whose family ruled Ossory happily until the neighboring clan of the Corca Laighde muscled their way in and evicted the Osrithe clan, taking over as rulers. When you lose your kingship, you also lose your castle, lands and other possessions, so this battle for kingship was a pretty big thing. After being displaced for over a hundred years, the Osrithe clan regained their kingship.

St. Natalis' life coincided with the Corca Laighde rule, so emotions would have been running pretty hot, with one group stinging over their defeat, but fighting to regain control. His lifetime also coincided with the latter days of the Tuatha dé Danann, who were persecuted by Christians such as St. Patrick, who made it his personal mission to take down the heathen Manannán mac Lir. The St. Patrick/Manannán battles would have taken place during St. Natalis' early childhood, or before he was born. This sets the stage for a bizarre event that took place roughly 600 years later, long after these royal and religious feuds had ended.

An Irish priest, accompanied by an assistant, was traveling from Ulster to Meath, and when night fell they built a campfire and made camp in the woods. Soon after, a wolf approached and before they could react, the wolf started speaking as if it were human. The wolf told them not to be afraid, and added some godly words to make sure that they understood that he meant them no harm. Of course, the concept of a talking wolf was beyond belief, and the priest questioned the wolf about what manner of beast it was.

The wolf said that he was from a pair of wolves, male and female, and that they were actually humans from Ossory. Their entire village had been cursed by the abbot, St. Natalis. Every seven years, one man and one woman from their village were transformed into wolves, and remained in that form for seven years. If the wolves were lucky enough to survive, they'd regain their human form, and two more humans would take their place as wolves. This curse had been in effect for centuries.

Then the wolf explained his reason for approaching the priest. His mate was very ill, and she was about to die. The wolf begged the priest to give her the consolations of his priestly office so that she could die in peace. They went to the she-wolf, who laid on the ground emitting moans and sighs which sounded completely human, and the priest gave her last rites, during which the priest was able to see her in her true human form. Then they all spent the night around the campfire together, and in the morning the he-wolf led the priest and his assistant out of the forest.

Two years later, the priest was asked to attend a synod to discuss the awful curse that the long-dead St. Natalis had set in motion, and its more ominous repercussions. The concept of a human-wolf creature led to a debate on whether killing one of these wolves should be considered the same as a human murder.

On the surface, this legend sounds like a fairytale — a fictional story with no basis in fact. However, there's another aspect that you don't hear about in relation to St. Natalis — his lineage. Bloodlines dating back to the early centuries can be difficult to unravel, because everyone had at least a half a dozen variants of their name, and historical documents often seemed to conflict with each other because of the name variants.

When you compare the genealogies of St. Natalis, to those of the Tuatha dé Danann, and the various clans who battled for rule over Ossory, and then take into account the comments that historians attached to the genealogies, you come up with a strong likelihood that St. Natalis was descended from Lugh — the son of the doctor who created the prosthetic arm. If Tuatha dé Danann blood, even diluted, was coursing through St. Natalis, he may indeed have had the power to inflict such a curse.

He was born as the Tuatha dé Danann were being evicted, stripped of their strongholds, and persecuted for their Celtic beliefs which so inflamed the Christians. Some Tuatha fell by the sword, some fled to their hidden island or other safe-houses, and those who were willing to embrace Christianity were absorbed into the world of humans.

Throughout history, there've been legends of humans taking animal form, usually in relation to witchcraft. Perhaps the shape shifting abilities of the Tuatha dé Danann and the Norse gods spawned the beliefs that were called up during the witch hunts. Thus, the witch hunts would have been targeting humans with an extraterrestrial lineage who were not following a Christian path as St. Natalis had done. Unlucky humans were also targeted for the misfortune of being different, making enemies, or suffering birth defects or diseases which would have been seen as demonic in nature, such as epileptic fits.

An estimated 100,000 were killed as alleged witches across Europe and the United States, and at the heart of the battle was magic and religion. Two forms of magic were believed to exist: natural magic which came from God, and demonic magic which came from Satan. As you can see in the comparisons, both sides seemingly had the same magical abilities, so the real issue was in your personal beliefs. Hence the bloodlines that fed the magic were decimated during the witch hunts, which is why you don't see much evidence of the miracles today. The legends, however, live on to remind us that these beings did exist in our history, such as the following legend which may have also spawned from the Curse of St. Natalis.

A bizarre disease broke out in England in 1315 that came to be known as *Barking Mania*, which caused its victims to bark like dogs. This was not an isolated incident, nor was it limited to a single region. One of the more detailed accounts comes from the 1609 outbreak in Labourd, France.

King Henry IV received a report that Labourd, France was infested with witches, so he sent judge Pierre de l'Ancre to investigate. Pierre fully believed in witches, and was of the opinion that we wouldn't still be plagued with witches if previous generations had killed them off when we first learned about them. Instead, we'd sent them back to the priests in the hopes that their beliefs were just illusions that could be set straight. As far as Pierre was concerned, the only way to get rid of witchcraft, was to get rid of the witches, and to this effect he burned 600 of them.

These Labourd demons had obviously come to France when Christian missionaries expelled them from India and Japan. Wine merchants from England and Scotland had seen the demons with their own eyes, flying over their vessels toward France, as they sailed across the ocean.

Once in Labourd, the demons recruited local women and even priests, to do their bidding. Every single household was contaminated, and the witches were everywhere, proven by the many confessions he received when he tortured suspected witches. The entire countryside was sorely afraid of both the witches, and the Inquisitors who might point a finger at them next. Sons accused parents; brothers accused sisters; husbands accused wives; and the townsfolk accused their neighbors.

The convulsions and barking caused by Barking Mania were proof of demonic possession and witchcraft. Oddly, the women who fell into convulsions were spared the barking, and the women who barked did not suffer convulsions. In Labourd it was called *Barking Malady*.

The convulsions were initially diagnosed as epilepsy, but these fits were far more severe. People fell to the floor, sprawled out, and then beat on the floor with their bodies and limbs like savage animals, banging their heads against the roughest object they could find. As if they couldn't help themselves, the afflicted turned these powerful forces against their own bodies, causing injuries.

Then there were the barkers, forty of them in a small church one day, all barking like dogs. They raised such a ruckus that no one could focus on their devotions. It was especially bad during a full moon, and for some inexplicable reason, as if they recognized one another, the barking started up every time one of their own came near.

The oddest aspect was the barkers' penchant for calling out other barkers by name, making it easy to know who was afflicted. If a victim started to bark in her own home, everyone else would run to the window to see who was walking by, as barkers set each other off. If the passerby matched the name she uttered, they ran out and grabbed that person and held them for the authorities.

This bizarre malady was contagious, and it erupted in several countries over several centuries. When the diagnosis of witchcraft fell out of favor, it was pegged as a mental illness, spread by hysteria, in spite of breakouts in regions that had no contact with one another.

1491, Cambrai, France: The nuns at Cambrai believed that they were possessed by demons. Some sort of animal spirit would take hold of them, causing them to run across the field like dogs, or fly through the air like birds, or climb up trees and hang from the branches like cats. The Cambrai nuns imitated the voices of many animals.

1566, Amsterdam, Netherlands: Thirty homeless boys and girls suffered convulsions that lasted up to an hour, which they later had no memory of, and believed they'd just slept. During the same outbreak, the children literally climbed walls and rooftops as if they were cats, without coming to any harm. They spoke in tongues, and had knowledge of events taking place elsewhere. Exorcists were called in, and during the exorcisms they vomited violently, expelling objects such as needles and shards of pottery. Lacking a better explanation, it was labeled hysteria and kids pulling pranks.

1673, Hoorn Orphanage, Netherlands: So many children were afflicted that there wasn't enough staff to take care of them all. Their bellies pounded so forcefully that it appeared as if a living creature were moving around inside. During a fit, it took six adults to hold down one child.

1700, Blackthorn, England: Five sisters in Oxfordshire suffered symptoms similar to those of a convent in Amou, which is 63 miles from Labourd, France, from a century earlier. Another Blackthorn family was also afflicted, which was related by blood to the first family.

As an alternative to blaming it on demon witches, could the human-to-wolf curse of St. Natalis, a Christian abbot, have sparked a full blown epidemic known as Barking Mania? St. Natalis wasn't the only person to inflict such a curse.

A Jesuit priest from the Canary Islands, the very region where the last sightings of St. Brendan's hidden island was said to be, also blasted some folks with an animalistic curse. Father José de Anchieta wanted to teach some people a lesson after they'd shot a bunch of monkeys, so he caused them to act like monkeys in order to mourn the monkeys they'd shot. Father Anchieta was prominent for his many miracles such as levitation, glowing with light, and communicating with animals.

As for Barking Mania, the legend doesn't end here. Another epidemic broke out in Ireland, in the middle of a war that involved a strange event in the sky. Remember how the wine merchants had seen "demons flying overhead" while they were at sea? Is it possible that they'd seen UFOs, and that UFO sightings in conjunction with general fear of the unknown had sparked the witch legends?

Ireland was mired in a nasty war with England, who'd sent English overlords to rule Ireland. Scotland had been under the English yoke as well, but they had fought, and gained independence in 1314. This spurred the Irish princes to believe that maybe they could shake off the yoke as well, and regain control of the kingdoms that had been stripped away from them.

The Irish enlisted the aid of Robert Bruce, the newly crowned king of Scotland, and promised that his brother Edward could rule Ireland if they helped chase the English off their soil. They'd had their fill of England, who among other atrocities had plundered churches and confiscated church lands. Irishmen weren't even allowed admittance into the monastic institutions that their own ancestors had built.

To insult them even further, the Irish were under English rule, but they were not protected by English law. Thus, an Englishman could murder and Irishman with full immunity.

Meanwhile, Robert's brother Edward was clamoring for a piece of the action, and the best remedy was to give him Ireland, if they could wrest it free from England. So in May 1315, Edward Bruce brought an army to Ireland.

It was a long and bitter battle that lasted for decades. This war wasn't simply Ireland fighting England, it was the English who'd been granted lands in Ireland versus their own countrymen, sitting on the fence as to which side they should be fighting for. If they fought against the Irish and lost, they'd lose everything they'd built-in Ireland. If they fought against the English, they'd be committing high treason.

In the middle of it all, Ireland was being devastated, castles destroyed, entire towns burnt to the ground. Whole families were decimated to the point that ancient Irish families were being slaughtered to near extinction. Homes were plundered, and even tombs were plundered for treasure. Churches were burned to the ground, sometimes with parishioners and priests locked inside. Not since the Anglo-Norman invasion had such complete devastation taken place.

The result of this lingering war was famine, pestilence and disease, not only for the Irish, but the English and Scotch armies as well. Warriors fought without having eaten for days, and all over Ireland people died from starvation. Some even reverted to cannibalism, such as prisoners who killed and ate the newcomers, and these horrors went on uninterrupted for 85 years.

With death all around, and their immune systems at low ebb for lack of food and clean water, diseases started coming in waves: epizootics (plagues that affect livestock,) then smallpox, then influenza, then Barking Mania, and pestilences. Wave after wave of debilitating and deadly disease hit them hard, until finally the dreaded Black Death came knocking on the door. Black Death was so contagious that entire villages became ghost towns, and it wasn't limited to Ireland. Across Europe, an estimated 200 million people died from this single disease.

As if war, famine and disease weren't devastating enough, in the middle of it all came the witch hunts. The religious persecutions started in 1325, at the beginning of the dark years. Ancestors of the very beings that might have been able to help feed and heal the people were mercilessly killed off, and again, humans used the witch hunts to eliminate anyone who got in their way for other reasons.

A wealthy, respected Irish woman named Alice Kyteler was accused of witchcraft by the children of her former husbands, probably to prevent her money from going to her favorite son — Robert Outlawe. Because she had powerful friends and lots of money, she was able to escape to England. One of her alleged witch-friends did not fare as well, and was burnt as a sorceress.

Religious wars were raging as well, with Christians still fighting to erase all vestiges of the old gods — such as the Tuatha dé Danann and their followers. In 1327, Adam Duff O'Toole was convicted of professing certain "blasphemous and anti-Christian doctrine." He was a Celt who denied the incarnation of Christ, the Trinity, and the chastity of the Blessed Virgin. He asserted that the Holy Scriptures were fables, and that the Holy Apostolical See was false. For his wicked heresy, he was burned alive after the octaves of Easter at Hogges Green in Dublin.

A year later, several others tried to spread heretical opinions in the diocese of Ossory, the very place where St. Natalis had issued his curse. Included among the heretics were Arnold Power and Roger Outlawe, the brother-in-law of Alice Kyteler. Their crimes included sympathizing with innocents who were falsely accused of witchcraft. Roger was cleared of all charges when nobody showed up to testify against him, and Arnold was convicted but spared the death sentence, and instead thrown into prison for the rest of his life. Even in death he was not given peace. His body was not allowed to be buried until it had become an object of horror to the living.

Even the Bishop of Ossory was accused of heresy, and thrown into prison for several weeks in 1339. He pleaded his case well, and in spite of repeated accusations in the years that followed, managed to live out his life and regain the favor of the king.

These were some of the darkest years that fell over Ireland. Over 100 years after Ireland had set out to gain independence from England, and after decades of devastation, plagues, and horrors beyond imagining, an odd event took place which suggests that someone was hanging in the sky, watching. This event took place in 1421, during a battle near Athy between Sir James Butler (4th Earl of Ormond) and O'Moore.

A historian named Edmund Campion stated that "the sun standing still in his epicycle and hastening not to go down for about six hours" until the English had defeated the Irish army in the red bog of Athy in a terrible slaughter. Another text described the event in more vivid detail:

> "In the Red Bog of Athy (the sun almost lodged in the West, and miraculously standing still in his epicycle the space of three hours, till the feat was accomplished, and no pit in that moor annoying either horse or man, on his part), he vanquished O'Moore and his terrible army."

How do you explain what happened in the sky that day, where *the sun stood still* for several hours, not moving across the sky as it should have? Perhaps the "sun" that they witnessed was a UFO, like the one seen by Queen Numbi that lit up her village one night as if it were daylight.

These visitors may not always get involved in our wars, any more than we would if we were exploring the universe, but you can bet that they were watching. Can you even imagine what they think of us, witnessing our own actions against one another? If you were hovering over a distant world, watching all of these horrors, and this is the *sanitized* version of events, what would you be thinking?

Shining with light:

Even during our darkest hours, humans have been visited by entities who literally shined with, or were made of light. These light-beings take two different forms: those who appear to be made of light like Queen Numbi's visitors, and flesh-and-blood beings who occasionally glow.

For example, the Tuatha dé Danann were described in very human terms, but one of their leaders, Eochaidh Ollathair, had been given the title *the Dagda*, which means "shining divinity." King Yima seemed to have the same distinction. On one hand, he was a king with a physical kingdom, but he was also described as "Yima, shining with light." Even among the Norse gods, there's a story of Odin sending an emissary whose name translates into "the shining one" or "the one giving light." This concept of glowing, which is usually depicted visually as having a halo, is not limited to otherworldly beings. Humans have the ability to glow as well, under certain conditions.

St. Columba frequently glowed with an "immense blaze of heavenly light" and his voice could be heard for eight miles off when he preached.

St. Francis Hieronimus who was known for passing through closed doors, also shined with light. On one occasion, his face was so bright that it was too dazzling for people to look at, and it was compared to the light of Moses which had to be covered with a veil.

St. Francis of Paola with his many miracles such as sailing on his cloak across a river, invisibility, and resurrecting his pet lamb, was also known to glow. This glow took the form of three "crowns" over his head as if wearing the Pope's tiara.

St. Philip of Neri not only became illuminated with light, but genuine sparks of fire flew from his eyes, and he wasn't the only saint to shoot sparks. St. Samson's face looked like it was on fire. Flames of spiritual fire actually burst from his mouth, ears, and nostrils, and angels were often seen at his side.

Father José de Anchieta, a 16th century Jesuit who became known as the "Apostle of Brazil," was born on the largest of the Canary Islands. During Anchieta's life he was considered a supernatural being for his many miracles. He caused humans to act like monkeys in order to mourn the monkeys they'd shot. He summoned birds to form a flock over his head, and hover there, to shield him like a parasol from the hot sun. He could travel for miles while levitating "at the height of several palms above the ground" which allowed him to shorten a several hour journey into a matter of minutes, and he was occasionally crowned in a halo of light.

Controlling elements of nature:

Rather than summoning a flock of birds to use as a living parasol, some chose to control the very weather itself. For example, just by saying a word, the Norse god Odin could put out a fire, calm the sea, and turn the winds in any direction he wished. The Tuatha dé Danann were also credited with power over the weather. They could control the wind, ride the wind, or raise up wicked storms. They could also create a wall of fire, or a wall of water.

A few humans were also credited with weather control, including Jetsun Milarepa, one of Tibet's most famous Buddhist yogis, who studied sorcery prior to embracing Buddhism. He admitted to committing "black deeds" in his youth. One involved summoning a giant hail storm to punish his aunt and uncle for stealing his family's wealth when his father died. The storm demolished their house, killing 35 people. This angered the villagers who went looking for him, so he sent another hail storm which destroyed their crops. He quickly regretted his deeds after realizing that he'd harmed innocent people, and so he chose a more harmonious path in life through Buddhism. He was also known for his skill at Wind Meditation, which allowed him to run faster than a horse.

Wind is an instrument of destruction that will rise up at the end of the world during Ragnarök, according to Norse mythology. Ragnarök begins with a giant named Eggther playing his harp, which will signal the cocks to crow and wake up the gods in the Nine Worlds to prepare for the final fight. Earth will shake and mountains will crumble, setting loose various creatures such as the Fire Giants who will come forth to do battle.

We don't know what type of harp Eggther played, but there is a harp known as the Aeolian Harp, which is so delicately stringed that it's literally played by the wind. You can put it in a window to entice the wind to blow across its strings, and it's the only stringed instrument that can play itself in this manner. It's also the only stringed instrument that plays solely harmonic frequencies. It was named after Aeolus, the Greek god who controlled the winds.

The Dagda owned a harp, among his many magical possessions. His was an oak harp that produced three types of music. One put people to sleep, another made them laugh, and the third made them cry. Like a boomerang, the enchanted harp would return to the Dagda if he called for it, though apparently he needed to be in its vicinity.

Once it was stolen, and hung up on the wall of his enemy. When the Dagda spotted it, he called out, "Come apple-sweet murmerer. Come, four-angled frame of harmony. Come, summer, come, winter, from the mouth of harps and bags and pipes." The harp sprang from the wall and rushed toward the Dagda, killing nine men as it flew through the air. Some believe that Dagda's harp could summon or change the seasons, due to his way of calling for the harp in reference to seasons, though the legends don't offer any supporting stories.

Neither the Norse harp that signals the beginning of Ragnarök, nor the Dagda's magical harp, are credited with actually controlling the weather. One of the biggest conspiracy theories today involves a government program known as *High Frequency Active Auroral Research Program*, or HAARP. Conspiracy theorists believe that HAARP can be used to manipulate, or control, the weather.

The official description is that it's designed to analyze and investigate the ionosphere, in order to develop more advanced technology for radio communications and surveillance. Whatever its nature, HAARP is a joint program funded by the U.S. Air Force, U.S. Navy, University of Alaska, and the *Defense Advanced Research Projects Agency* (DARPA).

The ionosphere is a region of Earth's upper atmosphere, which includes portions of the thermosphere, mesosphere, and exosphere. The thermosphere is where ultraviolet radiation causes ionization, and which is dominated by atmospheric tides. It's also a layer that radio waves can bounce off of, and it's where the Aurora Borealis originates. The mesosphere is a region in between standard aircraft and orbiting spacecraft. It boasts strong zonal winds, atmospheric tides, planetary waves, and night clouds which are those brightly shining clouds that you see at twilight, which are made of ice crystals. Then we have the exosphere, which is the outermost layer that sort of blurs with outer space. This layer is made mostly of hydrogen, with a bit of helium, carbon dioxide, and atomic oxygen.

Conspiracy theories link HAARP to earthquakes, floods, hurricanes, thunderstorms, and droughts, among other things. Some believe that it could cause Earth to flip its magnetic poles. Then there's the claim that it could turn the upper atmosphere into a lens that would make the sky appear as if it were on fire.

Articles from various sources, which are sponsored on an educational website through the University of Connecticut, give us the scoop on what the program is all about. Theoretically, HAARP will utilize the ionosphere to expand long-range radio communications, including communication with submerged submarines. It should enhance surveillance which could detect cruise missiles, aircraft, and nuclear warheads. In addition, it's designed to "see" down under the earth and detect underground tunnels and bunkers. It does this by transforming portions of the atmosphere into antennas, mirrors, and giant lenses.

Also mentioned is that HAARP could be a *first step* in building a full global shield that could destroy ballistic missiles, as well as the ability to manipulate the weather.

Giant sheets of cloth:

Few would be surprised if humans succeeded in weather manipulation on a grand scale, but this next legend so odd, and echoed in so many places, that it bears mentioning. It existed in Norse, Christian, and Persian legends.

From the Norse gods you'll find it in the legend of Otter, who was the shape shifting son of a dwarf king. He frequently took the form of an Otter, hence the name. Unfortunately, Otter was killed while in his animal form, and his father, the king, flew into a rage. The king demanded that the otter killers recompense him with enough gold to cover the skin of the slain otter inside and out. However, the otter skin stretched itself out to such a great size that no ordinary treasure could ever cover it.

Our Christian saints have a similar story — the extraordinary birth of St. Columba, also known as Columb Cille. His mother's name was Eithné, which is coincidentally the same name as the wife of Conn of a Hundred Battles in Tuatha dé Danann history. Columba is Conn's direct ancestor several generations removed, and Conn is also the ancestor of Lugh, one of the Tuatha dé Danann high kings. His lineage suggests that Columba had Tuatha dé Danann blood flowing in his veins when he performed his many miracles, though St. Columba was no friend of the Tuatha dé Danann, who sent up clouds and mists to hinder both St. Patrick and St. Columba.

As to the strange story of St. Columba's birth, one night his mother Eithné had a prophetic dream where an angel came to her with a robe that was embroidered with beautiful flowers in every color. Eithné touched the robe, but the angel took it back and spread it out up in the air, where it floated. Eithné cried out, wanting the robe back, but the angel said that it was too important a robe for her to keep.

Eithné watched as the robe grew larger and larger until it covered all of the plains, woods and mountains as far as the eye could see. Then a voice came from Heaven and told her not to be sad, because her unborn child was destined to be numbered among the holy prophets, and soon after she gave birth to St. Columba, who became one of the Twelve Apostles of Ireland.

St. Columba himself owned a cowl which, like the robe that his mother had touched, possessed expansive powers so great that it could be made to cover an entire acre of land, which it once did on the Isle of Arran.

Even the *Bible* had references to giant sheets. Simon Peter, one of the biblical Twelve Apostles, had an offering of food presented in an unusual fashion. He fell into a trance, and saw a vessel descending to Earth from an opening in Heaven. The vessel looked like "a great sheet, let down from Heaven by four corners." Inside this sheet/vessel was all manner of four-footed animals, creeping animals, and fowls of the air for him to eat, but Peter refused to eat as they were unclean. The Lord commanded him three times to eat, explaining that what God had cleansed was okay for him to eat. Finally, the vessel went back up into Heaven untouched, and Simon Peter's vision ended.

Another legend comes from King Solomon, the man who controlled the Jinn. He instructed the Jinn to weave giant carpets big enough to accommodate Solomon, his servants, throne, and entire kitchen, when he was exhausted from traveling. Once his retinue and possessions were situated on the carpets, he instructed the wind to blow and raise the carpets up into the air, toward whatever direction he wished to travel.

During a similar journey, his Jinn provided carpets big enough to carry every Israelite who wanted to join a pilgrimage to Mecca, including their camels, oxen, and sheep. Solomon ordered the Jinn and demons to fly in front of the carpets where he could keep an eye on them, as he did not trust them, and he ordered "birds" to fly over the carpet to provide shade for the pilgrims.

When this flying assemblage approached a town, Solomon made a sign, the "birds" *depressed their wings*, and *the winds abated* so that the carpets sank gently to Earth, which sounds suspiciously like a ship powering down for a landing. When the time came to travel again, he gave a sign for the "birds" to spread their wings, and then *the winds gathered force and lifted the carpets*, and the entire caravan sailed off to Mecca.

These were the *flying carpets* of legend, and King Solomon was revered not only in Christian texts, but Persian texts as well. As the gold digging ants were actually humans, one can't help but wonder whether the birds were literally avian, or whether they were some type of flying machine.

The Saints and the Otherworlders

It seems that virtually every magical trait that the Otherworlders were known for, our very own saints also possessed in the early centuries. If it's possible that some of the saints' miracles were enhanced by having blood ties to their enemies, such as the Tuatha dé Danann, it would explain the comments made by Richard Trench, who was the Archbishop of Dublin from 1864-1884.

Archbishop Trench wrote several books, including *Notes on the Miracles of Our Lord* in 1862, in which he theorized as to why the many miracles of the early saints seemed to have dwindled as time passed: "Few points present greater difficulties than the attempt to fix accurately the moment when these miraculous powers were withdrawn from the Church, and it entered into its permanent state, with only its present miracles of grace and the record of its past miracles of power." He added that this diminishment happened gradually, ebbing away by degrees.

If some of the Tuatha dé Danann converted to Christianity and used their vast array of powers and technology to further the cause of the Christian church, while others of the Tuatha were either killed off or retreated, this would give us a scientific explanation for the puzzle of dwindling miracles. With every century that passed, the Tuatha dé Danann bloodline became more diluted until it lost all of the power that it once had.

In another book by Walter Richard Cassels in 1879 regarding the Archbishop's quote, Cassels described this lessening of miracles as an act of division of the power. First it was divided among the Apostles, and then further divided by the ever-multiplying members of the church, until by subdivision, the power to perform miracles became virtually extinct, leaving us with the memory of the standing wonder of the church. He added that the miracles had been well authenticated.

PARADISE FOUND

Another oddity that surrounded the early saints was their belief that a physical paradise existed that humans could travel to. The Christian saints may have believed in Heaven and a spiritual life after death, but they also believed in the physical paradise of the Tuatha dé Danann and the Norse gods, which for some of them, would have been where their own ancestors, or enemies, retreated. An island paradise was the object of searches all around the world, most of which were in vain.

Juan Ponce de León and Alexander the Great both searched for it. So did Governor Juan de Mur y Aguerre of the Canary Islands. They were among the multitudes whose searches were unfruitful. A lucky few, however, not only found it, but came back to tell the tale — Norwegian Prince Eirek, Ogier the Dane, the Merddin Emrys, Bran, Cormac mac Airt, and several monks including St. Brendan and St. Machatus.

For Prince Eirek, it was called Deathless Acre, a legendary place in Scandinavian mythology. Eirek was the son of King Thrand of Drontheim, Norway, as well as being the great-grandson of the Norse god Odin, so he would have known that places existed outside of our normal realm.

Eirek made a few stops before the big journey, one to pick up a friend by the same name, and another to talk to the emperor in Constantinople for advice on how to get to Deathless Acre. Remember that traveling in those days wasn't as simple as "go south on I-75 until you get to I-20, and then head west." Maps were estimations drawn by hand, and didn't always include roads.

The emperor was a wiz at geography, and he told Eirek that the distance between Heaven and Earth was 100,045 miles. To put this in perspective, that's less than halfway to the Moon. He also told Eirek that Deathless Acre was east of India.

It was a long journey over land and sea until the two men finally reached India. Eirek and his friend traveled on horseback through India until they came to a forest so dense and gloomy, that attempting to look up at the sky was like looking up from the bottom of a well. Even during the day you could see stars twinkling as if it were the dead of night.

On the other side of the spooky forest they came to a river which separated them from a land so beautiful that they knew it was the place they'd been searching for. The trouble was that they had to cross a stone bridge to get to Deathless Acre on the other side of the river, and this bridge was guarded by a fierce dragon.

Eirek's friend took one look at the dragon and bailed out, refusing to cross the bridge, but Prince Eirek was fearless and determined. He drew his sword and walked unflinchingly across the bridge, straight into the cavernous mouth of the dragon.

Imagine his great surprise when, as if by magic, the dragon vanished as if it were just a holographic image, and Eirek was "safely placed" in Deathless Acre, apparently nowhere near the bridge. The land was flat as far as the eye could see, and the grass was purple with the many flowers blooming which filled the air with the scent of blossoms. There wasn't a cloud in the sky, and a gentle breeze blew. Joy and happiness prevailed in this paradise where night never fell, Earth was as bright as the Sun, and a half a year slipped by in just a few moments.

Eirek walked a short distance and spotted the most remarkable object — a tower suspended in the air, without any support whatsoever. The only way in was to climb a slender ladder, which he did.

Inside he found a meal laid out, as if it had been waiting for him, and he ate. There's no mention of his encountering people, only the food being laid out, after which he fell asleep and had a vision. In this vision, he talked to a guardian angel who promised to take Eirek back to Drontheim, but warned that after ten years, the angel would come for Eirek to take him away from his homeland forever. Even today it's common for beings to "visit us" or "communicate with us" when we think we're asleep.

Back in Drontheim, Eirek told everyone of his adventures in Deathless Acre, and of the floating tower. True to the guardian angel's word, in the tenth year Eirek was "caught up" by God's spirit and carried away, never to be seen again.

Some versions state that this is a Christian rewrite of an older heathen story about a place called Odainsakur (Deathless Acre) in Gloesisvellir, which refers to the Shining or Glittering Plain of Jötunheim, and that Eirek was a heathen rather than a Christian, so whatever being he encountered may not have been a Christian guardian angel.

The entities that were most associated with Gloesisvellir were beautiful women sometimes called *trolls*. The king who ruled over Odainsakur was a friendly giant, and Jötunheim itself is one of the Nine Worlds in Norse mythology. We know that there was a bridge between Earth and Asgard, another of the Nine Worlds which was Odin's home world, and Eirek's journey indicates that there was also a bridge from Earth to Jötunheim.

So this Deathless Acre had a tower suspended in mid air, where the sun shined brighter than our Sun, a half a year slipped by in just a few moments, and whose entrance was guarded by a holographic dragon. The description of Eirek's passing through the dragon stated that he was "safely placed" in the Deathless Acre after walking into the dragon's open mouth. In other words, he didn't walk the rest of the way across the bridge, he was transported after entering the dragon. This indicates that the dragon could have been a portal or transporter, and the gloomy forest that blocked out all sunlight could have represented the mist that you often traveled through to get to these Otherworlds.

In addition, before Eirek even started the journey, he was told that the distance between Heaven and Earth was halfway to the Moon, which was a really odd detail when the goal was to get directions to Deathless Acre.

When you compare the details from the paradise stories, such as Prester John's story with a sun that shined seven times brighter than our Sun, a meeting with a celestial being, and a paradise that "hangs" between Heaven and Earth — this whole concept of an Otherworld paradise looks more and more like an extraterrestrial planet on the other side of a wormhole. Through this wormhole, Eirek witnessed advanced technology in the form of a floating tower, or could the tower have been a hovering spacecraft?

Another lucky man was Ogier the Dane during the reign of King Charlemagne, whose story you read one version of in the *Island Paradise* chapter. Perhaps that was the shortened version, because it could have happened that way once he reached the island in this version.

Ogier was the son-in-law of King Gudfred of Denmark, though the king's daughter Astritha was Ogier's third wife which meant that he was a busy man. The legend of Ogier and Morgana doesn't mention the names of his family back home, nor do we know exactly what became of him, except that his date of death is listed as 817 A.D. One legend claims he is "sleeping" in the castle of Kronberg until some future date when Denmark needs him. Another claims that he's living in Avalon with Morgana, so does the year 817 represent the date of his death, or the date of his disappearance? And could a disappearance into Avalon to await a future date be misinterpreted as "sleeping"?

Ogier and an army of men were at sea when a wicked storm rose up with such ferocity, that it shattered the ship's mast and they all expected to die. Ogier and a handful of men escaped in a lifeboat, watching helplessly as the ship was smashed to pieces.

The lifeboat was drawn toward a lodestone (magnetic) rock, and once they were close enough, the lifeboat attached itself to the magnetic rock as if it were cemented there. Believing themselves to be stranded, they divided up the provisions.

Ogier warned the others that as their food ran out, he'd throw them into the ocean, and he did, until he was the sole survivor. Expecting to follow his shipmates to their deaths, he heard a voice which told him to wait until nightfall, and then make his way to the castle which would be visible. The voice, which he didn't know whether it was real or imagined, told him that no matter what he saw, not to be afraid.

He'd seen this castle on previous nights though never during the day, and did not realize that he could get to it from his location. Night came, and the castle "shone wondrously." He discovered that several ships were anchored to lodestone rocks as his was, and he could walk from ship to ship across the water to the island. Then he scaled a hill and when he reached the castle gate, two great lions stopped him and threw him to the ground. He remembered the instructions given by the voice, jumped to his feet, grabbed his sword and fought them off.

Finally he arrived at the Castle of Avalon, and went inside where he found a table set for dinner, complete with food. There were no people, but there was a horse sitting at the table as if it were human, named either *Papillon* or *Psyche*.

Papillon gave him a golden goblet to drink from, and led him to a bedroom so that he could sleep. The fairy-made coverlet was made of cloth, and gold, and ermine. He slept soundly and when he woke, there was no sign of people, or the horse, and he attempted to leave the room.

However, a giant serpent stood in his way, ready to attack him. Like the lions, he drew his sword and killed it. Then he went exploring and found a garden in its own little paradise, with trees

131

yielding every manner of fruit, and sweet smells which he'd never smelled before. He saw an apple tree with fruit like gold, plucked an apple and ate it, but immediately became so sick and so weak that he couldn't even stand up.

In that moment, a lady appeared, richly adorned and clothed in white — a glory to behold. He thought she must be the Virgin Mary and said as much, but the woman smiled and said no, her name was Morgue la Fée (Morgan the fairy, aka Morgana) and that she'd allotted him a gift that would make him famous. Then she gave him a ring which restored his youth to the age of thirty, though he'd been an old man when he landed.

She took him to Avalon and introduced him to King Artus, and Auberon, and the sea fairy Malambron. That's when she gave him the crown of forgetfulness, which made him forget all of his troubles, and his old life, so that he would remain with her. They even had a son, but while he was living this life of bliss with Morgana in Avalon, great battles were being fought back home.

This is where the story diverges. One version claims that Morgana realized that Ogier needed to go back home to help Christendom fight their battle, so she awakened him from his forgetfulness and returned him to Earth. In another version, the crown of forgetfulness fell off and he begged Morgana to let him "return to Earth" and she did.

However, nothing was as he'd left it. His friends and family were long dead, King Charlemagne was long dead, and those he encountered were astonished at his strange clothes and bearing. The generation below him was full of old men, and yet Ogier was like a man of thirty. He was out of place, and out of his time, and "his talk excited suspicion."

Finally he convinced the king of France to let him join their army, and he went into battle. He'd forgotten his life with Morgana as if she'd never existed, and fell in love. Before he could act on this newfound love, Morgana reappeared, and carried him back to Avalon.

His request to *return to Earth* makes it clear that Avalon was not on Earth, and that wherever it was had a time differential like Deathless Acre. The two Ogier legends could combine, as he could be in Avalon during this "long sleep." Both Ogier and Eirek would have visited their paradises in the early 800s.

Allegedly Merlin visited the same island as Ogier, although Merlin's many legends are so muddled that we don't know what really happened, and some of them were told under his other name — the Merddin Emrys. In the old texts, his name was written as "the Merddin Emrys" as if *merddin* were a title, rather than a proper name, and it had multiple spellings including "myrddin" which translates as *rowan*.

Rowan refers to a species of mountain ash tree, which had magical powers that protected you from all forms of witchcraft. Our ancestors must have forgotten to use the rowan tree in the era of the witch hunts, else none would have been harmed. In Norse mythology, the tree which connects the Nine Worlds is called Yggdrasil, which is interpreted as a giant ash tree. Using a tree may have been how the olden gods illustrated wormholes to us piddly humans, because its three supporting roots connected to Asgard (Odin and the Aesir gods), Jötunheim (giants), and Niflheim, which is also known as *mist world*, or *abode of mist* — where a goddess named Hel reigns over the dead, and humans have traveled back and forth to at least two of these worlds.

"Emrys" was linked to a Greek word which translates as *divine* or *immortal*, according to Lewis Gidley in his 1873 book about Stonehenge, though this connection may have been wishful thinking on his part. Still, it represents an interesting possibility when combined with merddin and the rowan tree that connects the Nine Worlds, this tree being the divine tree that stands tall until the end of our world, after which even the immortal gods die.

One monument stands as a testimony to the life of Emrys — that of Stonehenge, which Emrys allegedly built according to the *History of North Wales, Volume 1* by William Cathrall in 1828.

Stonehenge was erected on the site of what had been a circle of ambrosial stones, a sacred type of stone which Pliny claimed was oracular, like the "rocking stones" of the Celts, according to *Faiths of Man* by James George Roche Forlong in 1906. These rocking stones would wobble at the slightest touch, and yet all the force of men could not move a rocking stone from its perch. In Britain, they were erected by the Druids, and possibly used to demonstrate the Druid's power to move stones, which in the case of Stonehenge, would have been Emrys.

The Logan stone in Cornwall weighs 70 tons, to give you an idea of the mass of these strange stones. Sacred rocking stones exist all around the world, and their legends include massive stones floating in the air to get to their destination. So here we have another stone mover legend.

Ossian wrote how bards walked around a rocking stone singing, which made the stone move as an oracle to predict the outcome of a battle. Emrys was also a bard, which were Celtic singers and poets whose job it was to tell the story of the exploits of their tribe. In the company of nine other Cylveirdd bards, Emrys traveled across the sea in a *vessel of glass*, and in some versions this vessel was a *house of glass* or *crystal ark* that he and the nine bards traveled in. A similar vessel was attributed to Alexander the Great, which was called a *diving house of glass* or crystal in which he could dive under the water like a submarine, and watch the fish.

Emrys was also described as a powerful miracle worker, fathered by a "demon" with a human mother. This trip in a glass ship may have been to escape from the Saxons, possibly to the realm of the fairy queen, who would have been none other than Morgana in Avalon. Another reference to Emrys' *house of glass* claims it was the place where he took the thirteen treasures of Britain for safekeeping, which included: a cloak of invisibility, a flaming sword, a container which multiplied food, a drinking horn which always held whatever you most wanted to drink, a magical vehicle that would take you wherever you wished to go, a crock which produced whatever food you most desired, and seven other treasures.

The stories that surround Emrys are varied, especially as there were people with similar names whose histories got mixed up with his, but another legend involved a *floating house of crystal* which Emrys entered for the love of the Lady of the Lake, who is associated with Avalon — a house which he never came out of.

Some link it to the Isle of Glass, also called Scalpay which is located in the Outer Hebrides islands that were associated with the Tuatha dé Danann and Midir's revolving castle. The entire dimension of the Isle of Glass is 2.5 square miles. Others describe Emrys' destination as a *floating island with a strong door*, which sounds more like a floating spaceship.

Both Emrys and Ogier have another legend in common — that they are "sleeping" in some hidden location to be awakened at a future date. Singing someone to sleep starts the next legendary visit to the Otherworld. Bards were known for their singing, and so were the Otherworlders.

In the voyage of Bran, our traveler's journey began when Bran heard a strange song as he was out in the neighborhood — a song which put him to sleep. When he woke up, there was a silver branch (or wand) next to him covered in white blossoms. He took the branch home, which was a royal castle, and a strange woman appeared inside in spite of the ramparts being closed, so her entry was not made in an earthly manner.

The woman began to sing to Bran, telling him that the branch was from an apple tree on the beautiful island where she lived. Everyone there was happy, nobody ever got sick or died, and it was a place filled with beautiful music and colors. She sang of several islands, one being the Island of Women, and suggested that he journey there.

After the song was finished, the silver branch sprang from Bran's hand into the woman's hand, and he couldn't prevent it.

There was no strength in his hand to hold the branch. Then the woman vanished.

The next day Bran set out with 27 men to search for these islands that she sang about, and they encountered Manannán mac Lir along the way, who was traveling to Ireland to father a son who'd be named Mongan. He told Bran that the Island of Women was not far and that he'd reach it before sunset.

Bran passed the Island of Joy full of people laughing, and he let one of the men off there while he and the rest continued on to the Island of Women. The men landed and were treated to a great feast, where every man was given his favorite food, and the food on their plates never dwindled.

They stayed for a year until one got homesick and begged Bran to go back to Ireland with him, if only for a visit. The women warned that they'd sorely regret attempting to go back home, but the men were determined. She told them not to set foot on land under any circumstances, and to pick up the fellow they'd left on the Island of Joy.

They sailed back to Ireland and once they reached shore, Bran had a conversation with someone on the beach. He did not exit the boat. Apparently the "voyage of Bran" was now famous and everyone was familiar with it, except that it was considered ancient history, an event that happened a long time ago.

In that moment, one of the men jumped out of the boat, and as soon as his feet touched ground, he disintegrated into a heap of ashes as though he'd been dead for hundreds of years, and his body had turned to dust. Bran and the others remained in the boat, while Bran related everything they'd encountered in the islands. Then they sailed off, and nobody knows if they went back to the islands of the Otherworlders.

This story differs from the story of Ogier the Dane on one key point. For some reason, Ogier had been able to "return to Earth" though so much time had passed that everything was changed. He did not turn to dust, so why in Bran's story did a man disintegrate? The primary difference was the destination. The islands that they journeyed to were not the traditional Avalon, Otherworld, Yma, etc., so perhaps they went to a different world where the laws of time were even more accelerated. Instead of a year, or a hundred years, they'd stayed so long that several hundred years had passed on Earth. Or perhaps this got added to the tale in the hopes of warning men NOT to travel to the Otherworld, for whatever reason.

The concept of returning to Earth is echoed in the tale of Conn and the Tuatha woman who'd been banished from the land of the Tuatha dé Danann for having an adulterous affair. Her name was Bécuma and she rode up in a self-propelled boat to where Conn was sitting, watching out over the ocean, after the death of his wife Eithné.

The descriptions of her banishment clearly show that the realm of the Tuatha dé Danann was not on Earth. A book called *Ériu, The Journal of the School of Irish Learning, Dublin, Volume III* published in 1907 describes her journey: "Accordingly, she was banished beyond the expanse of the sea and the great deep; and it was into Ireland in particular she was sent, for the Tuatha dé Danann hated the sons of Mil after they had been driven out of Ireland by them."

From another text: "Bécuma was banished from the gods' land because of her sin with Manannán's son. She *came to Earth* in a self-moving boat..."

And another: "Bécuma had been discovered in an intrigue with Gaiar, a son of Manannán, and, banished from the Land of Promise, crossed the sea that sunders mortals and immortals to offer her hand to Conn."

She was banished *beyond the expanse of the sea*, she *came to Earth* in a self-moving boat, and *crossed the sea that sunders mortals and immortals*. How much clearer can you get in stating that wherever she came from, it was not of this Earth? Does that mean that a portal between worlds existed somewhere out to sea?

Conn had already lost his son, Connla, to a Tuatha woman who'd come in a similar boat. A lady had appeared to *Connla of the Golden Hair* as he was sitting on a hill (Uisnech) with his father, and the woman spoke to Connla. She was dressed in strange garb, and she was invisible to all except Connla.

She promised him kingship in the Plain of Pleasures, where he'd never have grief or woe again, at least until the awful day of Doom (dreadful Judgement.) Did the latter get added to the story to revise a heathen tale, or like the Norse gods, did the Tuatha dé Danann have an end of the world scenario such as Ragnarök?

If Connla joined her, neither death nor age would touch him, and together they'd remain young and beautiful. His father Conn, realizing what was taking place, had his druid drive her away with wizardry. Obviously there's something we're not being told, because why would you want to prevent a loved one from living in a blissful paradise? Why would you deny them a chance to remain forever young and healthy?

Before she left, she threw an apple to Connla. He ate from this apple for a month, disdaining all other food, and the apple never diminished in size. At the end of a month, she came back to Connla and gave him grief for being content to "await death amid the assemblies of the short-lived mortals" rather than become a prince in the Land of the Ever-Living. She sang of a land "which draws down the bright sun at eventide" — a land of maidens and of all delight.

That must have done it, because he leapt into her boat of pearl, sometimes described as a ship of glass or crystal. Together they sailed away in "the well-balanced gleaming skiff" and at the time, nobody knew where they'd gone, though we meet up with them again later.

This woman came in a shining ship to take Connla to a place where there were allegedly only women and girls, and though it was already dusk, they'd reach this place before nightfall. Connla's family watched as he sailed far off *as if into a mist*, as far as their eyes could see. Conn never saw his son on Earth again, but a man who Conn knew visited this Otherworld briefly, and saw Connla who appeared to be happy, healthy, and young. That visit tells us that Connla would indeed see his son at some point, as he was destined to join his son on an island.

Tadg (the son of Nuada of the silver hand) and his men landed by boat in a country where the air felt comfortable, not too hot or cold, where you didn't feel hungry even if you hadn't eaten, because the smell of crimson branches satisfied your hunger. The land was plush with wooded areas, apple gardens with red apples, leafy oak trees, and hazel trees with yellow nuts. It was summer in this place but winter back home.

They came to a sweet smelling wooded area with purple berries that were bigger than a man's head, and beautiful shining birds eating the berries. These were strange birds with white bodies, purple heads and golden beaks, singing such sweet music that a sick or wounded man would instantly fall sleep.

Beyond the woods was a great, smooth, flowery plain with a dew of honey over it, and three steep hills, each with a strong fort on top. One had walls of white marble around it, which was the fort of the royal kings of Ireland, from Érimón, son of Miled, to Conn of the Hundred Battles, who'd be the last to go in it.

This island was called Inislocha — the Lake Island — with two kings over it: Rudrach and Dergcroche, who were sons of Bodb. Here a woman told Tadg the entire story of Ireland. He asked who was living in the golden fort, and she told him to go there and find out for himself. She left and went into the fort of white marble.

In the middle fort was a woman, Cesair, who was "the first to reach Ireland." Since then, she and the men she traveled with had come out of that dark, unquiet land, and were now living forever on this peaceful island.

She told him that the golden fort was full of every noble person who had ever held a high position in Ireland — Partholón

139

and Nemed, Fir Bolg and Tuatha dé Danann. The fort of silver walls was empty, waiting for the kings who had yet to rule Ireland. The island itself was considered the fourth paradise of the world. Three others were Inis Daleb to the south, Inis Ercandra to the north, and Adam's Paradise to the east.

Then Tadg met Connla, who was enjoying a golden apple that never diminished. Connla was sitting with his sweetheart, and both appeared beautiful and gentle. They were so alike that you'd think they had the same parents. Connla explained that this was the *girl of many shapes* who had brought him here, another indicator that the Tuatha dé Danann can take on the appearance of anyone they wish.

Finally Tadg and his men traveled back to Ireland. They'd been on Lake Island for a day, but an entire year had passed. As they sailed away and looked back at the island, they couldn't see it any more because a magical mist had come over it and hidden it from them.

To recap the connections between Conn's family and the Tuatha dé Danann, Conn is descended in part from the Tuatha. Conn's son Connla had gone to live with his Tuatha wife on Lake Island in the Otherworld. Conn's wife Eithné died, leaving him with one remaining son named Airt. The banished Tuatha adulteress, Bécuma, had actually fallen in love with Airt from afar, and it was Airt she'd come looking for when she landed in her motorboat. Once she found out that Conn was the widowed king of Ireland, she changed the plan and married him instead, becoming the new queen of Ireland. In the meantime, Airt went on to marry and had a son named Cormac, who became the king who traded his wife and children for a magical wand, and then went searching for them where he met, and became friends with, Manannán mac Lir.

Apples have a strong connection to many of the island paradises. Manannán mac Lir was also known as Manannán of Emhain of the Apple Trees, where three apple trees existed: one in full bloom, one shedding its blossom, and the third covered in ripe fruit. The Norse gods were kept young by Idunn's apples of immortality. The legend of Epimenides who fell asleep for 57 years in a cave may have been linked to a race of nymphs called Epimelides who protected apple trees. Avalon was called the Isle of Apples. Connla was visited by a Tuatha woman who gave him an apple that never diminished, just before she lured him to join her in the Otherworld. Bran's voyage started with the silver branch of an apple tree, as did Cormac mac Airt's journey to paradise which began with a glittering silver branch with golden apples dangling from it, that made you forget all your troubles. We've already followed Cormac's journey which took him to the house of Manannán in the Otherworld in 248 A.D., which was on the other side of a "dark magical mist."

One of the most enduring legends of an island hidden in the mists, however, is attached to the Island of St. Brendan, which was positioned in various locations on ancient maps. Several people either traveled to the island, or saw it appear or disappear with their own eyes.

Brendan was one of several monks who set out in search of this island, along with St. Machatus, who was known by many names in the old texts. In those days, you didn't carry an ID card, or even spell your name when you gave it to someone. Chroniclers wrote down what they heard, so it was common to find a story told and retold with several name variants, especially when you add translations to the mix. There are no less than three spellings for Brendan, and thirteen variants for Machatus, and even a suggestion that Brendan's voyage was a mythical journey based on Bran's voyage, in spite of the many sightings of Brendan's island since then.

St. Brendan would have been 8 years old when St. Patrick died, and 37 years old when St. Columba was born. The early saints were intricately linked to one another, as well as to the Tuatha dé Danann either by blood, or as enemies, and sometimes both. When St. Brendan the Navigator set out on his journey to look for a legendary island paradise, he would have known full well that this island was connected to the Tuatha dé Danann.

Brendan's fellow traveler, St. Machatus, wrought marvels right up there with the other thaumaturgists. His miracles started when he was just a child, and it was said that not since the biblical Apostles had anyone wrought greater miracles in the name of Christ than Machatus. He expelled devils, restored sight to the blind, quenched the poison of serpents, calmed the tempests, and even raised the dead. In addition, he received messages from an angel of God.

Machatus was born a Welsh nobleman, and later became a monk under the tutelage of St. Brendan, who was the abbot of Lancarvan at that time, but later became a bishop. Together these two monks, along with several other monks, journeyed in search of a mystical place which was called variously Yma, Celtic Terrestrial Paradise, Avalon, Isle of the Blessed, and the Fortunate Islands.

The entire concept of "Fortunate Islands" would suggest that it was a group of islands, and not a single island, which makes sense in light of the legends which describe multiple, Otherworld islands such as the Isle of Joy and the Isle of Women. There are numerous versions of St. Brendan's legend, some of which claim that they never found the island, and others which included several unusual islands that they visited, including one that turned out to be the back of a whale. Regarding the claims that they never found Yma, the ancient maps that point to specific locations indicate otherwise.

The monks reached Yma after a long and arduous journey, and only with the help of a local guide whom St. Brendan had met on a previous voyage. As they approached the region where the island was supposed to be, they were enveloped in a cloud so dark that they could barely see their shipmates, and they sailed through this thick cloud for an hour. Finally, they arrived on the other side of the "cloud" and a great light shone around them. They were near the shore of an island encircled with a *bright wall*, or a *golden wall of great height*, or a *wall of mirror-like gold with no visible entrance*, and this wall encircled the island paradise.

Somehow they must have gained entry, because hidden behind the tall wall was a magnificent castle, whose halls were lighted with self-luminous stones and adorned with precious jewels. They must have told an amazing story about their stay on the island, but unfortunately, if there's a more detailed story about the castle, or what sort of people they encountered inside, it's not readily available.

The monks remained for fifteen days on this mountainous, thickly wooded but fertile island where the sun never set, and when they left the island, they discovered that an entire year had passed in the outside world. They clearly traveled through a portal to somewhere — and this portal likes to move around.

The island came to be known as St. Brendan's Island, or the Island of San Borondon, or Lost Island for the inability to find it again. The island garnered quite a reputation because whenever someone found it, and could place it on a map, everyone would make maps with the location — only the next travelers who attempted to go there would find the location empty, and when the island was finally rediscovered, it was someplace else entirely.

Christopher Columbus was aware of the legends, which he'd heard on Ferro Island, which is also known as El Hierro or Meridian Island in the Canary Islands, and this may have been the last location that Lost Island was ever seen.

In the 12th century, geographer Honoré d'Autun said that there was an island, now unknown to men, once discovered by chance and then lost again, which St. Brendan had visited. In the 16th century, mapmakers were calling it Hidden Island because it "changed its place through enchantment."

St. Brendan's discovery took place in the year 512 A.D., but sightings of the island continued in the vicinity of the Canary

Islands off the coast of Africa even into the 1900s, when the monk Sigebert de Gembloux spotted it in 1719, and Don Matea Dacesta saw it in 1721, though both from a distance.

After these two sightings, the governor of the Canary Islands, Juan de Mur y Aguerre, sent a ship to the island but by then, the island had disappeared again. As if toying with them, the island reappeared behind a low cloud in 1723 and this time, a priest performed an exorcism toward the island. I kid you not, they attempted to exorcise this island as if it were a demon.

The exorcism failed because in 1759, a Franciscan priest named José de Viera y Clavijo, who lived in the Canary Islands, published several sketches of the island as seen from a distance, including one that he drew in the presence of 40 witnesses, all of whom watched the island for an hour and a half as he drew it. Sightings continued into the 19th century, but they became less frequent. One of the last sightings occurred in 1958, when photographer Manuel Rodríguez Quintero allegedly captured the island in a photograph.

None of the Canary Island sightings involve a golden wall, nor can we be certain that the island that St. Brendan visited is the island in the Canaries, especially since we know that there are other, mysteriously hidden islands near Ireland and the Hebrides where the Tuatha dé Danann lived.

So we have an island that is sometimes surrounded by a tall, golden wall, and that seems to change its location as if through enchantment. The island appears and disappears, and hides in a dark mist. Is the mist a portal and if so, are there multiple portals around the world that would explain the belief that the island relocates? Or could the island with the golden wall be a space ship/city, such as the one depicted in the television series *Stargate Atlantis*, that has the ability to fly as well as float, which allows it to move around? Is it possible that a spaceship city landed on an island, and left again? Or is the whole thing just a mirage, imagined in the thick clouds that descend over the Canary

Islands and other regions? If it's a mirage, then how do you explain several people, including monks, claiming to have seen or visited this Hidden Island?

There's another Canary Island connection, one which began in Australia. On October 21, 1978, Frederick Valentich was piloting a Cessna 182L over Bass Strait in Australia. The sky was clear and the winds were light. At 7:06 p.m., he asked air traffic control for information on a craft that was flying 5,000 feet below him. He said he could not confirm the type of craft, but that it had four bright lights that he thought might be landing lights. Then it was 1,000 feet above him, moving at a high speed. Then it was approaching from the east, and he speculated that the other pilot was playing some sort of game with him.

At 7:09 p.m., he reported that the strange craft seemed to be chasing him. Then he was orbiting, and the object was orbiting above him. Since it wasn't zipping all around but instead positioned above him, he got a better look and described it as having a shiny metallic surface and a green light.

Then Valentich went silent for 28 seconds, and when he spoke again he said that the aircraft had vanished. He went silent again for another 25 seconds, and then reported that the craft had reappeared, this time coming in from the southwest. At this point, Valentich's engine was "rough-idling" and "coughing." Now the UFO was hovering on top of him, and he said, "It is hovering, and (long pause) it's not an aircraft."

For the next 17 seconds, all that came over the radio was an unidentified noise, described as "metallic, scraping sounds." That's the last that anyone heard from him for twelve years. Neither Valentich, nor the plane, were ever officially found.

A search and rescue alert was issued immediately, and the search continued for seven days. All that they found was a fuel slick near his last known location, which was not aviation fuel.

While Valentich was encountering the UFO, a local resident had set up a time-lapse camera to photograph the sun setting over the water. When the pictures were developed, they showed what appeared to be a fast moving object, surrounded by a cloud-like vapor or exhaust residue, coming up out of the water about 20 minutes before Valentich's encounter. Its speed was estimated to be about 200 mph.

Several ground witnesses had also seen Valentich's plane being "chased" by an object, which they described as an erratically moving green light in the sky, and one of them saw the green light trailing or shadowing Valentich's plane, which by then was in a steep dive.

You can't have a major UFO event without a conspiracy or cover up close on its tail, and the Valentich disappearance was no exception. A lot of hype surrounded his disappearance, casting shadows on his piloting skills, and claiming that he often flew into regions where he wasn't supposed to be flying.

Valentich's flight plan was scrutinized, and discrepancies were found. He stated that he was going to pick up passengers on King Island, but investigations showed that there were no passengers waiting to be picked up. He told his family that he was going to pick up crayfish as well, but there was no indication that he'd ordered crayfish, which were out of season and unavailable.

Some believe that he'd staged his own disappearance, which sounds oddly familiar. Another plane disappeared, and the same story got peddled afterward that the pilot simply stole the plane and ran away with it, intentionally staging his own disappearance, as detailed in the *Gateways to the Otherworld* chapter.

This would have been the end of Valentich's story, and officially it was. However, UFO researcher Manuel Carballal has more information about the Valentich disappearance. Carballal is not only a UFO researcher, he's also a criminologist who specializes in crimes associated with beliefs, as well as paranormal fraud. In addition, he graduated from the Theological Institute of Compostela with a degree in theology. In other words, he's pretty well grounded in all aspects of UFO phenomena.

Carballal took testimony from several people who claimed to have encountered Frederick Valentich in 1990 at the Plaza del Charco on the island of Tenerife, which is one of the Canary Islands. Valentich was alive and well, and apparently quite willing to share what he'd been up to for the twelve years since his disappearance. He showed his Australian passport to prove his identity, and the witnesses reported that physically there were no signs of aging from the time that he'd disappeared. He claimed that he now belonged to a group of humans who had been recruited by extraterrestrials.

Presuming that this sighting even happened, exactly what did he mean, "recruited by extraterrestrials"? Someone may have been posing as Valentich on a lark, or the alleged witnesses may have been having a little fun off an old story. Valentich may very well have staged his own disappearance, and was recognized, and came up with this UFO cover story. Or maybe he is indeed now living among extraterrestrials, visiting Earth on occasion.

Tenerife Island is part of the same group of Canary Islands which includes the sometimes hidden island that priests attempted to exorcise, and it's nowhere near Australia. What are the odds that an alleged sighting of this missing pilot, alive and well, just happened to occur in the same vicinity as the island that seems to appear and disappear in conjunction with a foggy mist or cloud?

During the 12th century, an island appeared off the Irish coast which had never been seen before. They didn't know what to make of it, and some thought that the island was a resting whale, but it remained stationary so they decided to investigate. A boat load of men approached the island and they were so close, that they could have stepped onto its shore, except in that moment the island sank into the water and vanished out of sight. The next day, it appeared again, but quickly vanished when they got close, so they dubbed it the Phantom Isle. On the third day, following the advice of an old man, one of the bowmen struck it with a barbed arrow of red-hot steel which caused the island to become stationary.

This enchanted island long haunted the memories and imaginations of fishermen and mariners, especially those living along the northwestern coasts of Ireland. From the coastal town of Donegal, Ireland, which translates as *fort of the foreigners*, the inhabitants often assembled to discern the shadowy outlines of the enchanted island off the coast.

Some believed that the Fomorians or Tuatha dé Danann lived there under a magic thrall, and that adventurous or wrecked voyagers had been cast onto its shores, where they found chieftains and warriors acting like sleepwalkers, being incapable of giving any information about themselves.

Another enchanted island is that of Hy Brasil, or Isle of the Blest, which has nothing to do with Brazil. Perhaps it was the same as the other legendary islands, because several maps show it off the coast of Ireland dated 1375, 1513, 1570, and 1595, along with another mysterious island called Demar. Neither island exists today in the locations shown on the old maps, so either the mariners got it wrong, or the islands disappeared.

GATEWAYS TO THE OTHERWORLD

Most of these cities, castles, islands, and other worlds were hidden beyond a mist, which you had to pass through in order to reach the destination. Sometimes you could barely see the person standing next to you. There were a couple of exceptions, like Eirek's holographic dragon, though they did travel through a very dark forest where they could see stars even though it was daytime.

Today we still have paranormal mists where boats, planes and people disappear, or experience otherworldly phenomenon, and the mists are often located over water. Today's paranormal mists are linked to places such as the Bermuda Triangle, and like the islands of old that changed location, they aren't limited to a single region of the planet. We don't know what lies on the other side, because the people who encounter them rarely return to tell the tale. So what are some of the stories we hear about today involving these mists, or glimpses into an Otherworld?

One pilot experienced a "low altitude cloud" over the Bermuda Triangle, and all we have are a few cryptic clues as to what he encountered. On February 11, 1980, pilot Peter Jensen was flying a Beechcraft Baron 58 from St. Thomas to Miami. He reported that he was lost in a cloud just 150 feet above the ocean. There was no reason for a cloud to have formed at this low altitude. His next transmission came eleven hours later and 600 miles away, long after his fuel would have run out. Then he vanished without a trace.

Jensen was a 14 year old aviation enthusiast, described as a "good pilot" by professional pilots who knew him. After his disappearance, reports surfaced that he'd been unhappy about his mother putting a halt to his flying lessons, and that he'd taken the plane from Harry S. Truman airport without permission. He'd been seen loading the plane with baggage.

Two hours after takeoff, a plane was spotted that matched the description of the Beechcraft, refueling in South Caicos Island. Four hours after takeoff, three pilots flying near Bermuda heard a distress call from a plane which matched the Beechcraft's number. The plane was about to crash into the ocean about 6.5 miles southeast of Miami. Later, the Beechcraft was allegedly seen in Jamaica, which suggests that the teenager had simply stolen a plane and run away from home. Neither the plane nor Jensen ever reappeared, and were presumed lost at sea.

Was Jensen simply a runaway who staged his own disappearance, laying the blame on a Bermuda Triangle legend where no one could follow? Did he crash into the ocean? Or did officials concoct this convenient cover story, not wanting to frighten people that "clouds" existed that you could disappear into? Did Jensen run off to start a new life where no one could tell him what to do? Or was he whisked off through a portal to another world? One could only hope that his destination was as pleasant as the paradise legends and not Davy Jones graveyard.

Like Jensen's story, most Bermuda Triangle disappearances are never seen again, and we're left guessing as to whether they sank to the depths of the ocean, or were pulled through a portal. Sometimes, decades later, we find physical evidence of a sunken vessel to dispute the otherworldly possibilities.

One thing that both believers and skeptics agree on, however, is that magnetic anomalies exist in the Bermuda Triangle that affect navigational controls. Magnetic anomalies also exist in other locations, such as the Great Lakes Triangle, and the Michigan Triangle within it. Inside these regions, planes disappear, ships disappear, and people see "ghost ships" sailing across the water. Time speeds up or slows down, and navigational systems go haywire. Some of these anomalous zones are even associated with tall, blond humanoids whose descriptions match the Tuatha dé Danann, such as the Zone of Silence in Mexico.

The Great Lakes are comprised of five lakes: Erie, Huron, Superior, Ontario, and Michigan. Unlike the Bermuda Triangle where Jensen disappeared, airplanes passing over any of the Great Lakes are never more than 20 minutes from land, and could easily glide to an emergency landing if the engine shut down. Yet, no less than 200 aircraft have disappeared over the Great Lakes, from helicopters to military aircraft.

To minimize the danger when flying over the Great Lakes, the Federal Aviation Administration created a special *Lake Reporting Service* where pilots continually check in. Pilots who utilize the service are expected to "check in" every ten minutes, and a five minute delay is all it takes to trigger a search-and-rescue operation. Most disappearances can be attributed to storms, but there are always questions and on occasion, hints that paranormal answers are possible.

One such hint came from a Lake Michigan experience which involved a mysterious fog, and this time Kathy Doore came back to tell the tale. In 1978, three sailboats were practicing for a sailing competition on Lake Michigan. The lake was calm and the skies were clear on a beautiful summer day.

Out of nowhere, a thick, freezing cold fog descended over the sailboats, and strange winds blew from multiple directions. Visibility dropped to zero. None of the seasoned sailors had experienced this phenomenon before.

On Kathy's boat, the crew was all together in one place prior to the fog, but suddenly they were in different locations as if they'd been moved. At the same time the sailboat began to rotate, as if it were on an axis, and it made three full rotations. Then, as quickly as the strange fog had appeared, it vanished, and Kathy could see that all three sailboats had been rotating in exactly the same way. Time anomalies also came into play, where each person reported that a different amount of time had passed. These time anomalies continued as they sailed for shore. One minute she saw a boat pulling into its mooring, and the next minute the boat was nowhere to be seen, only to reappear again a few minutes later.

Ships that appear and disappear out of an otherworldly fog include "ghost ship" sightings, and witnesses to this phenomena include Prince George of Wales, who later became King George V, along with his brother Prince Albert Victor of Wales and eleven others.

Their story began on a clear night with calm seas off the coast of Australia when a ghost ship appeared, seemingly engulfed in a strange red light. The ship was clearly visible about 200 yards off their port bow, but suddenly the ship vanished and they could not find it again. Two other ships that had been sailing nearby flashed them to ask whether they'd seen the strange red light. All believed that they'd seen the *Flying Dutchman* — a ghost ship that's been reported for centuries.

Another sighting more closely matched Kathy Doore's experience, though it took place thousands of miles away near the Cape of Good Hope at the southern tip of Africa, more than 150 years before Kathy's incident.

In 1823, a ship named *Leven* was surveying the seas around the Cape of Good Hope, when they spotted the ship *Barracouta* about two miles distant. *Barracouta* was a ship that the *Leven* crew was familiar with. Not only did they recognize her peculiar rigging, but they also recognized the faces of the crew when they sailed closer. The *Leven* sailors knew that the *Barracouta* wasn't supposed to be anywhere near the Cape of Good Hope, and they were surprised to see her nearby.

The *Leven* sailed closer and attempted to make contact, but the *Barracouta* simply sailed on, ignoring them. At one point the *Barracouta* lowered a boat into the water, and the *Leven* crew assumed that a man had gone overboard and a rescue attempt was underway. Then night fell and the *Barracouta* was hidden in the darkness.

The next morning, the *Leven* anchored in Simon's Bay, and the *Barracouta* joined them a week later. Finally they could compare their log books and get to the bottom of this puzzling mystery. The log books of the *Barracouta* showed that she was 300 miles away from the *Leven* on the day of the sighting, and had not lowered any boat. Further investigation showed that no other ships had been in the vicinity of the *Leven*.

What did the crew of the *Leven* see that day? Did they encounter a time slip where they witnessed the *Barracouta* on some other date in the past or future, lowering a boat in that exact same spot? Did they pass into some alternate dimension where the *Barracouta* was nearby, and then reenter our own dimension? Did they experience a mass hallucination?

This was not the first time that a ghost ship had been seen in the area. Two years later in 1825, an article appeared in *Mechanic's Magazine and Journal of Science, Arts and Manufactures*, which mentioned the *Flying Dutchman*. A footnote to the article was as follows: "The *Flying Dutchman* is a meteoric cloud, which is seen off of the Cape of Good Hope, occasionally, by sailors." Ghost ships are explained away as clouds, refractions, mirages, or optical illusions. Weird things just aren't possible, and we have to explain them away as being a figment of the imagination.

One factor that these experiences have in common, both in ancient history and modern times, is the appearance of a strange mist or fog. If it really is some sort of portal, and it was prevalent enough in history to spawn legends that survived for thousands of years, why aren't more people reporting incidents today? Well, a few people are.

One is known as the Moberly-Jourdain incident that took place in Versailles, France in 1901. Charlotte Moberly and Eleanor Jourdain were walking and got lost, while looking for a particular road, though they had a guidebook. As they walked, a feeling of oppression and dreariness came over them. The atmosphere changed, and everything suddenly looked unnatural and lifeless. There was no light or shade, and no wind stirred the trees. It was as if they'd been transported into a shadow of the past. The people wore clothing from a bygone era, and the two women walked across a bridge that didn't exist anymore.

Skeptics claim that they stumbled into a costume party, though it doesn't explain the bridge that was long since gone. Did the women make up a story for the fun of it? Did they encounter a costume party? Or was this a genuine time slip, where for a short time they witnessed life as it existed in the past?

Sometimes time slips are more like time travel. In 1979, two couples were vacationing together, and stayed in a motel that did not exist. The Simpsons and the Gisbys rented a car to explore France. Around 9:30 p.m. they pulled into a hotel hoping to rent a room, but the hotel was booked and they were sent to a smaller motel down the road.

As they drove along an old, narrow, cobbled road, they passed circus posters which advertised an old-style circus, and then pulled up in front of a long, low building with men standing out front. They asked if this was the motel, and were told it was an inn. Maybe they didn't like the looks of it, because for whatever reason they kept driving, and found an old-fashioned building with a hotel sign next to a police station.

Inside, everything was made of heavy wood. The windows had no glass, just wooden shutters. There were no elevators or telephones. The rooms had wooden catches for locks, and did not have private bathrooms. Everything in the shared bathroom, including the plumbing, was antique. There were no pillows on the beds, and the bed sheets were of some heavy material.

In the morning, they ate breakfast in the dining room, and drank coffee that was "black and horrible." At a nearby table sat a woman wearing a silk evening gown, carrying a dog under her arm. Two policemen entered, wearing old fashioned uniforms with capes over their shoulders, and large, peaked hats. Everything about the hotel and its people seemed out of time and out of place, but they enjoyed the old-fashioned atmosphere.

After the travelers finished breakfast, they asked a policeman for directions, but the policeman did not understand the word "autoroute." When they paid for the rooms and breakfast, the bill was so low that they argued it must be a mistake, but it wasn't. Except for the hotel, everything else about their trip was normal.

They drove to Spain, and on the way back through France decided to stay at the quaint hotel again. They found the road, and passed the first hotel, but the old-timey hotel they'd stayed at was gone. There was no sign of it.

They went back to the hotel that had been booked originally, but the staff was not dressed in the same uniforms as before, and when they asked about the man they'd spoken to previously who'd sent them down the road, no one had heard of him. They finally gave up and stayed at a different hotel, which cost them 247 francs, compared to the quaint hotel which had only been 19 francs.

When they later developed their photos, all the photos came out except for those taken at the mysterious hotel. They researched what they remembered, and identified the policemen's uniforms as being from 1905, yet their trip was taken in 1979!

The bigger mystery is why the quaint hotel accepted their modern currency, and failed to question their modern vehicle, unless a time slip "lives" in a particular location and the hotel was accustomed to "odd" visitors. If the story is true, you'd have to wonder, could they have remained in 1905? Apparently they interacted with this earlier time for an entire night, sleeping in the beds, eating in the dining room, and talking to people. Could they have traveled further into this earlier era and gotten stuck there, rather than coming back out again?

The other side of the equation is what happens when you encounter someone "popping in" from another time, and then "popping out" again, presumably back into their own time.

Bold Street in Liverpool, England, is shrouded in mysterious time slips. One woman sat on an outdoor bench to eat her lunch. As she sat down, the sun seemed to dim as if there were a partial solar eclipse. A man was on the bench next to her, and he started up a conversation. They chatted pleasantly, and she noticed his odd clothing from the 1950s. Just as she was about to throw her sandwich wrapper away, he asked her a question. She turned away just long enough to toss her trash into the garbage can, and when she turned back around to answer, he was gone. There was no sign of him anywhere. He couldn't have gotten up and ran off in that brief moment, based on the layout of the street. He simply vanished. In that same moment, the sun's brightness returned to normal.

This time slip is not an isolated incident. Bold Street has "sent" numerous people back in time briefly, including a policeman and his wife, which indicates that there may be one or more time portals present in that area.

Changes in perception during a paranormal event are known as the *Oz Factor* — a term coined by ufologist Jenny Randles, who was the director of investigations at the British UFO Research Association. This occurs not only with time slips, but UFO close encounters as well.

Effects of the Oz Factor include a feeling of isolation and changes to the environment, such as a noisy street full of people that suddenly seems quiet and deserted. In the time slip stories, the sunlight dimmed, everything appeared flat and lifeless, and there was no breeze.

A UFO event from the book *Alien Nightmares: Screen Memories of UFO Alien Abductions* gives a different aspect of the Oz Factor:

"The flying saucer lent an unearthly feel to everything surrounding it. In my back yard, the flying saucer had left behind a glowing set of concentric circles near the weeping willow tree. I wanted to go out and see the glowing circles. I very much wanted to touch them but I was afraid. The whole back yard had an otherworldly feel and the very air was different. The air itself seemed to glow, kind of like what you experience with a black light in a room full of black light posters, only in a milky-silver-white color instead of purple. It was as if the air itself were a milky-silver color. It was spooky."

It often takes a personal experience to become a believer, and Air Marshal Victor Goddard of Britain's Royal Air Force had several paranormal experiences. Not only did he start out believing that UFOs were a hoax, but through an intermediary, he tried to convince U.S. President Harry Truman to abandon UFO investigations. A series of paranormal experiences turned Goddard into a believer, and one of them involved an otherworldly mist.

The year was 1935, and Goddard was flying a Hawker Hart biplane from Edinburgh, Scotland to Andover, England. He passed over an abandoned airfield. Drem airfield was weedy and overgrown, the hangars were falling apart, and cows were grazing on what had once been the parking area for the planes.

He flew over Drem and continued toward Andover, but out of nowhere, a storm materialized with high winds and strange, brownish-yellow clouds. Goddard's plane started spiraling out of control toward the ground, and almost crashed. He managed to regain control, only to find that he was turned around and headed back toward Drem.

As he approached the abandoned airfield, the storm vanished, and it was all sunshine and blue skies. Drem was completely transformed in front of his eyes. The broken down hangars were brand new, and four planes were parked where the cows had been grazing. All four planes were different than the planes that should have been at an RAF airfield.

Three were biplanes, which he was familiar with, but they were painted a yellow color that he'd never seen before. The fourth was a monoplane, which the RAF didn't have in 1935. Even the mechanics were wrong in their blue overalls, which should have been brown. None of the men at the airfield looked up as he flew over, which was also odd.

Then the strange brownish-yellow storm reappeared, he reentered his own time and flew on to Andover. Four years later, the RAF began to paint their planes yellow, switched their mechanics to blue overalls, and acquired a monoplane like the one Goddard had seen. Had he traveled several years into the future and back again when he passed through the otherworldly brownish-yellow clouds?

Many of these time slips seem to be one way — you can see them, but they can't see you, as with the Moberly-Jourdain incident, the *Leven* and the *Barracouta*, and Goddard's flight over Drem. In the story of the quaint hotel, however, they physically interacted with the other timeline, which opens the door to the question: Could you travel backward or forward in time, into another dimension, or through a portal, and get stuck there?

The only clues would be in the stories of people appearing where they don't belong, because permanently missing persons could indicate any fate. The trouble with a missing person's report is that we have no way of knowing what happened. In a few cases, such as with the young pilot Jensen, we have radio contact prior to the disappearance which can give us a clue, but with most missing people, that's it. They are missing, nobody knows how or why, end of story.

We can speculate based on the testimony of family and friends, such as trying to figure out if someone ran away from home, had been afraid of a stalker, or had a mental disorder such as Alzheimer's that could cause them to get lost. Sometimes their dead bodies are found decades later and the mystery is solved, but for some, the mystery is never solved.

The only place we can look for clues regarding inadvertent time travelers stepping through a portal, is in the stories of people who "pop in" to our timeline, and that's where living John Doe's come in — "persons of any age who are living and unable to determine their identity" — which are listed as EULs in the FBI-NCIC missing and unidentified person's database.

At the end of 2012, the database listed 7,885 "active entries" for these unknown people, which get listed as amnesia victims, or infants too young to communicate, or people who are "mentally unable to give consent." They become living John Doe's. If they stepped through a portal, you'd expect them to claim coming from a different time or place, so that it would be obvious that they just "popped in," but what do you think would happen to a person making such a claim? Here's a scenario:

> One day a man knocks on my door, in a panic because he's lost and can't find his way home. His speech is unusual, archaic. If I was a Good Samaritan and not afraid that he was an axe murderer, I'd invite him in, offer him a beverage to calm him down, and ask him questions hoping to help. Maybe we'd get in my car and drive around looking for his home. As soon as I start the car, he flies into a panic — sheer utter terror. Cars hadn't been invented yet so he freaks out. Even if I could get him to calmly stay in the car, we'd never find his home because it's long gone, built over with a subdivision.
>
> While we search for a location that he recognizes, we're talking, and if I believe his story that it's the year 1625 and that somehow, he got transported into 2013, I've got two choices. If I allow him to stay in my home because he's got nowhere else to go, sooner or later he's going to be discovered, and I run the risk of the authorities accusing me of kidnapping, and mentally harming this man, or labeling both of us as being *schizophrenic bizarre delusional* and carted off to the nuthouse. If I take him to the authorities, he will probably end up with that label anyway and be institutionalized.

If, on the minuscule chance, a policeman believes us, and we attempt to research this man and see if we can find his ancestors, who probably wouldn't believe any of this, let alone accept him into their fold, sooner or later it would end up on the higher government networks, and if THEY believe his claim of being from the year 1625, you can bet they'll whisk him away somewhere out of sight.

However, if a man pops in from the future and can't get back, he'd be better equipped to think on his feet and stay off the radar. However, you cannot function in our society without identification. You can't rent, buy, work, or get medical care without a verifiable ID, or at the least a fake ID. Whatever he'd be carrying from the future wouldn't pass muster, so he wouldn't be able to quietly rent an apartment while he "figured it out" unless the first person he encountered believed his wild story of being from the year 2189, and attempted to help him.

So you see how someone "popping in" would likely end up institutionalized, or taken into government custody, where ordinary folks like you and I would never know about him.

Once I understood how time travelers might get labeled — *schizophrenic bizarre delusional* — I attempted to research whether anyone had made such claims and been thus labeled, where it made its way into the news. I found claims of alleged time travelers, such as Eloi Cole appearing at the Large Hadron Collider in Switzerland on April Fools' Day, but none of them had a ring of truth.

I did not find anything related to time travel claims in the dozens of online articles I read on schizophrenia. I did, however, find several references to aliens and extraterrestrials, particularly for claims of implanted chips or alien abductions. I also read several public discussions on schizophrenia, which included debates on whether many of our mainstream religious beliefs should have been labeled *bizarre delusional schizophrenia*.

What I read was no different than burning the so-called witches in the Salem witch hunts, but instead of burning you at the stake for having an otherworldly experience, they wanted to slap a label on you as having *bizarre delusional schizophrenia* and pump you up with pills or lock you away. Wow.

So what about the living John Doe's who made the news without alleging time travel? These John Doe's exist, and one of the most famous is using the name Benjaman Kyle. On the surface, his story appears pretty straightforward. He was found in 2004, lying behind a dumpster as if left for dead, covered with ant bites, badly sunburned, with indications that he'd received blows to the head. He didn't know his own name and didn't recognize his face in a mirror. A massive media campaign followed which attempted to find someone who knew this man, but as of 2013, his identity remains unknown.

There were exhaustive searches in fingerprint databases and missing person's databases hoping to match him up with someone. They even searched DNA databases tried to figure out who he might be related to. In the meantime, he has a few random memories which indicate that he is familiar with places in three different states. He remembers a 2% sales tax, milk for a nickel, and grilled cheese sandwiches for a quarter, but these are believed to be childhood memories, and several of his memories place his life in our timeline. In other words, I'm not suggesting that Benjaman Kyle popped in through a portal. What I'm demonstrating is that these John Doe's exist whose identities cannot be determined in spite of fingerprints, DNA, and mass media coverage.

Benjaman Kyle was diagnosed with *schizophrenia* and *dissociative amnesia*. I have no idea what he may have told the doctors to generate a schizophrenic diagnosis, but common symptoms include: hearing voices that nobody else can hear, and delusions. A delusion is a belief which is held "with strong conviction" despite evidence to the contrary, no matter what evidence is presented to you, and despite the implausibility of that belief. In addition to delusions and seeing or hearing things that aren't there, you might experience a sense of unrealness where the world seems hazy, where you feel as if you are in a dream-state.

The time slip incidents are perfect matches for seeing or hearing something that isn't there. Goddard saw an airfield in a condition that couldn't have existed, and if he took someone back there and described the brand new hangars and strange planes, nobody would have believed him. Ditto for all the other time slip cases, and the ghost ship sightings. In addition, all of these experiences had the feeling of being "unreal" while they were occurring — the Oz Factor.

The public debates on what should get labeled as schizophrenia (mental illness) and the subsequent discussions about religious beliefs, which currently fall outside of the schizophrenic umbrella only because of the sheer numbers of believers, bring up an interesting point.

A paranormal event from a thousand years ago versus one that happened yesterday have one thing in common — you must believe these stories solely on faith. Once an experience is proven scientifically, it's no longer considered paranormal, and there's no question about whether to believe it. Nobody today (barring aboriginal tribes) would think twice about hot air blowing from a vent in your house, without an actual fire to explain where the heat was coming from. We take HVAC for granted. Two thousand years ago, they might have described it as "leprechauns blowing hot air with magic." Today's technology would have been yesterday's magic — or witchcraft.

In addition, history, fact and fancy are all mixed up together which muddies the waters, because no doubt some of our ancestor's stories would sprout Pinocchio's nose. A few of these stories, however, have become legends that have taken on a life of their own, such as the *Philadelphia Experiment* that alleges that our government was tinkering with cloaking technology, and that the experiments went awry. Volumes have been written about the *Philadelphia Experiment* including interviews, but one of the more interesting mentions comes from the National Investigations Committee on Aerial Phenomena (NICAP) database.

"1908: Coast of Delaware. The English ship *Mohican*, piloted by Capt. Urghart, was going to Philadelphia when it was surrounded by a thick, luminous cloud which 'magnetized' everything on board. The compass was observed to swing wildly. When seamen tried to move some chains on the bridge, they found that they (the chains) were glued to the metal floor. Suddenly the cloud rose and was seen above the sea for some time. — NICAP"

Another version of this event was published in 1904. Presumably, the report was made to NICAP in 1908 for an event that had happened in 1904, making it difficult to find the corroborating source by year.

A more expanded version was published on August 5, 1904, on page 181 of *The Electrical Engineer, A Weekly Journal of Electrical Engineering, with which is incorporated Electric Light, Volume XXXIV*. The publisher clearly believed that the story was pure hogwash, and this appears to be an original source for the phenomena described in the *Philadelphia Experiment*.

"In a magnetic cloud — The following has received the credit of a good evening paper in this country, and it speaks volumes for the knowledge of the sub-editor of the same. Obviously the story has crossed the Atlantic, and we presume that the writer was either approaching or receding from a 'bar' at the time he was delivered of the paragraph. We admire the vivid description of the magnetic, electric, and gravity storm cloud quite as much as we do the transparent veracity of the writer.

"The British ship *Mohican*, which has arrived at Philadelphia, reports having passed through a magnetic cloud while approaching the Delaware breakwater. Fire played across the metal ship from stem to stern, the needle of the ship's compass flew around like an electric fan, and everything was magnetized. It was impossible to lift even light chains or bars, which clung tightly to the iron deck. The captain says: 'The hair of our heads stuck out like bristles, and it was difficult to move the arms or legs. Suddenly the magnetic cloud lifted, and the phosphorescent glow around the ironwork vanished, and things became as usual.'"

This story also appeared in *The New York Times* on August 1, 1904. The NYT version listed the captain's name as being Captain *Urquhart* rather than *Urghart*, along with a few additional details. The captain saw a strange, gray cloud at a distance, and watched as the cloud approached. In the meantime, the vessel *and crew* had a fiery coating before the sailors saw it (the story wasn't clear whether *it* referred to the cloud, or the fiery coating.)

The compass needle flew around like an electric fan. Captain Urquhart ordered the panicked crew to move some iron chains, hoping to divert their attention. However, they couldn't move the chains, or bolts, or spikes, or bars, because everything was stuck tight to the deck as if the objects had been riveted.

Their hair and beards stuck out like bristles, and it was difficult to move their arms and legs. The frightened sailors fell on the deck and prayed. Suddenly the cloud began to lift, and the phosphorescent glow started to fade. The magnetism of the steel faded away gradually. After a few minutes, the cloud had passed over the vessel, and they watched as it moved off over the sea.

Did the difficulty in moving their arms and legs indicate that they experienced a change in Earth's gravity? Could this magnetic cloud explain some of the incidents associated with the Bermuda Triangle, and its numerous disappearances? The cloud seemed to be drifting over the ocean, and they got caught in it for a few brief, frightening moments. While this story doesn't mention anything that would resemble a portal or time travel, it does suggest that strange phenomena occurs that we can't explain. Nor does it discount additional possibilities, as there is undoubtedly a more detailed account either in the ship's logs or headquarters, which may not have gone public at that time.

One anomaly may link this event to the portals that connect us to paradise. The phrases "fire played across the ship from stem to stern" and "the vessel and crew had a fiery coating" are similar to portal descriptions that don't involve clouds or mist.

Prester John's kingdom was surrounded by a moss-covered wall with a single entry that was "closed with burning fire so that no mortal man dared to enter."

The "bridge" that connected Earth to Asgard, the world of the Norse Aesir gods, was called *bifröst*, and the gods traveled across it every day. Descriptions of bifröst included the phrase: "for Heaven's bridge burns all in flame." The bridge consisted of three colors, including red, and the red was "burning fire" which prevented the giants from using the bridge to get to Asgard, and yet the Aesir gods had no trouble crossing this fiery bridge.

The "fire" on the ship *Mohican* did not burn the crew, so this was a different type of fire than we'd normally think of. References to fire that doesn't burn appear in the *Bible* as well, such as the burning bush in *Exodus* where "the bush burned with fire, and the bush was not consumed." Another biblical reference comes from *Acts 2*, where the sound of a mighty wind came from Heaven, and fire appeared which sat on each of the Apostles, and did not burn them: "There appeared unto them cloven tongues like as of fire, and it sat upon each of them."

The "burning fire" of the bifröst bridge to another world did not burn the Aesir gods who crossed over the bridge every single day. Is there a connection between magnetic clouds, fire that doesn't burn, portals to paradise such as the bifröst bridge, the fire that protects Prester John's door, and the clouds that you had to pass through to reach hidden islands?

Magnetic Wormholes

There's a phenomenon known as *electronic fog*, which is described as "chasing and trying to capture vessels" as if attracted to them magnetically. Electronic fog is a gray cloud of electromagnetic fields that form over large bodies of water, seemingly in an instant. Once formed, they seek out nearby ships or planes and attach themselves, completely engulfing the craft, and they move right along with the vehicle.

Navigational controls go haywire, controls cease to function, and sometimes the craft simply disappears without a trace. No one knows whether the ships sink, the airplanes crash into the ocean, or whether they are transported someplace else. We simply do not know. Every opinion at this point is pure speculation, no matter which side of the debate you fall on.

Despite a history full of descriptions such as that of the ship *Mohican*, and genuine SOS calls from veteran pilots as well as the Coast Guard, all of them describing this bizarre fog, such stories get dismissed as hoaxes like the comment in *The Electrical Engineer* which implied that whoever told the story had obviously been drinking at the bar. However, NASA has discovered wormholes in Earth's magnetic field, though they are far out in space where the average human is not likely to encounter them. Still, it opens up interesting speculation.

NASA found evidence of magnetic wormholes which they refer to as *X-points* or *electron diffusion regions*. These are places where the magnetic field of Earth connects to the magnetic field of the Sun, creating an uninterrupted path between the two. When a portal opens, high energy particles and solar wind can flow through the wormhole from the Sun to Earth. This is called a *flux transfer event* (FTE). These magnetic portals are unstable, and they may open and close dozens of times a day. NASA has a mission planned for 2014 called *Magnetospheric Multiscale Mission* (MMS) to study this phenomenon.

Here we have absolute evidence that wormholes exist in Earth's magnetic field, and Einstein believed that wormholes through the space-time continuum were possible. While we haven't proven the science of space-time wormholes that can transport us to another planet or dimension yet, it's simply a matter of time before we do. Who will be the first to achieve the breakthrough? A brilliant researcher from the Max Planck Institute for Extraterrestrial Physics, perhaps?

We have indications that magnetism goes hand in hand with traveling through a portal to another world — the UFO connections to magnetic fields. UFOs have a long history of magnetic anomalies like the one on the *Mohican* that caused the ship's compass to spin around like an electric fan, and magnetic fields have been measured after UFO sightings such as the one in Gulf Breeze, Florida on September 11, 1992.

According to ufologist Bruce Maccabee, who has a Ph.D. in physics, investigators swept the area with a fluxgate gradient magnetometer which indicated a strong magnetic field, or magnetic cloud, just above the tree tops. This machine is designed to measure Earth's magnetic field, and detect anomalies and distortions to the field.

Project Magnet, under the direction of Wilbert Smith, was created in 1950 to research the possibility that UFOs were extraterrestrial craft which manipulated magnetism for flight, and how we might exploit Earth's magnetic field as a source of propulsion for vehicles. While this particular project was shut down in 1954, the belief that UFOs manipulate magnetic fields was just beginning.

Ufologist and nuclear physicist Stanton Friedman wrote an article entitled *UFO Propulsion Systems* which suggested that the manipulation of electric and magnetic fields would allow the rapid acceleration and tight turns made by UFOs. He referred to our own research in this area, such as an electromagnetic submarine designed in the 1960s by Dr. Stuart Way, and the highly classified research into magneto-aerodynamics.

Ufologist Jacques Vallée and French astrophysicist Claude Poher co-wrote an article about the UFO-magnetic field connection entitled, *Basic Patterns in UFO Observations*, which analyzed data from years of UFO research in multiple countries. There's a worldwide network of stations that record fluctuations in Earth's magnetic field, day and night. They studied the measurements for the year 1954, which coincided with a major UFO wave in France, and estimated that the magnetic field produced by a UFO might be 150,000 ampere turns per meter in its immediate neighborhood.

THE ANCIENT ONES

By whatever manner that the Otherworlders came to Earth, whether through portals such as the bifröst bridge between worlds, or via some sort of magnetic or electronic fog which posed as a gateway to the hidden islands of paradise, there is no doubt that they were here. They lived among us, interacted with us, married us, had children with us, did battled with us, and taught us.

All through the ancient world, you've seen evidence of advanced technology, and extraordinary visitors, many of whom left a positive mark on the world. What seeds of wisdom and knowledge did these beings leave behind?

King Yima started out as an ordinary human, who was chosen by the god Ahura Mazda to rule over men, and to ensure that all living things prospered. To carry out this mission, Yima was endowed with the royal *farr*, which imbued him with a radiant splendor, and he came into possession of a magic mirror. Under Ahura's guidance, Yima taught farming, weaponry, weaving, mining, construction, and navigation, and thus raised humanity out of its primitive origins.

His reign also brought health, youth, long life, peace, and prosperity to his people, but the benefits of a youthful long life backfired, and he was repeatedly warned about the perils of overpopulation, and a world that had become materialistic. Apparently he'd been feeding humans with the forbidden fruit of immortality from the Tree of Life, by one interpretation of the ancient texts.

One day, Ahura Mazda and a group of divine beings met with King Yima. The king was instructed to build a vara to prepare for a great flood, which held approximately 2,000 people in addition to animals and plants to be saved from the flood. He was instructed to populate the vara with the best cattle, seeds of fruits, men and so forth, and he was specifically forbidden to include anyone or anything that was less than perfect, such as deformed or diseased humans, or those with mental aberrations.

His vara would not be the only survivor of the flood. Others would survive who lived in remote regions on mountaintops. Some equate Yima's flood with Noah's flood, while others believe that Yima's flood is still pending and that Yima's vara is hidden away to repopulate the world after the final big battle.

Somewhere along the way, Yima got really full of himself, and stopped giving credit to Ahura Mazda for the benefits to mankind, taking all of the credit for himself. He began to act as if he were the creator, as if he were a divine being. For his pride, the royal farr was stripped away from him, and the glory never returned. The people began to rise up against King Yima after a successful several hundred year reign, and his rival, Aži Dahāka, took advantage of Yima's fall from grace.

Aži Dahāka was the son of a destructive spirit named Angra Mainyu — an enemy of Ahura Mazda — who was associated with evil thoughts and evil deeds. He was the polar opposite of the good King Yima, and together with his brother, they killed King Yima and took over his rulership with the aid of the Daevas. This takeover plunged civilization back into a Dark Age. However, even if mankind succumbed to a mental evil, they still would have retained Yima's teachings on farming, navigation, construction, and so forth.

On the other side of the world, and many centuries later, Hiawatha came and provided seeds and grains, and taught farming and other skills. He gave instructions on how to make, and use, weapons, and how to protect ourselves in the forest from both giants and "monsters." He provided fishing and hunting grounds. In addition, he brought several warring tribes together in peace. Like King Yima, he was a good ruler, who brought peace and prosperity, and made the world a better place.

Hiawatha gave a farewell speech, which explained that he'd been "allowed" by the Great Spirit to communicate with us, and now it was time for him to leave. His mission had been fulfilled.

This is one of the few clues we've been given regarding the beings that came to us long ago. For most of these ancient visitors, we can look at the evidence of what they left behind, though we don't get the benefit of a parting speech.

As with most of the history that includes otherworldly visitors, the stories did not get written down until long after the visitors had gone. History was preserved orally, with each generation telling the next generation, until one day it got written down. Unfortunately, some of the transcribers did not embrace the stories that they were preserving, so we don't know how true to the original that history ended up being. In addition, so much of our history was burned or destroyed during religious wars, territory wars, and hostile takeovers.

The Norse gods are one of the more cryptic, because much of their history was pieced together in the 13th century, hundreds of years after the gods themselves had come and gone. We can only guess at how much of their follower's advancements came directly from the teachings of the Norse gods. What we do know is that the Vikings were followers of the gods which included Odin and Thor, and we have clear evidence that the Vikings possessed advanced technology. For example, Visby lenses were found in Viking graves on the island of Gotland from the 11th or 12th century, though the lenses are much older.

Made of quartz crystal, their design demonstrates optical knowledge far in advance of what the Vikings were thought to possess. Theories of what the Visby lenses were used for include magnifying glasses, fire starters, and maybe even telescope lenses — hundreds of years before traditional history tells us that telescopes were invented!

The image quality suggests that whoever made the lenses knew more about what they were doing than the scientists and mathematicians of that era. Whatever knowledge went into the production of these Visby lenses was then "lost" for hundreds of years, until Descartes came onto the scene in the 1600s and added his mathematical knowledge to the field of optics.

The quality of the Visby lenses is comparable to lenses that we use today, such as those used in projectors and eyeglasses, and it's possible that the manufacture of Visby lenses was limited to "a single craftsman." So who was this advanced craftsman? Was it one of the Norse gods who lived among us? Did the Vikings possess telescopes? Or were the lenses acquired through trade routes with other civilizations? The Vikings had contact with much of the known world, which in itself was amazing.

Gotland is a small island off the coast of Sweden, and its town of Visby was one of the most important Hanseatic cities in the Baltic Sea. A commercial and defensive confederation of merchant guilds banded together to form the Hanseatic League, possibly dating back to 1358 A.D., which had its own legal system and armies to protect cities along its trade route. The league did not "own" the cities that it protected, in the sense of being a country, but these cities did come to each other's defense when necessary. The importance of Visby itself, however, predated the Hanseatic League, as it was already an established trading center in 900 A.D.

The island of Gotland traces its descendants back to the son of Pjalfi, who was literally a servant of the Norse god Thor. According to legend, the island itself was hidden underwater during the day and appeared only at night, until Pjalfi "broke the spell" which hid the island by lighting a fire. This story is very similar to the Phantom Isle of Ireland, which was stabilized after someone shot an arrow of red-hot steel into it.

Along with the Visby lenses, hoards of silver coins from Arabian countries were discovered on Gotland that when combined, rival the number of Arab dirhams found *in the entire Muslim world*. Also of interest are the grooved stones which are called "the grinding grooves of Gotland." These stones represent an *unknown industrial process*. Over 3,600 of these grinding grooves have been found on Gotland dating back as early as 3300 B.C., according to astronomer Göran Henriksson, and their purpose is an unsolved mystery. Theories include that they were made while sharpening axes and blades with a suspended grinding wheel, or even that they were some sort of celestial calendar whose importance should be ranked as highly as Stonehenge and the Mayan calendar.

Here we have an island once believed to be hidden, whose descendants trace back to a servant of the Norse god Thor, on which advanced Visby lenses have been discovered, along with mysterious grooved stones, and massive hoards of Arabian silver coins. Archeological finds are shattering what we thought we knew about the Vikings.

Their nautical achievements were exceptional. Viking distance calculations were so precise that when compared to today's satellite measurements, they differed by only 2-4%. The Vikings used other optical technologies as well, including an optical compass for navigation, which could pinpoint the location of the Sun even when it was hidden behind clouds. With their stable ships and advanced navigation, they traveled everywhere, predating Christopher Columbus' voyage to America by 500 years. We did not discover the Viking village in Newfoundland, Canada until 1960, completely altering the history of both the North American continent and the Vikings. Were their nautical technologies, Visby lenses, or Gotland island mysteries, the product of interaction with visitors from one of the Nine Worlds?

Hidden islands seemed to be a theme for these long ago visitors. Gotland was a once-hidden island off the coast of Sweden, associated with (a servant of) the Norse gods, and the Isle of Man was the once-hidden island off the coast of Ireland, associated with the Tuatha dé Danann.

Most of what we read about the Tuatha dé Danann involves their arrival in Ireland, battles, quarrels, love affairs, technology, magical abilities, and their demise at the hands of both the Milesians and Christians, neither of whom wanted anything positive written about their common enemy. A few seeds have survived to give us an inkling of what benefits may have come from these beings.

The Tuatha dé Danann were described as "the gods of human civilization" versus their predecessors the Fomorians — who were "the gods of chaos" or "wicked gods." The knowledge of astronomy, astrology, and natural philosophy that the Tuatha dé Danann possessed was so revered, that the sons of kings were sent to them for education. Considering their likely origins, it's no wonder that they were well versed in astronomy and astrology!

Manannán mac Lir was one of the most renowned of the Tuatha dé Danann, and there is evidence that he shared wisdom in the form of parables. Remember Cormac mac Airt, the high king of Ireland who disappeared for seven months in 248 A.D. to search for the wife and children that he'd traded for a silver branch? The entire trade was a set up from the beginning, designed to lure Cormac to visit Manannán, where Cormac could witness a visual representations of life lessons.

Cormac was one of the most beloved of the high kings. He was wise and courageous, and unlike some who ruled before him, he was not needlessly bloodthirsty. Could Manannán's influence have contributed to Cormac's wisdom, considering that Manannán mac Lir took Cormac under his wing?

The first "parable" that Cormac saw was a great dun (fort) in the middle of a plain, surrounded by a wall of bronze, and inside the fort was a house of white-silver which was partially thatched with the wings of white birds. The house was surrounded with people carrying armloads of white bird's wings for thatching, but no sooner would they install the thatch, than a great blast of wind would blow it off and carry it away.

These were all the men who had looked for a fortune, chasing after riches, but as soon as they turned away the riches disappeared, so that they were forever chasing after riches. Presumably this means that earthly riches disappear as soon as you do, so if you wanted to leave a legacy behind, earthly riches isn't the way to go.

Then Cormac saw a man throwing a thick oak tree onto a fire, and when the man came back with another big tree to keep the fire going, he found that the fire had already burned out, so the man was forever restarting the fire. This man was a young lord who was more liberal than he could afford to be. While he was restarting the fire and getting the feast ready, everybody else was being served, and everybody else was profiting from his labors.

Cormac walked on until he came to a royal fort encircled in a wall of bronze. Inside the fort were four houses. One was a great king's house with beams of bronze, walls of silver, and the outer walls were thatched with the wings of white birds. Neatly trimmed, emerald green grass stretched out in front of the king's house. In the center of the grass was a shining well with five streams flowing from it, and armies drinking water in turn. Nine lasting purple hazels of Ruan were growing over the well. They dropped their nuts into the water, and five salmon would catch the nuts and send their husks floating down the five streams.

The sound of those streams was sweeter than any music that a man could sing. The well was the Well of Knowledge, and the streams were the five streams through which all knowledge flows. No one will have knowledge who does not drink from the well itself, or out of the streams, and the people of many arts are those who drink from them all.

The third parable follows a completely different train of thought than the other two, and I was curious as to whether *Ruan* had any significance. The journey the third parable led me on made me realize how incredibly powerful this seemingly simple story was, and that Manannán mac Lir was indeed wise beyond his years.

The number *five* seemed to be significant, especially when it came to learning, so it could represent making full use of all five senses, and not just one or two. Sight, sound, touch, taste, and smell are the senses we currently hold as the Big Five. However, extrasensory perception has long been called "the sixth sense." Knowing that kings sent their sons to Manannán's people for advanced learning, the entire concept of learning and knowledge was obviously important to the Tuatha dé Danann.

Another contender for the number five, especially with the nuts being sent down five rivers and the reference to armies, was that it designated five clans, or was connected to five physical rivers, so I looked up "five rivers" in both Ireland and England, because Manannán is associated with Ireland, and Ruan turned out to have a fascinating link to both Ireland and England.

Manannán's parable spoke of "nine lasting purple hazels of Ruan growing over the well," and deciphering what he meant with *Ruan* led me down a twisted, winding path. I figured it would either be a type of tree, or a prominent family name in the history of Ireland, but it didn't seem to fit either hypothesis. I thought maybe it was another spelling for the Rowan tree of Norse mythology — the giant tree that links the Nine Worlds — but Ruan does not equal Rowan in any text that I researched.

Then I hit pay dirt for the name *Ruan* in England, which is how England came into the picture. There was a St. Ruan connected to Tavistock Abbey in Devon, England. Unlike the many other saints whose histories are prominent, you really need to dig to get into the life of St. Ruan. The historians of old couldn't even determine whether he was Irish, Scottish, or Saxon, or who his family may have been, or where he was born, and there are quite a few theories. It's as if he appeared one day out of nowhere, and made such a name for himself that towns, parishes and churches were named after him in several countries. The old texts credit him with many miracles, but they don't offer details of what those miracles may have been, with one questionable exception.

There was a legend that claimed that St. Ruan was a sorcerer who could turn himself into a wolf. So here we're back to this wolf business like the curse of St. Natalis and Barking Mania. As the story goes, a pagan woman who didn't like St. Ruan's Christian teachings was afraid that her husband would leave his husbandly duties and run off to become a monk, so she denounced St. Ruan to the king as being a werewolf in the hopes of getting rid of him. The king did arrest Ruan, but quietly worked behind the scenes to ensure that the monk was found innocent.

Some texts have this legend taking place in Cornwall, England where Ruan settled. However, he also lived in several cities in France, where he was revered as Ronan of Locronan. He lived in the French cities of Léon, and Hillion, and the French king who assisted him after the werewolf accusation was King Gradlon, sometimes written as Grallo. Once you bring King Gradlon into the picture, it gets weird again. Gradlon fell in love with a sorceress named Malgven, a woman he'd met during his travels. She was a red-haired beauty with blue eyes and creamy white skin, who was linked to the kingdom of Alban, and the Alban Isles, which refers to a portion of Scotland, along with the Shetland, Orkney, and Hebrides islands.

This woman, like the Tuatha dé Danann of the Hebrides and the Isle of man, not only possessed powerful magic, she owned a "horse" that could gallop across the sea causing the sea to boil underneath him, whiles flames or lightning flashed from his nostrils. This "horse" rushed to shore with such power and speed that it actually shook the shore. Not only does this sound like a powerful speed boat fashioned to resemble a horse, it goes hand in hand with the water-horse legend from the Isle of Man. Was Malgven a member of the Tuatha dé Danann, or a similar race of beings?

The legends of King Gradlon are all mixed up with hidden or lost underwater cities, a wife who possessed magical abilities, amphibious water vehicles, along with Merlin the wizard and the Arthurian legends, and this king was good enough friends with St. Ruan to ensure that he was found innocent of werewolf activities. For some reason, Ruan's name was also important to Manannán.

As with most names in history, Ruan's name is linked to several alternate spellings, including Rumon, Rumoni, Ruadan, and Ronan. Manannán specifically used Ruan, however, and in Cornwall, England, three church parishes were named after St. Ruan which still exist under his name. This saint lived around 500 A.D., which puts him right at the tail end of the Tuatha dé Danann legends in Ireland, along with the other early Christian monks and their miracles. Some of Ruan's constituents believed that he came to England from Ireland, and that both he and his parents personally knew St. Patrick.

St. Ruan settled in the Nemean wood in Cornwall, a forest that was full of wild beasts, and "haunted by wolves" according to local legends. Whether the wolf legends were already in existence before he moved into the forest is unknown. Once he came into the picture, few dared to enter the haunted forest, and from there shared his Christian wisdom.

Nemean comes from Greek mythology, being the son of the Greek god Typhon. Nemean was the Nemean lion — a shape shifter who could take on the appearance of a beast or a human. As a lion, Nemean was swathed in golden fur which no mortal weapon could pierce, and equipped with claws so sharp that they could slice through armor. It took the strength of Hercules to slay the mighty Nemean lion who was then placed among the constellations in the sky as Leo the lion, because the Nemean lion was the king of beasts. What frightening beasts lived in the Nemean woods of Cornwall besides wolves isn't mentioned, but Ruan was the only man courageous enough to travel these woods.

St. Ruan was the only contender that I could find for the name *Ruan* of Manannán's story. Now that I'd found a Ruan, I wanted to know more about him, such as why he was important enough to be named in a parable, and this is where it got even more twisted than his connection to shape shifters, werewolves, and kings who married otherworldly women with speed boats.

King Gradlon was connected to Merlin, and Ruan had a hill in Cornwall — Polruan Hill — which is only 33 miles from Merlin's Cave, a place long associated with the wizard Merlin.

Many strange legends surrounded St. Ruan and his parishes including haunted Nemean forests, werewolves, and ghost ships. Several parishes in England were named after Ruan including Ruan Major and Ruan Minor, along with the church of Ruan-Lanyhorne. The parish of Ruan Major consisted of 2,325 acres with no village, chapel, or public house in the olden days, but it did have three ponds: Hayl Kimbro, Leech, and Croft Pasco.

The latter was located in the weird, dreary, melancholy wasteland known as Goonhilly, which was so lonely and haunted that few humans dared to cross over it after sunset. In the center of Goonhilly was Croft Pasco, a pond known for a ghost ship called "the ghostly lugger of Croft Pasco" which sailed at night with its sails spread.

Today, Goonhilly is the home of gigantic satellite dishes named Merlin, Guinevere, Tristan and Isolde, whose legends are all linked to the region. Goonhilly is also the location of a tall, upright stone, or *menhir*, which is an ancient monolith of unknown significance.

Also in Ruan's parish was the Chapel of Pol Ruan, which combined with Polruan Hill led me to consider that his full name was Paul Ruan. I found no connection to the name *Paul*, but Polruan itself translates as "harbor of a man called Ruveun" or "Ruveun's harbor" according to three dictionaries of place names published variously by Penguin, Oxford, and the University of Michigan.

Pol actually means "pool" or "harbor," which leaves *Ruan* as being equivalent to "Ruveun." In Icelandic, Polruan is the same as Hróvinshöfn, with *Ruan* being "Hróvin," but I did not find a Hróvin in the Norse legends of Odin, so that path petered out, which left Ruveun.

When you plug Ruveun into Google, the hits you get are a location in South Africa, and a reference in a French text called *Celtic Review*, which equates Ruveun with Ruven. In addition, a page comes up in the old Norse texts that relates to the history of Odin, the Nine Worlds, and so forth, where Ruveun shows up as *'ru enn* with a connector between *'ru* and *enn*. The exact phrase turned out to be: "pau eru enn sva at ek man manna." *Pau* doesn't seem to translate so it must be a name, and the rest translates as "are still so that I can remember people." What made me follow this trail was the "man manna" as it was so close to Manannán's name, that I thought there might be a connection. *Man manna* means "remember people" in Icelandic.

Since I was really only trying to track down the name Ruan/Ruveun and not an entire phrase, plugging Ruveun into an Icelandic/English translator brings up the name Ruven, just like in the French *Celtic Review*, and this is where it got seriously twisted amazing.

I searched old books hoping to shed light on what I thought might be a long forgotten St. Ruven, but what came up completely floored me. *Ruven* comes from an ancient language and it translates as the word "man" according to one of the most important archeological discoveries in the Middle East.

Carved into the rock on Mount Behistun in Iran is an inscription known as the *Behistun Inscription*. It was inscribed in three languages — Old Persian, Elamite, and Babylonian — and it unlocked the keys to deciphering ancient texts in those languages. The inscription was written by Darius the Great, who worshipped the Zoroastrian god Ahura Mazda, and it has been compared to the Rosetta Stone that helped us decode the Egyptian hieroglyphs. The Behistun Inscription dates back to sometime around 500 B.C.

Manannán tells a story which specifically talks about learning from the Well of Knowledge, and not to limit your learning to one stream or another, but to partake of all of the streams that flow from this Well of Knowledge. He links this water to Ruan — the equivalent of Ruveun/Ruven — which comes directly from the Behistun Inscription that was used as a Rosetta Stone to help us decipher ancient languages. Is that what Manannán meant by Ruan? I don't know, but it sure is an interesting coincidence, especially when no other connections exist to explain the *Ruan* in his parable.

St. Ruan was revered in England, and his parishes were in England, so I continued on this vein of research by looking up "five rivers in England" to see if the five streams in the parable might have referred to an actual, physical location. This search immediately brought up the city of Salisbury, England, which *sits at the confluence of five rivers*. Eight miles north of this confluence is Salisbury Plain — which is the location of Stonehenge, a place that links not only to England, but also to Ireland, where the Tuatha dé Danann legends all took place. Stonehenge in England is connected to one of the most sacred places in all of Ireland, along with the number *five* in Ireland.

Manannán referred to five nuts that fell from the nine lasting purple hazels of Ruan which grew over the Well of Knowledge. This seems to be an almost perfect reference to an ancient tale called *The Settling of the Manor of Tara*, which was told in the same series of texts where the many Tuatha dé Danann histories come from. The gist of the Tara story is that a

183

mysterious man appeared in Ireland one day (the day that Jesus was crucified) whose description reminded me of Moses in the *Bible*, only this man's name was Trefuilngid Tre-eochair.

Trefuilngid wore a shining crystal veil, just as Moses had done after encountering God, because Moses' presence became so bright that people couldn't look at him without the veil. Like Moses, the man who came to Tara also carried stone tablets, though the story doesn't give their purpose.

Trefuilngid brought all the people of Ireland together and asked them to relate their history to him, which then became permanent record by being told in the story. Once he'd heard everyone's concept of history, his goal was to settle land boundary disputes in Ireland for once and for all, which resulted in the division of Ireland into five provinces. Along with dividing Ireland into five provinces, Trefuilngid also handed out five berries, which were planted and grew into five sacred trees named Tortu, Rossa, Mugna, Dathe, and Usnech.

Mugna can be traced directly to Jesus, and Usnech to Stonehenge, though I'm not sure about the significance of the other three trees and beyond family names and local history. Mugna is the Gaelic word for "salmon" which was also the fish that appeared in Manannán's parable — "Five salmon caught the nuts and sent their husks floating down the five streams." As a fish, salmon plays a prominent role in Celtic mythology, Norse mythology, Native American mythology, and the name Salmon appears in the *Bible* as a person. Salmon was a *direct ancestor* of Jesus! If we embrace the possibility that Manannán's parable is connected to the personage of Trefuilngid and *The Settling of the Manor of Tara*, then we can follow the trail of Usnech as well, the sacred hill of Ireland which has many relevant connections.

Under the spelling *Uisnech/Uisneach*, this is one of the most significant locations in all of Ireland. On this sacred hill sits the *Ail na Mireann*, which is the "stone of divisions" that once marked the meeting point of the borders of the five provinces that

Trefuilngid divvied out. The Irish stone of divisions is listed as an *omphalos,* or mystical navel, and it's one of the few in the world.

According to legend, the *Hill of Uisneach* in central Ireland is where some of the stones for Stonehenge came from. The Hill of Uisneach was once called Killara Mountain (aka Killagha/ Kildare) and on this mountain was an ancient monument called the Circle of Heroes. This consisted of "stones of immense size of which no one can give an account."

It was none other than the Merddin Emrys (Merlin the wizard) who set out to steal these sacred Irish stones from the Circle of Heroes in order to build what became Stonehenge in England. A battle ensued between King Gillamori of Ireland, and Merlin who was fighting on behalf of England, over possession of the gigantic stones.

The powerful wizard prevailed and by his own magic, Merlin transported the stones "without labor" to ships, and finally to Salisbury Plain. Remember the other legends of stones being transported through the air? The Fenodyree on the Isle of Man which was a Tuatha dé Danann stronghold, the Jinn who transported stones in Heliopolis in Ancient Egypt, the Aymara legends of the stone movers who built Tiahuanacu and Pumapunku in South America, and the Cherokee legend of Spear-finger in North America, all referred to magical beings who could transport stones through the air. Now we have the wizard Merlin moving stones from the Circle of Heroes in Ireland to Stonehenge in England — without labor.

This gives us a clear connection between the number five, the sacred hill in Ireland which represents the convergence of five provinces, and the confluence of five rivers in England. Both are very sacred locations. Coincidence? I don't believe so.

Another point of interest in the division of Ireland into five provinces was the personage of Trefuilngid Tre-eochair. His name is often linked to Christianity and the Holy Trinity, along with the concept of a three leafed clover, but I dug a bit further knowing that old legends were often rewritten to glorify Christianity and erase whatever came before.

His name breaks down to Tre-fuil-ngid Tre-eochair. *Tre* represents "three." *Fuil* is the old Irish word for "blood." *Ngid* is the Hebrew word for "prince" or "ruler." *Eochair* means "key." So what you end up with is "three blood princes/rulers who are the three keys." Manannán's parable specifically mentioned "nine lasting purple hazels of Ruan growing over the well" whose nuts were carried down the five streams, and I believe that this is also a reference to family trees or bloodlines. I followed every bloodline that seemed remotely relevant, and the one with the most connections was a trio of kings who ruled Ireland together.

These kings were brothers, and they were the last of the Tuatha dé Danann to rule over Ireland. They were grandsons of the Dagda, who has a connection to the Hill of Uisneach. Their names were MacGreine, MacCecht, and MacCuill, each being born with a different name which was later changed to reflect the gods that they followed. MacCuill was named for his god Coll, which means *hazel*. You can get into a whole bunch of other legends relating to this trio of Tuatha dé Danann blood brothers who ruled Ireland, but I'll forego writing another book in this chapter. Suffice to say that I believe that somehow, the name of Trefuilngid Tre-eochair is linked to this band of Tuatha dé Danann blood brothers.

They were grandsons of the Dagda, whose daughter Brigit was one of the most prominent saints of Ireland, but before we get to their aunt Brigit, we're going to veer off into another direction for a moment. Manannán mac Lir told a simple story that turned out to be extremely complex. It linked the division of Ireland into five provinces, the location of Stonehenge in England, the hill in Ireland where the stones for Stonehenge were excavated, the Irish *omphalos* or navel stone, a shape shifting saint that turns into a wolf, Norse and Celtic mythology, the Behistun Inscription, and lord only knows what else.

Another mystery from ancient history comes from the word *dun* in Manannán's fables — the word *dun* means fort, or hill fort — and there's something known as a *vitrified* dun or fort, whose dates range from approximately 800 B.C. through 900 A.D., which puts their dates in range with the Tuatha dé Danann.

More than 200 of these vitrified forts have been found around the world in Scotland, Wales, Ireland, Hungary, Turkey, Iran, Germany, England, and France, but the majority seem to be in Scotland, which shares an island with England and Wales, across the Irish Sea from the Isle of Man and Ireland.

A vitrified fort is a fort that's been subjected to such intense heat that the silicate rocks turn to liquid, and then harden into crystalline or glass-like rocks. These rocks are literally melted, and fused back together, by temperatures *in excess of* a thousand degrees Celsius, which is 1,832 degrees Fahrenheit.

Vitrified forts were often located in strong defensive positions, and some had double or triple walls for defense. Entire forts were not vitrified, however, only portions were. Sometimes pieces of rock were enveloped in a glassy, enamel-like coating which bound them into a unified whole. Sometimes, an entire wall was a solid mass of vitreous substance.

Nobody knows how or why the walls were subjected to vitrification. Temperatures had to be hot enough to liquify both iron and stone. Even today our attempts to duplicate the process demonstrate the sheer difficulty of such an undertaking. We have to maintain the intense heat in close proximity over a significant period of time, and apply it consistently to a large area, in order to duplicate the vitrification of these forts.

In 1934, archeologists V. Gordon Childe and Wallace Thorneycroft showed that forts could be set on fire which would generate enough heat to vitrify the stone, but they had to set it up just right in order for their experiment to work. They had to construct a wall that they specially designed for the test, which did not match the walls of the forts that were actually vitrified.

When they attempted to duplicate the experiment in 1937 using an actual, ancient fort in Rahoy, Scotland, the same problem was exposed. Modern attempts to vitrify a fort do not match the conditions that actually existed in the ancient forts, and we're only successful if we change the conditions.

Vitrification success takes a great deal of planning. A super structure must be built around a fort using a large quantity of wood and other flammable materials to concentrate the heat. None of the experiments answer the question of *why*. Vitrification makes the rock brittle, not stronger, so it makes no sense for defense. Battle damage from traditional weapons is unlikely, because the process isn't a hit-and-run technique — it requires intense, sustained heat.

Archeologists and ancient astronaut theorists have come up with several suggestions. Theories include the forts being deliberately destroyed with fire following their capture by enemy forces, or the use of ancient volcanic stones in building, or natural plasma discharges which could have caused Noah's flood.

The most interesting theory involves ancient astronauts and powerful weapons blasting down from the sky, a concept echoed in several religious texts. The Hindu goddess Shiva called down "fire-rain" from the sky. Then we've got the biblical cities of Sodom and Gomorrah that were blasted with fire and brimstone from Heaven, which left the cities smoking as if burned in a furnace. We've even got witnesses to ancient aerial weaponry.

In the UFO battle over Nuremberg, Germany, humans woke up on April 4, 1561, to a bizarre aerial battle taking place in the sky, which included a large, triangular UFO that crashed. Literally *hundreds* of UFOs of various shapes and sizes were seen in the sky that day, engaged in a battle against one another.

If extraterrestrials were living on Earth, and their enemies were flying the skies, it could explain how various locations were blasted with fire from the sky, with vitrified forts being the remnants of these ancient battles. It also bolsters the theory that multiple alien agendas exist out there, and that these battles may have taken place to determine the fate of humans, or determine which alien species was allowed to fly Earth's skies.

The red-headed Malgven with the speed boat horse was linked to Scotland, where many of the vitrified forts are located. Is it possible that Malgven's people warred with the Tuatha dé Danann of Ireland causing these vitrified forts? Or were the Fomorian giants, who were also worshipped as gods, and whose legends suggest that they possessed magic and the ability to shape shift, in an aerial war with the Tuatha dé Danann or Malgven's people? It's something to think about.

There is another theory which connects the vitrified forts to the legendary glass or crystal castles, although the remnants of what we've found at these forts don't represent transparent glass. However, one particular vitrified fort exists in Shielfoot, Scotland, that shares a common aspect with both the glass castle stories and the various Tuatha castle legends.

Off the coast near Shielfoot are the Hebrides islands, a region long associated with the Tuatha dé Danann. The Shielfoot fort sits on top of a knife-edged ridge known as The Torr, and there is *no apparent entrance* to the heavily vitrified fort, which may have been accessed by a ladder. Tuatha castles were renowned for their hidden entrances, as were others such as the castle that Norwegian Prince Eirek found, that involved climbing a ladder into a floating glass castle.

That brings us to the goddess Brigit, who was the daughter of the Dagda, which made her one of the Tuatha dé Danann. She was also the half-sister of Midir with his revolving castle. Brigit was so beloved by the people (humans) that the Christians had to adopt her as a saint, because her followers absolutely refused to abandon their love and worship of her. This indicates that at least some of the Tuatha dé Danann were worshipped as gods.

According to *The Irish Mythological Cycle and Celtic Mythology* by Henry Arbois de Jubainville in 1903, the most ancient beliefs about the arrival of the Tuatha dé Danann were that they literally came down from heaven "on the wings of the wind." They were men of learning, and of medicine. One historian described them as "a people of superior intelligence and artistic skill" who were conquered, and then driven into remote districts by the "warlike Milesian tribes who succeeded them."

In virtually all of the stories that involved their battles, they appeared to be men of honor, sometimes giving lands to those they'd conquered, and frequently making battle bargains which they generally honored. That seems to be how the Milesians took possession of Ireland, rather than by killing off such an all-powerful race of seemingly omnipotent beings.

Among their contributions to humanity, it's possible that the Tuatha dé Danann put an end to the concept of human sacrifice. The Fomorians who came before them, and who were also worshipped as gods, required human sacrifices from their followers. The Fomorians were called the gods of Death, Night, and Storm, while the Tuatha dé Danann were called the gods of Life, Day, and Sunshine.

When you read the various legends of the Tuatha dé Danann, human sacrifice is never involved. They engaged in the very human pursuits of battles, adultery, and so forth, but human sacrifice just didn't seem to be part of it. When St. Patrick destroyed a pagan idol that had been used for human sacrifice, there were no current sacrifices being made to the idol, as they'd long since been abolished prior to the coming of St. Patrick.

That suggests that the Tuatha dé Danann, who were the "good gods of life" that ruled after the Fomorians, had done away with human sacrifice, at least in their vicinity. That's not to say that followers of other gods weren't still engaging in the rituals, and the Tuatha dé Danann and Fomorians did intermarry or have affairs. Even Lugh was half-Fomorian and half-Tuatha.

Lugh was the grandson of Balor, a powerful Fomorian who locked his own daughter in a castle for her entire life to prevent a prophecy from coming true — that he'd be killed by his own grandson. Remember the doctor Dian who manufactured the prosthetic silver arm? His son Cian gained access to Balor's daughter through trickery, and impregnated her with triplets. Lugh was one of the triplets, and he did indeed end up killing his grandfather as predicted.

Due to the many interactions between the two peoples, it's possible that rituals attributed to the Fomorians may have erroneously been linked to the Tuatha dé Danann. In other words, several pre-Christian sects may have gotten lumped together as simply being the pre-Christian pagans, and by the time historians came onto the scene to separate the threads of truth, their stories had become so muddied that we may never know what really happened.

Both the Christians, and the Milesians who took possession of Ireland after the Tuatha dé Danann, referred to the Tuatha as *demons* to be obliterated, just as the Tuatha dé Danann had labeled the Fomorians, but prior to Christianity there was a specific term used to denote the form that the Tuatha took among men — *siabra*. The best translation is that of a phantom, which represented a god that took a human-like body in order to become visible to men. This is another way of calling them shape shifters. *Demon* is just a word that gets used to denote virtually any undesirable supernatural being in our history, and on the opposite end of the spectrum are the saints such as Brigit. It's hard to reconcile this beloved saint who everyone adored, with the notion of evil beings and demons. It just doesn't track.

The Dagda's daughter Brigit had a second name — Dana — and was believed to be the Dana that the Tuatha represented. Tuatha dé Danann means "people of the god whose mother is called Dana" which means that her son was a god as well, the one who begat the Tuatha dé Danann. Her father, the Dagda, was known as "the good god," so these beings were not just visitors that lived side by side with us, we worshipped them.

Midir of the revolving castle was also considered a god, as was Nuada of the Silver Hand, who was worshipped as a god long before his appearance as high king of Ireland. A temple was dedicated to Nuada in the county of Gloucester, *in England*, so Manannán's parables are even more noticeably linked to both Ireland and England, and their reign must have included Ireland, England, and the Hebrides islands.

Brigit was the goddess of fire, and of hill forts, and she was skilled in warfare. She also invented a whistle to communicate at night. The Celtic Brigit was combined with the Christian St. Brigid of Kildare, merging the two distinctly different personages into one, along with both of their legends.

An interesting tale regarding this dual St. Brigid involved a sacred flame barrier which produced no ashes, in the form of a hedge or which surrounded a hedge, *which no mortal man could cross*, because in doing so they'd go insane, become crippled, or die. This sounds a lot like the supernatural flame that protected the gate to Prester John's kingdom, and the flame that prevented giants from traveling the bridge between Earth and Asgard.

Another Brigid connection is that the Hill of Uisneach which holds the navel stone of Ireland, and where the stones for Stonehenge may have originated, was anciently called Balor's Hill. This sacred hill is located in Christian Brigid's parish of Kildare. It's the very same hill where the Fomorians and the Tuatha dé Danann battled, and on which Lugh fought and killed his own wicked grandfather, the Fomorian giant-king Balor of the Evil Eye. Even today, Balor's name is used to frighten children as if he were a bogeyman.

These legends represent just a handful of the Otherworldly beings who visited Earth. Now that we have an idea of who they were and how they interacted with us, along with evidence that their world may actually still be accessible, and even the suggestion that they might return, how does this impact our world moving forward?

GAME CHANGER

Should we embrace their return in the hopes that they'll "gift" us with their magic elixirs again? Well, that's a mixed bag. They advanced our knowledge in several areas while they were here. Ancient astronaut theorists are amazed at the star charts, astronomical data, advanced mathematics, and other knowledge that our ancestors possessed, as well as the giant leaps forward that we made with the help of our visiting friends. They were our mentors and teachers.

However, they also bickered with one another, just like we do, engaged in extramarital affairs, and they warred with one another bringing us right along into the wars with them as if we were just pawns. Sometimes they were arrogant and treated us badly. In other words, they were *human* in their emotional flaws. Only a handful walked among us with a perfect wisdom, or purity of heart and spirit.

The Norse gods and the Tuatha dé Danann were not *gods* by our definition of a perfect, spiritual being. They may have seemed like gods with their magic and technology, but emotionally they weren't any better than us. Even in their own ranks, saintly souls lived side by side with devilish ones. In other words, individually they had free will. Are these the other sheep who are "not of this fold" mentioned in the *Bible*?

Did perfect, spiritual beings exist? Yes. And that is a subject totally outside the realm of this book. We can embrace the possibility that extraterrestrials walked among us, and may have even gotten some of the credit for our spiritual beliefs, but it does not negate the concept of the human soul, the spiritual afterlife or rebirth, the concept of free will to do good or evil, or the holy beings who walked among us and founded our many religions.

The quest to rediscover an earthly paradise that may have been linked to extraterrestrial visitors with advanced technology does not mean that there isn't also a spiritual paradise, whether as a rebirth into the spirit realm or a reincarnation back into the physical realm. Our history may be a little different than originally thought, but this doesn't eliminate the existence of a human soul. And it sure doesn't negate the concept that choosing to do good or evil in our lives will in some way influence what happens to that soul.

As mankind gains knowledge of the universe, we have to revise our beliefs. Once we believed that Earth was flat and that we could fall off the edge. We thought that Earth was the center of the universe and that the Sun revolved around us. We believed that in order to fly, we had to paste feathers on our arms and mimic the birds in the sky. Humans were even afraid that mirrors stole the souls right out of our bodies.

Even our religions have evolved. At one time, many religions involved both animal, *and human*, sacrifice. If you could follow your own family or religious tree back far enough, you'd be horrified at the activities of your ancestors. Few of us live as our ancestors did, and even within the same religion. Few of us *worship* as our ancestors did, so adapting to new knowledge doesn't negate the core beliefs that we hold dear.

Consider the following: Early Christians believed in reincarnation. Later Christians burned witches at the stake. Hindu widows committed suicide on their husband's funeral pyre, being burned alive alongside the body of their deceased husband. Jewish men were allowed to have multiple wives. Every religion that's been in existence for a thousand years or more will have undergone some major change, whether from internal forces, or external influence or laws.

Acknowledging extraterrestrials is a game-changer for many of the world's religions, and this is one of the major reasons given as to why governments won't admit that UFOs are flying the skies and have been for thousands of years. The other reason is the possibility of sparking a worldwide panic, as was demonstrated by the *War of the Worlds* 1938 radio broadcast.

Incorporating UFOs and extraterrestrials into our mainstream beliefs is being done gradually. Educational television programs are exploring the UFO phenomenon, bringing science and archeology into the forefront in order to merge UFOs into our history. Science fiction has been "reprogramming" us for decades to look at the universe as being full of diverse beings that we may someday live side by side with, form intergalactic unions with, mate with, or go to war against.

Even the Vatican has come forward with statements that allow for extraterrestrials to exist within the Christian faith. Father José Gabriel Funes of the Vatican Observatory gave an interview in 2008 which became known as *The Extraterrestrial Is My Brother* interview. He stated that it's possible to believe in God, and in extraterrestrials. He explained how we did not have today's level of scientific knowledge at the time the *Bible* was written, so the *Bible* is not a science book, but rather a letter from God to his people.

Regarding extraterrestrials, he stated that God could have created other intelligent beings, and then he quoted St. Francis: "If we consider Earthly creatures as *brother* and *sister*, why cannot we also speak of an *extraterrestrial brother*?" He fueled the hypothesis that beings could exist who are similar to us, or more evolved than us, though he did not offer any indication or acknowledgement of past contact, stating that "until now, we have had no proof."

Moving forward is a series of baby steps, and logically so. An interesting point came up at the 2013 *Citizen Hearing on Disclosure*, where six former Congressmen were interviewed for a documentary regarding UFOs. What if the President appeared on national television and admitted to the existence of UFOs flying our skies? How would we handle an identified alien presence? With a Congressional hearing? A United Nations commission? Would we send a special emissary on behalf of the Children of Earth? We'd have to yield some sovereignty to the United Nations, as this would be a worldwide issue and not a countrywide issue, and that opens up a major can of worms. Are we ready to think in terms of a united world government in order to address the alien issue on a global level?

Valid points indeed. It's easy to get hung up on wanting to know what happened yesterday, without giving thought to how it might affect tomorrow. Even if we are ready for full UFO disclosure, are we ready for the decisions that must follow? Are we ready to throw our hats into an Earth-wide ring of decision makers, where individual countries may be overridden in their preferences? Are we ready to figure out how to "get along" with members of an extraterrestrial race whose histories may be radically different from our own, with little common ground?

Considering how difficult it is for humans to embrace one another — a goal that we still haven't accomplished — can you even imagine how difficult it would be for humans to enter into an overtly active relationship with extraterrestrials? We don't even trust our neighbors, let alone unpredictable beings who are parked on our front lawn in their spaceship.

In addition, humans are accustomed to being top dog in the neighborhood, ruling over every other species on our planet. Advanced civilizations usually take the lead when dealing with less advanced cultures. Extraterrestrials are more advanced, and guess where that leaves us? Our ancestors fought the visitors to be free of their rule, are we really ready to invite them back in?

Are we ready to step through an alien portal and bring back a *Giraffe for the Back Yard?* Here's a little story that demonstrates how it might go down.

One day, President Ross Wellian traveled to Africa and adopted a giraffe, an animal that he knew nothing about. He brought the giraffe home and installed it in his middle class, suburban back yard, which was about an acre square.

None of his neighbors had ever seen a giraffe in person, and the entire neighborhood gathered around the fence, curious about this strange looking creature which stood as tall as a tree. Soon, Ross was fielding his neighbors' eager questions:

"Hey Ross, what do you call that thing?"

"A giraffe."

"What does it do?"

"I don't know."

"What does it eat?"

"I don't know."

"Will it eat my apple tree, which is right next to the fence?"

"I don't know."

"Is it dangerous?"

"I don't know."

"That's a big animal. Will it stink up the neighborhood with giants mounds of giraffe poop?"

"I don't know."

"What will it do if my kids sneak over the fence?"

"I don't know."

"Will it get along with my dogs and cats?"

"I don't know."

"Can it jump over the fence?"

"I don't know."

"Is it noisy? Will it keep us up at night?"

"I don't know."

"Is it like a bunny rabbit? Will it start popping out babies and overrun the neighborhood?"

"I don't know. I doubt it. I didn't bring it a mate."

"How does it sleep? Standing up or laying down?"

"I don't know. Maybe it doesn't sleep at all, or maybe it hangs upside down like a bat. Maybe it sleeps for months like a bear. I just don't know."

"Is it friendly?"

"I don't know."

"Won't it get lonely all by itself?"

"Probably."

"Why did you bring it here, then?"

"Because it was interesting."

"Hey, do you think that birds will try to build a bird's nest on its head?"

"I don't know."

"Will it eat the bird's eggs out of their nests in the trees?"

"I don't know."

"Can it fly?"

"Not without a plane ticket."

"Can it swim?"

"I think it's tall enough that it doesn't need to."

"Does it bite?"

"No idea."

"It's really tall and it's got those long legs. Will it step on me if I get too close? Are you sure it was a good idea to bring this thing into our neighborhood?"

"You sure ask a lot of questions. If you don't like that I brought a giraffe home, maybe you should just move to another neighborhood."

"What if they have a giraffe, too?"

"Can't help you there."

"Can I pet it?"

"Only if you sign this liability waiver first."

"Well then, Ross Wellian, what the heck CAN you tell me?"

"It's a giraffe."

LOST CIVILIZATIONS

History is full of civilizations that were eliminated by their enemies, died off for natural reasons, were absorbed into some other group, or which simply vanished, coming down through the millennia as lost civilizations. Some were extinguished out of fear of being the misunderstood "giraffe next door" that frightened their neighbors for being different.

As humans spread out over the world, unclaimed lands diminished. Homesteads got smaller and there was just no place any more for giraffes. You had to get along, or move along. The extraterrestrial visitors had to either blend in, die out, leave if they could, or eliminate us, and there's no evidence that they were bloodthirsty enough to choose the latter, at least not the ones highlighted in *Ancient Aliens and the Lost Islands*. Even human tribes were displaced to become a people without a country, as with the Mycenaean Danaans, and the Lost Tribe of Dan.

The disappearance of the Mycenaeans, whose civilization existed from 1600-1100 B.C., usually shows up on lists of the top 10 most mysterious lost civilizations. For every historian there's a theory, and a handful even link the lost Mycenaean Danaans with the Irish Dananns. Were they related?

The *Danaans* or *Danaoi* were associated with the Mycenaean empire of Ancient Greece, which disappeared rather suddenly and nobody can pinpoint why. They were descendants of the Greek princess Danaë, and it was her son, Perseus, fathered by the god Zeus, who founded the fortress city of Mycenae. Princess Danaë had ties to Egypt, as did the Milesians who took down the Tuatha dé Danann.

Danaë was the great-great-granddaughter of the Greek Danaus, who was the twin brother of Aegyptus, the king of Egypt. Danaus had 50 daughters, and Aegyptus had 50 sons, who were supposed to pair off and marry one another. However, instead of allowing his daughters to marry their cousins, Danaus built "the first ship that ever was" according to the historian Pliny, and fled. Apparently they failed to escape their fate and married after all, but on their father's orders, they all killed their husbands except for one woman — Hypermnestra. It was from her pairing with her cousin Lynceus that the Danaid Dynasty arose, which founded the Mycenaean civilization of Danaans, and the fortress of Mycenae. Thus the Mycenaean goddess Danaë was descended from a Greek, and an Egyptian. She also ties in with the old wolf tales, as she was the great-granddaughter of Lynceus, whose name means *wolf*.

While it isn't generally recognized, a few believe that the Greek goddess Danaë and the Irish goddess Dana are one in the same, and that the Mycenaean Danaans of Danaë are connected to the Tuatha dé Danann of Dana. Some go even further and link the Dananns and Danaans to the Danites — who represent the Lost Tribe of Dan.

The Tribe of Dan, which is also spelled *Dann*, is one of the Twelve Tribes of Israel, and in the biblical *Book of Revelation*, they were excluded from the sealed tribes for their pagan practices, though the *Book of Ezekiel* gives them a portion of future Israel.

The *Torah* states that the name Dan derives from *dananni*, which means "he has judged me." Dan was the son of Jacob and Bilhah, and he was a black sheep for not following the traditionally accepted religious practices. Some early Christian writers even believed that the Antichrist would be borne of the Tribe of Dan, which gives you an idea of how he was perceived.

Like the Mycenaean Danaë, the biblical Dan had ties to the pharaoh of Egypt, though this pharaoh is never named. Dan's story takes place in Heliopolis, Egypt — the same city where the *Stone of the Pregnant Woman* was moved by the Jinn.

Dan's father Jacob had two wives, and two mistresses, which together produced twelve sons who became the Twelve Tribes of Israel. Four mothers meant that several of the boys were half-brothers, four of which were illegitimate, creating jealousy. Dan was illegitimate, and his brother Joseph was not only legitimate, he was also the favorite son, driving a wedge between them.

Dan wasn't the only brother who was jealous of Joseph. Reuben, the first-born son, was also not a fan of Joseph, because Reuben had committed an unforgivable act and his father handed over Reuben's birthright to his half-brother Joseph. So this was not a happy band of brothers.

Some of Joseph's half-brothers teamed up to get rid of him, with the original plan being to kill him. However, not all of the brothers were on board with such a radical plan, and instead he was sold into slavery to a traveling caravan for 20 pieces of silver. They presented his bloody coat to their father as evidence that he'd been mysteriously killed, so that Jacob wouldn't go looking for his son.

Joseph passed through several owners, finally settling in Egypt as the slave of a man named Potiphar, who was both a priest, and a captain of the palace guard, under an unnamed Egyptian pharaoh in Heliopolis. Joseph made a good impression on Potiphar, and rose up the ranks from menial slave to become the personal servant of Potiphar. Before long he was the overseer of Potiphar's entire household.

In the meantime, Potiphar's wicked wife Zuleika had set her sights on Joseph, coveting him as she'd done so many others. Her conquests never came to a good end, and unlike those who'd gone before him, Joseph refused her advances, which angered her into spewing lies so that he'd be thrown into prison. Instead of moldering away in prison, this set the stage for the pharaoh to discover Joseph's unique talents.

Joseph had the gift of prophecy and the ability to interpret dreams, gifts which were so beneficial to the pharaoh, that he released Joseph from prison and put him in charge of "all the land of Egypt" as vizier — which was the most powerful rank that existed under the pharaoh. Not only did he bestow Joseph with rank and title, he took the ring off of his own finger and presented it to Joseph, along with Potiphar's daughter Asenath to be his wife, and this put Joseph back on someone's hit list. The pharaoh's own son was in love with Asenath, so now Joseph had another enemy in addition to Zuleika and his own half-brothers, and this is where Dan reappears in the story.

Dan was keeping tabs on his brother, and seeing all those blessings showered on Joseph must have irked Dan to no end, because he teamed up with the pharaoh's son to kill Joseph once and for all. The plan failed and the pharaoh's son was killed instead. Joseph and his wife Asenath went on to become the rulers of Egypt, and with their hearts full of goodness, they forgave Dan for his plots against them. Thus the wicked Dan wandered off where his deeds and legacies were lost in obscurity. A list of his descendants was not preserved, and today we're trying to piece it back together, which is why they are known as the Lost Tribe of Dan.

At some point, Dan invaded the city of Leshem in what is now northern Israel, and the city was renamed Dan, and its residents were called *Danites*. It's likely that he left some of his seed behind in that city, as invaders often do. In this region, we're given a glimpse of the "pagan ways" that so irked his family, along with clues that this Dan may have been connected to the Milesians who took down the Tuatha dé Danann. Usually when people follow the clues, their goal is to demonstrate that the

Tuatha themselves came from the Tribe of Dan, probably because neither were popular for their choice of religious beliefs. As the Tuatha dé Danann clearly came from the Otherworld, and Dan was human, follow along with this alternate theory.

The city of Dan in Israel is roughly 30 miles from the city of Sidon whose residents worshipped Ba'al, and Dan had strong ties to Sidon. The city of Dan was also approximately 30 miles from Mount Hermon, the highest mountain in the region, and here's where the coincidences start piling up.

The palace of the evil god Ba'al was situated on Mount Hermon, and this mountain is specifically named in the biblical *Book of Enoch* as the place where the "fallen angels" descended to Earth from the Fifth Heaven. These fallen angels were called the *Grigori*, and they were human-like giants who took the daughters of men as wives. They begot the Nephilim — those biblical savage giants who pillaged Earth and endangered humans.

The Grigori were also called the Watchers, and their ranks included both good and holy angels as well as fallen angels, so they had free will to choose their path. You can't help but wonder if there's a connection between the savage giants of the Fifth Heaven who pillaged Earth, and the Norse giants who'll come from the world of Múspelheim during Ragnarök to pillage and destroy Earth.

So these Grigori, aka fallen angels or giants, came down to Mount Hermon, where their leader Ba'al had a palace, and here's where we get a coincidence of names. Hérimón was another name for Érimón, who was one of the Milesians who invaded Ireland. The Milesians founded the city of Miletus, which was 600 miles from Mount Hermon.

The Milesian Hérimón not only took part in the battle against the Tuatha dé Danann in Ireland, he became one of the first Milesian rulers of Ireland. Was this mountain that was associated with the Fifth Heaven named after the man who took down the mighty Tuatha dé Danann?

As for the suggestion that the Irish Dananns descended from the Tribe of Dan, there's no direct evidence. It's true that the Tuatha dé Danann often intermarried with humans, just like the giants who came to Earth, so any human bloodline could have been intermingled with theirs. For example, the Dagda's daughter Brigit married the Fomorian named Bres, whose father was Eladan, who was allegedly a descendant of Noah through his son Japheth and grandson Magog. This is not the same family tree that the Tribe of Dan comes from. Ellada, however, is another name for Greece, and the Milesians originated in Greece and Egypt.

In Ireland, a pagan Dan is connected to the regions where the Tuatha dé Danann ruled, in the form of a festival specific to Ireland, Scotland, and the Isle of Man. This festival is called *Beltane* or *Bel-dan*, according to *Ancient Pillar Stones of Scotland* by George Moore. *Bel* and *Ba'al* are both titles rather than names, and they mean "lord" or "master." Thus Bel-dan *could have* referred to Lord Dan or Master Dan, which Moore equates with Danann. He believed that the Tuatha dé Danann were the Lost Tribe of Dan, and had come to Ireland from Egypt.

While it's possible that Bel-dan represents a shortened form of Danann or Dana, the trouble is that Bel-dan is considered a druidic festival, and contrary to popular belief, the Tuatha dé Danann were *against* the druids. One of the biggest aspects of the Bel-dan festival was driving cows between two bonfires, which is associated with the Fomorian Bres, not the Tuatha dé Danann. Bres was a mean, miserly man who made everyone around him miserable. He was a rotten host, and if you dined at his house, you weren't treated to ale or entertainment.

During his kingship, he passed a law where the milk from all brown, hairless cows, would be given to him. Of course, you don't find many naked brown cows in nature, so Bres devised a method of ensuring that ALL cows became brown and hairless, by forcing them to pass through fiery bracken which burned their hair off and singed their skin. Later this morphed into the Beldan ritual of passing cows in between bonfires. In other words, if any one was associated with Dan, it was the Fomorians whom the Tuatha dé Danann battled.

Bres was a cruel overlord and when the Tuatha dé Danann took over kingship after him, the people were relieved, and delighted. In addition, as much as the people despised the Fomorian Bres, they adored his Tuatha wife Brigit, bless that poor woman's heart for marrying such a mean man!

The biblical *Ba'al* refers to any god who is a rival of Yahweh for the devotions of the people, and in that regard both Bres and the Tuatha dé Danann would have been associated with a Ba'al, as neither worshipped Yahweh.

Another city that was devoted to Ba'al was Sidon, which was also known as *Side*, which is, coincidentally, a word that's interchangeable with *Sídhe*. The latter has become synonymous for the fairies of Ireland who are believed to be the remnants of the Tuatha dé Danann. Thus the city of Sidon, which forms a 30-mile triangle with the city of Dan and Mount Hermon, was called Side; and the fairy race of the Sídhe in Ireland was also called Side.

Another link to Side was that Aegyptus' mother (ancestor of the Mycenaean Danaans of Danaë) was named Achiroë, but she was also known as *Side* for her association with Sidon. Achiroë's father-in-law was Belus, whose brother was Agenor, who ruled over Sidon. Agenor's wife was his niece Damno, and this brings us back to Ireland again.

According to the *Bibliotheca Ms. Stowensis, Volume I,* by Reverend Charles O'Conor in 1818, the Tuatha dé Danann translates as "the people of Damnonia" rather than "Dana." While this is not an accepted translation, it's another coincidence in a series of odd coincidences that may link the Mycenaeans to the Irish. There's another Damno link in Ireland which predates the Tuatha, in a people known as the Fir Domnann.

One of the Irish patriarchs who predated the Tuatha dé Danann was Partholón, and it is this man who descended from the Japheth branch of Noah. He defeated the Fomorians who are referred to as giants, but then they were all wiped out in a plague. His brother was the great-grandfather of Nemed from which the Tuatha dé Danann allegedly descended, as well as the Fomorian Bres. However, this brother went through several animal reincarnations between the days of Noah and the birth of Nemed, and therefore the lineage is sketchy.

Nemed came along and also battled the Fomorians, but most of their ancestors were wiped out in a flood, and the rest were scattered to the four corners of the world. One branch of Nemedians settled in Greece, and were enslaved. Later they made their way back to Ireland and split into three groups: Fir Bolg, Fir Domnann, and Fir Gálioin.

The Fir Domnann were linked to the "god of Domna" or "dé Domnand" and both the god, and his people, were hostile toward the Tuatha dé Danann. The Domnand's may have had sects in Cornwall, England, as well as France, just like St. Ruan.

These Fir Domnann ancestors of Nemed got lumped together with the Fir Bolg and Fir Gálioin, under the name *Fir Bolg* in most histories. The Fir Bolg and the Fomorians were the people that the Tuatha dé Danann encountered, and battled, when they arrived in Ireland. Some historians claim that all of these ancient Irish sects came from the same seed — the Fir Bolg, Fomorians, Partholóns, and Tuatha dé Danann — but this connection may have come from the notion that all humans derived from a single human pair. Considering that the Fomorians were giants, the Fir Bolg were diminutive in stature, and swarthy with jet black hair, and the Tuatha dé Danann were from the Otherworld and were NOT giants nor dark-haired, it's an unlikely assumption.

The Tuatha dé Danann of Ireland were a tall race of blond-haired, blue-eyed people. The Mycenaean Danaans of

Greece stood out as a blond-haired race living in a dark-haired region. Theirs is a likely match, and there is other evidence that links the Greek Mycenaeans to the Irish.

The blond Greek Danaans believed in freedom, and self-government, and apparently an island called Elysion — a paradise where life is easy, the weather is pleasant, and which is lit by its own sun and stars. This island of immortality was identical to the Isle of the Blest, the Fortunate Isles, and all of the other islands with similar legends. Elysion is also linked to the lost city of Dilmun, along with the Canary Islands. For the Mycenaeans, it was the giant named Cronos who ruled over Elysion. Cronos is associated with the Golden Age of longevity and morality, where everyone does the right thing so no laws are needed. If only Cronos ruled our world today!

The Greek Mycenaean civilization was very productive. They manufactured a quantity of commodities beyond what their people could use, and yet there is little written evidence of what was being done with it, such as export logs or distribution routes. Their products were found as far away as Great Britain.

This was a great civilization from their palaces down to their graves. Archeologist Emily Vermeule said of their graves, "There is nothing in the Middle Helladic world to prepare us for the furious splendor of the Shaft Graves." These were shafts sunk deep into outcroppings of stone, with rooms at the bottom for chamber tombs. *Grave Circle A* which was founded in 1600 B.C., at the beginnings of the Mycenaean civilization, was the burial site for the royal family of Mycenae. Ornate staffs, weapons, gold and silver cups, and even golden death masks were excavated from these royal tombs.

Mycenaean building was often done in a technique that we call *Cyclopean masonry* using massive boulders that were so big and heavy, that mythology attributed this stonework to cyclopes or one-eyed giants — the only beings believed to be strong enough to accomplish such stone-moving feats. One of the greatest cities was Mycenae itself, built of stone blocks, some of which weighed nearly 100 tons each.

The downfall of the Mycenaean civilization was sudden, taking place around 1100 B.C., and all of the Mycenaean centers were destroyed simultaneously according to Vincent Desborough in *The End of the Mycenaean Civilization and the Dark Age*. It was as if the upper echelon and literate rulers disappeared, leaving the peons to meet their demise at the hands of invaders. Whatever happened, it signaled the beginning of the Greek Dark Ages.

Mycenaean palaces were abandoned or destroyed, all vestiges of the government vanished, and the recognizable aspects of the Mycenaean culture disappeared. Simple, barbaric pottery replaced the ornate pottery, and entire villages were abandoned after the collapse of the palatial centers.

One theory is known as the *Dorian Invasion*. The Mycenaeans and Dorians were enemies due to old family feuds. If the Mycenaeans were related to the Tuatha dé Danann, and the Dorians were related to the Milesians, then this would have been a feud that traveled across the world.

The Dorians were the ancestors of Dorus, whose grandparents Deucalion and Pyrrha settled in Epirus, which was an inhospitable land unsuitable for cultivation. Their son Hellen fathered Dorus, whose son was Aegimius. There were three tribes of Dorians from the three sons of Aegimius — Pamphylus, Hyllas, and Dymas — though Hyllas was an adopted son, fathered by Heracles. When Aegimius died, his two natural sons allowed Hyllas to become the ruler of the Dorians.

The Mycenaeans sprang from the seed of Zeus with Danaë, through their son Perseus, who was the founder of Mycenae and the Perseid dynasty of Greek Danaans. Heracles was also the son of Zeus, by the mortal woman Alcmene, making Perseus and Heracles half-brothers. Heracles was also the great-grandson of Perseus, which pitted their ancestors against one another over who would control Mycenae.

Perseus' grandson Eurystheus was king of Mycenae, and when Heracles died, Eurystheus drove Heracles' son Hyllas out of Mycenae. This set the stage for the Dorian Invasion. It was Hyllas, and his adopted Dorian brothers Pamphylus and Dymas, who banded together to take over Mycenae. The Dorian Invasion was also known as the *Return of the Heracleidae*, meaning the descendants of Heracles.

The Dorians were living in the northern portion of ancient Thessaly, as well as Epirus which bordered Thessaly to the west. There was also a region called Doris immediately south of Thessaly which some associate with the Dorians, though there was a goddess named Doris who was unrelated to Dorus. All of these regions were part of Ancient Greece.

The Irish Milesians also came from Greece, though they are more commonly associated with Spain, which wasn't their origin, but rather their last stopover before Ireland. The Milesians descended from the three sons of Míl Espáine, which literally means "soldier of Hispania."

Their story begins with Scota, the daughter of an Egyptian pharaoh, and her marriage to the Greek Geythelos Glas, who was called Goídel Glas by the Irish. Geythelos was the son of Neolus, who reigned over Athens, Greece, so the Milesians were actually Greek/Egyptian, and they lived in Greece for awhile.

Neolus sent his son Geythelos to Egypt to help drive out the Ethiopians, as his father and the pharaoh were allies, and the pharaoh's daughter was given to Geythelos in marriage to seal the deal. This is not only in the history of Scotland and their first king Geythelos, it was also chronicled in *The Legend of St. Brandan* — that very saint that the mythical island was named for.

Geythelos was quite a troublemaker in his homeland, and they were happy to be rid of him according to most accounts. In Egypt, he helped the pharaoh keep the Israelites in bondage, and with Scota being the pharaoh's only child, Geythelos expected to take over the throne of Egypt someday. Geythelos and Scota were in Heliopolis when the pharaoh died, but the Egyptians had no intention of submitting to a foreign ruler. The only way to ensure that Geythelos would never take the throne was to kill him, and Geythelos and his wife Scota had to run for their lives.

Geythelos had already burned his bridges in Greece, and now he had to flee Egypt, so he gathered an army who was willing to follow him in search of a new land to conquer. They traveled through Africa, and then to Spain near the islands of Gades. From there they made their way to the northernmost point of Spain in Brigantia, where they built a great tower which was later called the *Tower of Hercules*. From this tower, they could see Ireland.

The reason it's called the Tower of Hercules is for the legend that Hercules killed the giant tyrant Geryon there, buried his bones and built the tower. Hercules is *the same as* Heracles, and Geryon is *the same as* Geythelos.

Geryon was the son of Chrysaor and Callirrhoe, which at first glance doesn't jive with Geythelos' parentage, whose father Neolus reigned over Athens, Greece. However, Callirrhoe had *three* husbands, one of whom was Neilus, son of Oceanus, which is almost identical to Neolus, son of Aeneas. That makes Neilus his stepfather, and Chrysaor his biological father.

Not only did Hercules/Heracles kill Geryon/Geythelos, the ancestor of the Milesians, he stole Geryon's cattle and gave them to Eurystheus, the grandson of Perseus, who was Heracles half-brother and grandfather. He also stole the golden apples of immortality from the Hesperides, which were siblings of Geryon's grandfather. This makes Heracles one of the Danaë, who killed Geryon, ancestor of the Milesians, giving them history long before the battles in Ireland.

Geythelos was not well received in Spain, and keeping his people alive was a constant battle. Ireland beckoned across the ocean, and Geythelos exhorted his sons to go to the green island, which is where the story intersects with the Irish account of the

Milesian invasion. Goídel Glas in the Irish versio̶r̶
Gathelus, so all versions come together, with the
that the Milesian descendants of Geythelos a̶
ancestors came from Greece and Egypt, evicteᴅ ᴜ.
Danann from Ireland, with Scota giving her name to Scotland.

This brings us to the fall of the Mycenaean empire of the Danaans being brought down by the Dorians of Greece. Thessaly, the Doric regions, Epirus, and the city of Miletus all belonged to Ancient Greece, with Miletus founded by the Milesians.

If the Dorian Invasion of Mycenae took place in 1100 B.C., and the Milesian invasion of Ireland didn't take place until several hundred years later, the hostility of the Tuatha dé Danann upon the arrival of the Milesians makes perfect sense. They'd already had a history as the Danaans being driven out of Mycenae by the Dorians.

The Dananns appeared in Ireland around 1500 B.C., and the Danaans in Mycenae around 1600 B.C. In other words, both civilizations started up right around the same time, though the latter was much shorter lived. In Ireland, their history continues to the time of St. Patrick around 400 A.D., while Mycenae went down in 1100 B.C. This could explain the legends of the people who "learned the black arts" in Greece, and brought this dark knowledge back to Ireland, if any of the displaced Mycenaeans joined their Irish counterparts.

The homeless Mycenaean Danaans were referred to as *Achaeans* by Homer, by which he meant "a name without a country," and he described them as being a blond-haired race in a dark-haired region. The Tuatha dé Danann was also a blond-haired race. Did the Danaans abandoned their Mycenaean kingdom and flee to Ireland? One historian seems to think so.

In 1786, Charles Vallancey in his book, *Collectanea de Rebus Hibernicus, Volume III*, puts forth this exact hypothesis. He was a British surveyor who was sent to Ireland, where he became an authority on Irish antiquities. His theories were not well received, his contemporaries stated that Vallancey "wrote more nonsense than any man of his time" calling his works "absurdities." Vallancey did, however, have access to some of the oldest documents of Irish history to draw his conclusions from, and he lived during an era where someone may have remembered what was in the lost nine folios of the *Great Book of Lecan*, which contained the pedigrees and history of the Norse-Gaelic Irish families. This information is now lost, and doesn't exist anywhere else. Vallancey wrote numerous books relating to the history of Ireland, including one which discusses Irish history and Sanskrit texts.

Vallancey drew parallels between the Mycenaean Danaans and the Irish Dananns, going so far as to claim that the Irish were none other than the Mycenaeans who had fled the city of Athens in the province of Achaea. He wrote that these "Dadananai" were using their magic arts to raise dead Athenians back to life as fast as they were slain in battle by the Assyrians. This was a very effective ploy, because their enemies were disheartened to kill an Athenian one day, and then be fighting that exact same Athenian again the next day.

The *General History of Ireland* expands on the story, stating that instead of giving up, the Assyrians sought advice from a druid on how to battle this type of resurrection magic, and the druid told them to drive a stake of *quick beam wood* through the body of the resurrected, after which they could no longer be revived. Vallancey's Dadananai, who were none other than the Tuatha dé Danann in this version, were no longer able to bring the dead back to life, and decided that it was prudent to move out of the country. They left Athens and sailed to Lochlon, and later made their way to Ireland, where they either burnt their ships upon arrival, which is a complete failure in logic, or flew in from the heavens in dark clouds.

Historians don't agree on the location of Lochlon. Some equate it to Norway and the Scandinavian countries, while others believe that it refers to the Hebrides islands or the Norse-dominated region of Scotland. Wherever it was, it's been designated as where the Tuatha dé Danann lived prior to their arrival in (or return to) Ireland.

A different narrative claims that they left Greece and traveled to Norway and Denmark, where the residents gave them four cities where they could build schools to teach the locals their magic arts. The cities were Falias, Gorias, Finnias, and Murias. The *Oxford Dictionary* lists Gorias as being a mythical city somewhere in Greece, and Murias is listed elsewhere as being a municipality in Spain, and that's about as far as you'll get. The trouble is that nobody knows where these cities were, because apparently there's no record of them in Denmark, and they are now considered mythical cities whose locations are unknown — just like the mythical islands associated with these visitors.

Vallancey believed that the Dananns started out in Ireland, and then left, and then came back. He claimed that the Fir Bolg were the druids that the Dananns left behind when they left Ireland previously, and traveled to Denmark, Norway, and Greece, and that on their return *from Greece*, the existing druids did not approve of the "new doctrine" that the Dananns brought back with them. He listed them all as ancestors of Nemed.

The *General History of Ireland* published in 1723 by Jeoffry Keating and Dermod O'Connor echoes Vallancey's claim about the Tuatha dé Danann in Greece, though this version corrects Vallancey in that they went to Achaea rather than Athens, which perfectly matches up with the Mycenaean history which equates them with the Achaeans. The displaced Mycenaeans were called Achaeans, even though they were not of the same stock as what later came to be known as Achaeans. This book also makes the distinction that "*some* antiquaries are of the opinion that the Tuatha dé Danann descended from him (Nemedius)." This is specified as being *an opinion of some*, rather than a statement of clear fact, and a few paragraphs later he talks about the "romantic writers who have been the bane and destruction of true history." Everyone had an opinion, and they didn't all agree. It all comes down to your personal beliefs, and what you're attempting to prove when you sift through the historical documents. Two people can tell the same story with completely different takes on that story.

There's a flaw that taints many genealogies — the belief that all ancestries absolutely MUST trace back to a single human pair. In order to make this theory fit, sometimes genealogists "fudged" an ancestral path into a direction that it didn't actually go. Another issue is the very human desire to trace one's ancestry back to a heroic figure. As any lawyer can demonstrate, two people can take the same pile of books and present two very different pictures of history, depending on what they're attempting to prove.

Ancient astronaut theorists believe that Earth was seeded with numerous "base pairs" and not just one. In addition, as we've seen with King Yima's mirror which was described as being "pre-Adamite," there are countless people who believe that human, or humanoid life, existed *prior to* Adam and Eve, and they offer competing historical documents prove it, just as the *Bible* is used to demonstrate a single originating couple.

Entire cultures and religions believe that other races existed on Earth before Adamic man, such as a race of giants, and that these beings co-mingled with Adamic man. We've discovered the bones of giants in Castelnau as well as smaller beings in Flores, so there is a very real possibility that everyone doesn't trace back to a single pair. You'll even find ancient astronaut theories that include dozens of extraterrestrials races dropping their "seeds" on Earth, so when genealogists attempt to trace back a varied group of ancient Irish to a single ancestor — Nemed — we need to be aware that genealogy is not always an exact science.

Consider the following: If you took away the internet with all of its genealogical information, and could only rely on a handful of books in your local library, or handwritten letters to distant librarians in the hopes of answering questions, how far do you think you'd get in tracing your ancestry? Complicate it further with entire libraries and churches being burnt to the ground by invaders, losing historical information that can never be replaced. Remember the Irish Dark Ages described in earlier chapters? Ireland was *devastated* in those days — decimated, burnt, ravaged, pillaged, plundered, and utterly destroyed.

On top of that, we didn't have computers and fancy ID cards, or birth certificates, or Social Security numbers. Names were written down *as they sounded*, and with different spellings for each country. Brendan had several spellings, including Borondon, so you see how tracing one's genealogy isn't a simple undertaking, the farther back you go.

Names also got skewed with descriptions, muddying the waters even further. There was a Fir Bolg king named Fiacha Cinnfionnan — *cinnfionnan* meaning "white head" to describe his fair hair. However, there was a Milesian king Fíachu Findoilches who also had fair hair, and was thus referred to as Cinnfionnan. Was this a single person with two identities — Fir Bolg and Milesian? Or was it two people who shared a name, confusing anyone who might later try to piece together their histories?

The Milesians who displaced the Tuatha dé Danann in Ireland were listed as descendants of Míl Espáine, which means *soldier of Spain*, which is not a name, but a designation. Some of their ancestors built the settlement of Miletus, a Greek city whose ruins are near what is now Balat, Turkey. Miletus was at the eastern edge of the Mycenaean civilization, so the Danaans of Mycenae and the Milesians of Miletus would have had history prior to either one arriving in Ireland.

RETURN OF THE GODS

They may not be living among us as they once did, but you can bet that they are still out there keeping an eye on us. Can we decipher the clues and match up any of today's extraterrestrials with these ancient aliens, based on their descriptions?

One of the most compelling match ups is that of today's Nordic aliens to the Tuatha dé Danann. The Nordics are described as six or seven feet tall, with long blond hair, blue eyes, fair skinned, and magical. The Tuatha dé Danann were tall, with yellow or gold hair, blue or gray eyes, and fair skinned. One description said that they had "manes of hair the color of gold" with far-seeing blue eyes, teeth which were bright like crystal, and thin lips. As we know, the Tuatha were definitely magical.

Coincidentally, there was a race who interacted with the Native American Cherokee that matched the Tuatha dé Danann in every way except in physical description, and with the Tuatha dé Danann ability to take on any appearance, you can't help but wonder whether this was the same race of beings.

The Nunnehi were a race of immortals whose name meant "the people who live anywhere" which was usually underground inside of a mountain. They were distinctly different from gods, but they were definitely supernatural, and like the fairies of Ireland who are thought to be the remnants of the Tuatha dé

Danann, the Nunnehi liked to sing and dance. They could appear and disappear at will, having the power of invisibility. They were immortal, and could bestow immortality on humans. However, if those humans attempted to return home, they could not, because they'd eaten the "immortal food" of the Nunnehi. Eating human food would strip you of the immortality you had gained. Unlike the humans who traveled to the Otherworld and had to remain there, you could live with the Nunnehi and travel back and forth to visit your friends and family on Earth.

They were friendly, kind, and they often helped people who got lost in their vicinity. When Europeans forced the Cherokee to leave their homes and resettle elsewhere, the Nunnehi offered sanctuary to members of a particular village. They knew what was about to happen and warned the village that an impending disaster was coming, far worse than anything that the Cherokee could imagine, and they offered sanctuary to anyone who wanted to live with them.

Villagers who accepted the offer were given seven days to pack up and get ready, and then the Nunnehi came and led them to a large stone that was hidden way up in the mountains. The gigantic stone rolled away, revealing an entrance to the most beautiful world the villagers had ever seen, and several families rushed in without looking back. Unfortunately, others chose to take their chances and from those who stayed behind, we're given the stories of the Nunnehi and their paradise world.

Even today we're discovering underground realms that we didn't know existed, such as the Son Doong cave in Vietnam which was discovered in 1991. Son Doong is the biggest cave in the known world, and inside the cave you'll find waterfalls, rivers, and a jungle which they call the *Garden of Edam*. The jungle is home to monkeys, birds, snakes, flying foxes, and a number of other species. This cave represents a true miracle on Earth.

The Cherokee/Nunnehi legend makes you wonder whether other vanished cities or civilizations were offered a new life elsewhere. We find evidence of ancient cities which were abandoned, but we don't know why. The Olmecs of Mexico, the Minoans in Crete, the Cucuteni-Trypillians of Romania and the Ukraine, and the Anasazi of New Mexico in the USA, all seem to have vanished.

The Anasazi disappeared at the height of their success, and new archeological evidence is wiping out the old explanations such as drought. We can speculate on whether they left their homes due to crop failure or climate changes, enemies at the gates, a plague, or maybe they just used up all the local resources and moved on. Maybe they were absorbed into some other culture, though you'd think the cities themselves wouldn't be abandoned. Even if they'd been invaded, you'd expect the invaders to take over or destroy the cities. What happened to these ancient civilizations?

The Cherokee rescue offers hope that somewhere, there's an open door of welcome for us in the event of an Earth-wide calamity, or even to evacuate one civilization who's about to fall at the hands of another. Granted, many civilizations have fallen in Earth's history without a lifeboat that we know of, but maybe a few managed to escape to a new world, such as a single Cherokee village. Who knows? Maybe every vanquished civilization has a few survivors on the other side of the wormhole.

The Nordic visitors demonstrate the possibility that the Tuatha dé Danann may still be visiting us, albeit with an arm's length approach. Considering our history with them if they were indeed the Tuatha dé Danann and/or Mycenaeans, you can't blame them for taking a giant step back and interacting from a place of safety. Humans aren't the friendliest species in the universe — as our own bloody history demonstrates.

While the Nordic visitors may be concerned for their own safety, another race of extraterrestrials appears to have been blocked from accessing Earth, in order to protect humans. This block is temporary, however, and they are predicted to return.

These were the giants, and unfortunately they were rarely painted in a good light.

The giants are sometimes called the oldest race, or the first race — an ancient race that carries the wisdom from bygone times according to Norse mythology. They also play a major role in the downfall of humans at the end of the world. They were the Nephilim of the *Bible*, the Jötnar of the Norse, the Daityas of the Hindus, and the Titans of the Greeks. They also existed in Native American legends both as monsters, and as divinities such as Hiawatha. They appeared in Prester John's kingdom, and solicited mentions in the Tuatha dé Danann histories.

Giants also existed in Persian history prior to, and during the early years of Adamic man, as ruled by the 72 Suleiman kings. These giants were the second race of the world, with the first being an ethereal race, and they were neither male nor female but instead, both sexes in one body. They were a long-lived race, as the last three Suleimans ruled for 1,000 years each.

While there's controversy as to whether King Solomon was a Suleiman of the second race, the parallels are uncanny. He wore a magical ring that held the same powers as a Suleiman's magical ring, his name was synonymous, and he wielded power over the Jinn and other supernatural beings.

Adamic man, which means us, was divided into sexes. Some believe that we started with a single pair — Adam and Eve — while others believe there were several base pairs with the males being called "the Adams." In both theories, Adamic man founded our existing race of humans.

It gets a little confusing because every culture numbers the ancient races differently. Humans were the third race, but there was also a race of giants in Atlantis which was considered the third race, and the sons of God which married the daughters of men were also known as the third race, so you'll get a different accounting of which race constituted the first, second, third, and so forth. No matter how you number it, the final tally is still the same — sooner or later our race of humans will come to an end, and we'll be replaced by a radically different form whose nature we can only guess at.

The extraterrestrial hybrid scenario may take us into that new form. Or perhaps we'll find a way to move our brains into cloned bodies and become a race of brain-men with disposable bodies. Maybe we'll rediscover the magic of the Jinn, the strength of the giants, or the longevity of the Tuatha dé Danann, and the next race of beings who inhabit Earth will be superhumans. The future of mankind is full of maybes, but first we have to survive the end of the world.

Several religions have beings that are currently imprisoned, and who'll bust loose at the end of the world to wreak havoc on Earth, including King Yima's enemy Aži Dahāka, and the Norse fire giants, also known as the sons of Múspell.

As with most end of the world scenarios, things are going to get really ugly before the big battle begins. Earth will be plunged into three years of winter where it just snows and snows with no sign of summer. The Sun will turn black, and the Moon and stars will seemingly disappear, which suggests that something will darken the sky such as volcanic ash. Earth will shake so violently that the very mountains topple over. Oceans will rise up to become devastating floods. Everywhere you look, you'll see flames and steam as high as the heavens, and Earth will become toxic. People will run for their lives, but there won't be anywhere safe to go. Humans will turn against one another other, and no man will have mercy.

Just when you think it can't get any worse, the sky splits in two and out come the sons of Múspell, with their shining battle troops riding across the bifröst bridge, and then the bridge breaks. These fire giants aren't here to save humanity. They're here to wage war on everyone and everything in sight, including the Aesir and Vanir gods who are currently holed up safe in their homes until this end of the world war known as Ragnarök.

The war will take place not only on Earth, but on at least some of the Nine Worlds as well. Odin will return, and Thor, and Tyr, and Freyr, and even Loki, to fight in this battle to end all battles. Thor will fight furiously as a protector of Earth, but most of the old Norse gods will be killed. This signifies the end of Earth as we know it. When it's over, there will be a new Heaven, and a new Earth, and humans get divided up between several afterworlds or afterlives, depending on how we lived. There are beautiful places, and repugnant places.

Virtually every culture and religion has an end of the world scenario which includes Earth being wracked by natural disasters, while a *good* versus *evil* battle takes place. For some strange reason, *good* always wins, which makes you wonder what the heck they aren't telling us. If it's all preordained to go down in a detailed, predicted manner, and *good* always wins, why the big battle? Unless it's for the benefit of determining our individual fates?

In Norse mythology, *evil* takes the form of fire giants, and in all likelihood, the giants of old were between ten and fifteen feet tall, so the Nordic/Tuatha can't be these Earth destroying giants. Some of the Aesir and Vanir gods claim to have giants in their lineage, and there were also frost giants and mountain giants, thus the races intermingled, which means you can't separate the sons of Múspell from those who'll fight on our behalf by height alone. Odin's father was Aesir, and his mother was a giantess. The benevolent Hiawatha was also a giant.

The Fomorians who were conquered by the Tuatha dé Danann were giants, and they intermarried and had children with the Tuatha dé Danann. Biblical giants intermingled with humans and produced children. It doesn't appear that giants are currently visiting Earth. However, when all hell breaks loose, they will make an appearance and be fighting on both sides.

On the opposite end of the spectrum are those who are generally smaller than humans. Norse legends include dwarves, who "groan by their stone doors" during Ragnarök. Historically, these Norse dwarves were credited with manufacturing magical weapons, armor, jewelry, ships such as Skidbladnir, and even being shape shifters.

The goddess Idunn with her apples of immortality was the sister of three dwarves, though she was listed as an elf, so we don't know if they were half-siblings, or whether there was a connection between the two species. Four dwarves in Norse mythology were given credit for "holding up the sky" which brings us to the next race of current visitors.

One of the most active races visiting Earth today are the gray aliens. They are between two and four feet tall, skeleton-thin, sexless, hairless, with gray or cream colored skin, and overlarge heads with huge, piercing black eyes. They lack protruding ears and noses but may have small openings where ears and noses would be. They have the ability to make themselves appear as virtually any other creature.

There are two aspects of the gray aliens: their physical appearance, and shape shifting ability. We have legends all around the world, and throughout the millennia, of little people, though few descriptions come close to the gray aliens. Most of the legendary beings were hairy, and we may have actually identified some of them. We have bones that prove that there really was a race of smaller beings, although analysis of the bones is steeped in controversy.

One set of bones comes from *Homo floresiensis*, commonly called Flores Man, though proposed scientific names included *Homo hobbitus* and *Sundanthropus floresianus*, but in the end *Homo floresiensis* won out, at least for the moment. We've discovered the remains of nine distinct humanoids of this species, all found on the island of Flores in Indonesia.

Analysis of the bones has the experts arguing, because some want to classify Flores as a new species, and others want to label them as *Homo sapiens* who suffered medical ailments such as microcephaly or thyroid disorder. We know they lived alongside us, but arguments exist over when they went extinct. One hypothesis puts it at 12,000 years ago, another claims they existed into the 19th century, and a third is open to the possibility that they may still exist in unexplored regions.

The latter is based on legends of a small, hairy cave dweller called Ebu Gogo in the Flores region, as well as the Orang Pendek of Sumatra. Ebu Gogo was hunted down for their habit of stealing food, and sometimes children. Orang Pendek isn't even given the benefit of being called a human, but is spoken of as an animal — a three to four foot tall, hairy, bipedal primate that lives underground but is often seen in trees. Local legends give Orang Pendek magical or ghost-like traits. Flores Man was three to four feet tall, and weighed about 55 pounds full grown.

Even more controversial than the debate over Flores Man is the debate over the Starchild skull. About the only aspect of Starchild that researchers agree on is that the skull is genuine. On the one hand, you've got claims that this skull represents an alien-human hybrid — with the alien representing an extraterrestrial species. Skeptics attribute the Starchild oddities to medical issues such as congenital hydrocephalus, similar to the arguments against Flores Man being a new species of human.

You'd think that we could settle both Flores Man and Starchild with DNA testing, but no such luck. In spite of having bones from nine different Flores beings, we've not been able to get a good enough DNA sample to definitively prove anything. As for the Starchild skull, both believers and skeptics are using DNA to promote their theories. If you read the skeptical analysis, you'll be fully convinced that it was a sickly human child. If you read the believer analysis, you'll be just as convinced that it's a genuine, alien-human hybrid skull. There's nothing alien about the Flores bones, however, but they do bring an interesting perspective to the Starchild debate. They demonstrate that even among experts with access to physical evidence, you'll end up with a lot of disagreement.

Indonesia wasn't the only region with legends of little people. The Native American Omaha, Otoe, Lakota, and Sioux tribes had legends of Stick Indians, which was a race of frightening dwarves about a foot and a half tall, with very large heads. These beings so terrified all the other tribes that none would willingly approach the Stick Indian's mountain, according to explorers Lewis and Clark. The Stick Indians were ferocious in their attacks, and their arrows could fly long distances. They were also believed to have wings for their ability to leap from crag to crag, sometimes disappearing down a yawning abyss, only to reappear again unharmed.

Yet not only are there stories of Stick Indians trading in towns and communicating with Europeans, there's a Crow legend about a boy who accidentally fell into a fire which left his face horribly scarred, earning him the name Burnt Face. Once he was healed, he left his tribe and went off on his own, and was approached by the Stick Indians. Instead of attacking and killing him, they healed his scars, gave him the power to heal others, and then directed him on how to get back to his people, where he became a great chief. If these Stick Indians had even remotely resembled gray aliens, the Europeans would have had a lot more to say about them in historical depictions.

Stick Indians have been compared to the Mannegishi of the Cree, the Memegwesi of the Ojibwa, the Itste-ya-ha of the Nez Perce, and others, though not all descriptions of these dwarf-like races match, and there's no way to know whether all the tribes were describing a single entity, or multiple entities.

The Memegwesi/Memekwesiw were about the height of a two year old, with a large head, and no nose. These beings were hairy all over, and had a strange voice that sounded like a dragonfly. They could appear in your dreams, or take physical form. They offered guidance on natural medicines, and how to live in harmony with nature. If you left a basket and requested herbs to treat a specific ailment, the next day the basket would have the appropriate medicine. They carved canoes out of stone, and they may be reappearing today to warn us of dire concerns over the fate of the environment.

The Makiawisug were knee high, could become invisible, had magical powers, and one of their women had long hair and tiny feet. The Wemategunis had a similar description, and were sometimes sent as messengers from the Great Spirit.

The Apci'lnic were magical little people about two feet tall, who could become invisible. They sometimes helped you find your way home if you got lost, or brought warnings to medicine men. They also stole things, committed sabotage, and kidnapped children, which sounds like they had free will.

The Ojibway Bakaak was a skeleton-like creature, as if it were made of bones draped with skin, which is how I described the beings that I encountered as a child in the book *Alien Nightmares: Screen Memories of UFO Alien Abductions*. I now believe that the beings of my childhood were the gray aliens.

The Bakaak was said to be emaciated, or extremely thin with translucent skin. The eyes were like two, glowing balls of fire. The Bakaak emitted a shrill, chilling cry as it flew through the air in search of a victim. It had the ability to paralyze or kill its prey using "invisible arrows" meaning that whatever the weapon, it couldn't be seen. Like Spear-finger, it ate your liver. Was this frightening being the same as a Stick Indian?

Not all of these little beings had big heads. The Manogamesak had narrow faces which suggests a narrow head, and their bodies were so thin that they could only be seen in profile, which sounds two-dimensional.

Then there were the Pukwudgies — knee high beings with gray skin that sometimes glowed, with enlarged noses, fingers, and ears. They were magical, could become invisible, and could shape shift into the form of animals. They brought harm to people *by staring at them*. They could confuse people, and make people forget things.

226

Another small humanoid was the Yunwi-Tsunsdi. Most of the time they were invisible, but when they did appear they were the size of children. Their bodies were weak, puny, and "unusually shaped" without further details. Sometimes they were handsome with long hair down to the ground, in direct conflict with the weak/puny/unusual description. They were magical, with the ability to cast a spell over you that bewildered you, and they could make you lose your way in the forest. If you did find your way back home, you were dazed. On the plus side, they sometimes helped you gather crops the same way as the Fenodyree did on the Isle of Man. Sometimes the Yunwi-Tsunsdi cared for sick people who they found wandering in the woods. Like the fairies of Ireland, they loved to sing and dance.

These beings came with varied descriptions. Some had no noses, and others had big noses. Most were about two feet tall, had big heads and were hairy all over, but one had a narrow face. They were all considered magical, with the power of invisibility. However, there were a few interesting traits from the various legends that are worthy of note, because these traits are also linked to the gray aliens. Remember that the following traits come from legends of different entities, rather than one legend of a single entity.

> Appeared in dreams
> Shape shifters who took the form of animals
> So thin they could only be seen in profile, weak, puny
> Gray skin
> Caused harm by staring at people
> Confused people, made them lose their way
> Left people bewildered, or dazed
> Made people forget things
> Carved canoes out of stone (remember Hiawatha?)
> Messengers of the Great Spirit (Hiawatha again)

In spite of their habit of frightening and bewildering people, they were also helpful, sometimes by providing medicine,

227

healing people who were ill, by gathering crops, or helping you find your way home.

The gray aliens are usually stereotyped as being the clinical beings who strap you to a table to perform medical tests, or engage in genetic manipulations to create hybrids, which is an interesting concept in itself that conjures up all sorts of speculation. I offered up one scenario in the book *Alien Nightmares: Screen Memories of UFO Alien Abductions*, and now I'm going to propose a different scenario.

Ancient astronaut theorists believe that the elusive *missing link* in human evolution came via extraterrestrial intervention, meaning that extraterrestrials manipulated our genetics in some way to nudge our very nature from an ape-like species toward the humans we are today. They may have even done this by adding themselves to our gene pool. This would have created a branch where the original ape-man continued on his evolutionary path, while the new hybrid alien-human (us) took off on a new path.

Generally speaking, humans are pretty full of ourselves, and we would scorn what we perceive to be a "lesser species" of ape-man. If you were to put a colony of ape-men next door to us, we'd treat them as non-humans even if they were our ancestors, just as we do with Orang Pendek or Bigfoot, neither of which is labeled *human*. Now what if our ancestral ape-men were self-aware enough to comprehend the concept of change, and were emotionally able to perceive our disdain of them, how do you think they'd feel about being genetically manipulated? They probably wouldn't like it, which brings me to another view of genetic manipulation.

What if extraterrestrials, gray or otherwise, are simply doing to us what the ancient alien visitors did to the ape-men? What if we're in the throes of a *missing link* being introduced, and today's humans will be viewed by this new species much the same as we perceive our distant ancestors? This could mirror human evolution where we went from ape-man to human, and now human to superhuman. If you distance yourself from an individual perspective and zoom out, so to speak, would you have stopped the missing link or links in our ancestry from taking place, because of how they may have been introduced? Would you have prevented us — modern man — from coming into existence? It's just something to think about.

What would this revised human be like? Would they be able to walk through walls, or float up into the air at will? Would they be super-psychic, or super-strong? Would they be smarter than we are? Maybe the extraterrestrials are adding a Genius Gene and the new humans will all be like Einstein. Perhaps it's about making the human body more resistant to disease and aging, so that future generations will be healthier and live longer, maybe with lifespans of a thousand years. Or maybe the whole experiment will bomb and we will become weak and die off. Who knows? The point is that this scenario is possible, and we can't even begin to know their true motivations. We're a world that loves to put a negative spin on every news story, twisting the truth into some tabloid media blitz.

We hear so much about scary alien encounters, but beneficial encounters disappear into a media void, probably because we're so geared toward the negative. Just pick up any newspaper and you'll get blasted with every negative story they can dig up, with positive stories being lucky to earn a paragraph on page fifty. For example, have you heard a single story where gray aliens healed people? Would you believe it if you did?

Spontaneous healing was one of the more prominent miracles of our saints. Even today, spontaneous healing occurs in people who've been told they are going to die. Sometimes, the miracle is attributed to a force within ourselves. Sometimes, the miracle comes through faith healers or angelic intervention. Sometimes, credit is given to extraterrestrial aliens. That's where Preston Dennett comes in, a man who knows a lot about UFO encounters from his work as a *Mutual UFO Network* (MUFON) field investigator. MUFON is one of the oldest and largest UFO organizations in the United States, with members worldwide.

Dennett published a book called, *UFO Healings: True Accounts of People Healed by Extraterrestrials* in which he presented over 100 cases which were verified by UFO investigators, doctors and other officials. He quoted some of the biggest names in UFO research to substantiate the claims of extraterrestrials healing humans. He came up with an estimate of the number of healings based on 270 cases listed in the book, *UFO Abductions: The Measure of a Mystery* by Thomas E. Bullard.

In 4% of abduction cases, humans were healed of afflictions which included arthritis, rheumatism, burns, heart disease, polio, muscular dystrophy, multiple sclerosis, and cancer, to name a few. Some of these healings were performed by the gray aliens, a surprising fact as you'd expect all of the healings to come from the shining beings such as those who healed Queen Numbi.

Another name linked to extraterrestrial healing is Christine Day, who claims that she was healed of systemic lupus after being told by doctors that she only had a short time to live. Her website doesn't appear to offer a description of the Pleiadian beings that she credits for the healing, but other experiencers describe the Pleiadians as being the Nordics.

Juan Osorio gives us another account of extraterrestrial healing, as reported by Luis Ramirez Reyes, a UFO researcher in Mexico and other Latin American countries. Juan's encounter took place in 1975 and it involved several tall, beautiful, human-like beings who arrived in a disc-shaped craft. These beings healed him of cancer. Without a more detailed description, we can't say without a doubt that his extraterrestrials were the same as Christine's Pleiadians and/or the Nordics, or whether they represent three races or a single race.

As for their benevolence, just because someone heals you, whether shining, Nordic or gray, it doesn't guarantee that the entire species is friendly, or are the guardians of Earth. In most cases they are simply galactic travelers and Earth is just a stop along the way. Our ancestors called some of these visitors gods, but they were technically astronauts, which is how the term *ancient astronaut theorist* derived.

In regards to the gray aliens who appear to be more than visitors passing through, the most compelling trait is their ability to make you see them as anything but what they are. People see spiders, owls, wolves, deer, dogs, cats, monkeys, rabbits, cows, and even humans. In other words, they can appear as any species.

They are not actually changing their nature, they are implanting a different image in our minds than we're actually seeing. These images are so realistic, and so detailed, that most experiencers never discover the true nature of what they saw, and that brings me to the old legends of shape shifters.

What's the difference between a shape shifter and a screen memory? Nothing. Our ancestors were fully aware that there were beings that came to us in different forms as they pleased. Is it possible that some of the shape shifters of our ancestors were gray aliens? Conversely, is it possible that the gray aliens don't look like that at all, and the gray alien image is a screen memory? Let's recap the shape shifters we've listed in this book, which does not encompass every shape shifting being in the world.

Buggane — giant, hairy ogre, Isle of Man
Glashtyn — hairy water goblin, or water horse, Isle of Man
The Little Folk — aka fairies, Isle of Man
Tuatha dé Danann — aka fairies, sídhe, Isle of Man/Ireland/
Hebrides
Merlin — aka Merddin/Myrddin Emrys
Spear-finger — Cherokee ogress
Hiawatha — Native American peacemaker of many names
Odin — Norse all-father god of many names
Otter — shape shifting son of a dwarf king
Nemean Lion — son of the Greek god Typhon
St. Ruan — allegedly took the form of a wolf
St. Natalis — cursed others to take the form of a wolf

Four of the shape shifters lived on the Isle of Man, whose total land mass is 221 square miles. What are the odds that one small island has four completely different races of shape shifters? I'm betting that one race of shape shifters — the Tuatha dé Danann — took some of the other forms.

While it's possible for the gray aliens to take on the appearance of regular humans, it's unlikely that they could sustain it to the point of living among us as Hiawatha, Merlin, the Norse gods, and the Tuatha dé Danann did. If the gray aliens were appearing in the old legends, they were probably the secret, sporadic visitors who made a grand entrance for an hour or two, but didn't live in the house next door.

Other legendary shape shifters included the Greek gods, who were notorious for "cursing" humans and the other gods to turn them into spiders, deer, cows, dogs or wolves. Whoever these shape shifters were, whether a single race or multiple races, they played a big part in our history. A more ethereal race impacted our history as well — the beings of light.

Queen Numbi encountered this species and it worked out well for her. They literally seemed to be composed of "yellow fire or light" that resembled humanoid ghosts. Most sightings are attributed to angels, unlike Numbi's which flew in on a spaceship. Halfway between humans and the light-beings are humans who occasionally glow with an inner light, a phenomenon that we don't hear much about anymore.

The Norse gods gave us several descriptions of this shining. The Jötun goddess Skaoi was the "shining bride of the gods." The Vanir, which were also magical beings, signified the "shining ones." Odin's favorite helper Liserus was another shining one. The name Liserus may have represented the Latinizing of a name that Danish historian Saxo found in the Norse records. No such root as "lis" existed in Old Norse, and as Saxo interchanged the vowels i and y, Liserus may be synonymous with Lysir which means "the shining one, the one giving light, or the bright one."

Another Norse reference is the word *Tiwar* which signifies celestial beings or gods who were known as "the shining ones." Then we have the Sanskrit *Deva* which derives from a word which means "celestial" or "shining," and Hindus call these deities "twinkling, unsleeping, eternal orbs of light." Buddhist Devas have the power of invisibility, can manifest the illusion of another form, can move great distances quickly, as well as fly through the air. The lower ranking Devas actually eat and drink, and the higher Devas shine with their own luminosity. Humans originally possessed many of these abilities including flying and shining by our own light, and not requiring food. However, once humans began to eat solid food, our bodies became coarse and the supernatural powers disappeared.

Not to be confused with the Devas, are the Daevas, which are the supernatural beings of shining light that the Zoroastrians battled under Ahura Mazda. As translated from the Avestan language, *Daeva* means "a being of shining light."

Belief in these shining beings is not limited to the Norse, Hindus, Buddhists, or Zoroastrians. Native Americans have their own version of a shining entity known as the gods of the sky — "the shining ones, those that soar on bright wings, those that are clothed in gorgeous colors, those that came from we know not where, those that vanish into the unknown" — and which are the supreme gods who are organized in tribes.

Queen Numbi in Africa encountered shining beings who came down in a glowing spaceship. Her shining beings appeared to be made of yellow fire or light, and although you could make out a body, limbs, and a featureless face, you could not see individual fingers. After touching one of these beings, Queen Numbi's eyes glowed with an otherworldly light, and she went off with the light-beings in their spaceship. She later returned with her failing health fully restored and her clock turned back to a much younger age. She went on to rule for a long time, and no mention was made of her continuing to glow after her return.

One human who shined with his own light was Moses, who directly encountered the Lord on several occasions, either in a thick cloud or cloudy pillar, or ascending/descending in a cloud. When Moses asked to see the Lord's face, he was told that no man could see the Lord's face and live, though he did allow Moses to see him from behind.

Moses spent 40 days and nights on Mount Sinai with the Lord, and then came down off the mountain with the stone tablets of the Ten Commandments, himself glowing. Moses was initially unaware that the skin of his own face was shining, and that the people were afraid to come near him. Moses had to wear a veil over his face, because his countrymen could not look at him for "the glory of his countenance." Maybe Moses by being blessed to carry out a sacred mission was transformed into some higher form of human.

Many of the early saints emanated light. St. Columba was bathed in "an immense blaze of heavenly light," and Father José de Anchieta was crowned in a halo of light. When we see a historic image of a person with a halo, that's what the halo originally represented — a physical light emanating from, or surrounding that person.

Shining Ones are referred to in the *Bible*, though their identity is debated due to various translations. Lucifer may have been a Shining One. We also have the angelic *Seraphim*, a word which derives from "seraph" which in turn, is usually translated as *serpents*, but which literally means "burning ones." Thus the Seraphim are either fiery, angelic beings with six wings, or fiery flying serpents. The Hebrew word for serpent, *nachash*, means "shining one" according to some translations.

The point being that the meaning of a single word can trigger a wide-ranging debate, and somewhere in this debate these fiery, Shining Ones exist. There are several ranks of angels, including the *Hashmallim* which are the "glowing ones" or "amber ones," and the singular *Hashmal* has come to mean "electricity."

Some of these light-beings are even linked to a specific celestial region, known as Empyrean or the Highest Heaven, and beings made of pure light or fire live there.

Sometimes the Tuatha dé Danann glowed with a blinding light such as Lugh during a battle scene:

> "Like to the setting Sun was the radiance of his face and forehead, and they were unable to gaze upon his countenance on account of its splendor... when the cathbarr (helmet) was off him, the appearance of his face and front was as brilliant as the Sun on a dry summer's day."

The son of the Fomorian king actually mistook Lugh for the rising Sun at one point, and yet the Tuatha dé Danann were not shining beings, but rather, tall, blond-haired, blue-eyed humans.

Another shining king comes from descriptions of King Yima, or breakdowns of the etymology of his name, which suggests that he was radiant, bright, or shining, and include phrases such as "radiant Yima" or "Yima, shining with light" or "Yima, the shining" or "shining Yima." Was this shining a byproduct of the royal farr that the gods endowed him with?

The Jinn are also glowing entities. Islamic texts list the Jinn as a unique class of beings, separate from humans and angels, with all three being creations of God. These Jinn consist of smokeless, scorching fire, but are also corporeal and can physically interact with humans. Jinn have the power of invisibility and shape shifting, along with the free will to be either good or evil. As the latter operating under the influence of Satan, they "whisper" evils into the heart of man so that we'll use our free will in bad ways, and thus destroy our own futures.

The entire concept of *free will* exposes the difficulty in passing judgement on an alien race. We want to pigeonhole extraterrestrial visitors as being "good" or "bad" but in all likelihood, these races are probably similar to humans with both *good* and *bad* individuals. A leader might create many beneficial accomplishments for his people, while at the same time committing acts that we perceive as evil, so how do you judge something like that? We could dissect any random world leader, or ordinary individual on Earth, and paint them as either a saint or a monster, depending on which of their acts we highlight.

It all comes down to the end times where we will be judged on our actions in life — a belief which spans many of the world's religions. The particulars may vary, but the concept is the same. The choices we make today are going to come back to either haunt us, or reward us, tomorrow. Whether we'll reap these punishments or rewards in spirit form, or in the flesh, is a subject of religious debate. However, here's an interesting addendum to what might become of humans in a physical resurrection.

Several of the magical beings possessed an odd ability, including the Jinn. According to legend, the Jinn could subsist on bones, because they could touch bones and cause them to grow flesh again. The Tuatha dé Danann were credited with this same ability. They could put the bones of a pig back into the sty, and in the morning it would be a live pig again. The Norse gods also had a regenerating boar called Saehrímnir, which after being eaten, was somehow brought back to life again to provide food the following day.

Our own saints have performed this amazing feat as well, both with animals *and humans*. St. Francis resurrected his pet lamb from bones, and the lamb reacted to him just as it had previously, recognizing words which he spoke as if even its brain and memories had been restored. This same ability is echoed in many of the saint's legends of humans being raised from the dead, even if their remains had been cremated or were several decades old. This suggests that a physical resurrection is possible.

Several religions include a concept of resurrection, whether physical or spiritual, along with how our actions in this life carry forward into an afterlife, a reincarnation, or a resurrected life. The Celtic belief offers an interesting parallel of what happens when you die. First, it's possible to be reincarnated, and second, your new life is a continuation of the life you just left. Whether or not you are reincarnated into another physical body, you still continue wherever you left off in this life. If you die leaving behind a lot of debts or bad karma, the debts carry with you, still needing to be settled.

EPILOGUE

Many of the stories that our ancestors told are pretty wild, and no doubt there are some tall tales marching side by side with the truth. However, the fact that cultures who had no contact with one another told similar stories of magical visitors, indicates that something extraordinary happened in our ancient history. Look past some of the flowery descriptions and focus on the details. What did these ancient stories have in common? Answer that, and you'll find the seeds of truth.

When you remove the word "magic" and stick to actual descriptions, it's clear that our ancestors witnessed advanced medical techniques, speed boats, cities suspended in the air, electricity, radios, remote controls, computers, aerial weapons, cloaking technology, and voice activated GPS systems.

Extraterrestrials set up camp here, if only for a little while, and shielded their camps with cloaking technology, or wormholes, or portals of some sort. A few lucky humans got to visit these futuristic cities. How blessed the humans must have felt to experience what surely seemed like paradise, whose technology was thousands of years more advanced than ours. What our ancestors witnessed was no different than what we're seeing with alien visitation today — advanced technology that we haven't invented yet. Back then they called it *magic*, but today we use the term *science fiction* to describe future technology. It's fiction only until our scientists unravel the secrets.

Every year, thousands of people witness advanced aeronautical spacecraft which we call *unidentified flying objects*, or UFOs. Abductees are transported through walls, and up into the air, into an extraterrestrial craft, and then returned home again. Are all of these people making up stories or hallucinating? If it's just a bunch of far-fetched stories with no merit, then why are scientists and governments attempting to unlock the secrets? You don't spend billions of dollars for secret facilities to research something that you don't believe in.

Einstein believed in wormholes, and the bifröst bridge from Earth to Asgard appears to be such a wormhole. Prince Eirek, King Gylfi, Ogier the Dane, Merlin, Bran, Connla, Tadg, St. Brendan, and others, all claimed to have traveled to places which by current knowledge could only exist through a wormhole that leads to another dimension or planet. In almost every case, they had to pass through a strange mist to get there, and on the other side they saw a sun that was different from our own.

What about the people who disappear in places such as the Bermuda Triangle? Are they taken aboard a spacecraft and carried off? Or do they stumble through a portal and get stuck on the other side? Do they find paradise and choose not to return to Earth? Or do they travel forward or backward in time on Earth itself? Do they all just sink to the bottom of the ocean to be buried in Davy Jones graveyard?

Our distant ancestors described technology that they called *magic*, but today it's common place. They claimed to have seen it, touched it, and ridden in it. They watched as people were whisked off into space in a magic boat or metallic craft, and sometimes those people returned to become great leaders.

The evidence strongly suggests that extraterrestrials have been visiting here since the dawn of man, bringing advances to our technology, spirituality, and human relations. Look at what

Hiawatha accomplished. He worked to bring several warring nations together. Under the guidance of the divine Hiawatha with his speed boat that could also rise up into the clouds, the warring nations were united in friendship.

We should not jump on the welcome wagon and embrace every extraterrestrial visitor who comes along, because with all the different races that are visiting us, there will be multiple alien agendas. Even our ancestors embraced some of the visitors, but rose up against others and chased them off.

We should, however, stay open to the possibility that we have friends out there who occasionally help us move forward. At the very least, we need to be aware that we are one species among many, and that for our continued survival, we should learn about these other species, form allegiances when necessary, and take our place in the intergalactic cosmos.

The universe is full of unique beings, both friends and enemies, and all that entails. Extraterrestrials exist, whether we want it to be true or not, and the next step is to learn about them, and develop our own spacefaring technology. Are YOU ready for humanity to step into the next level?

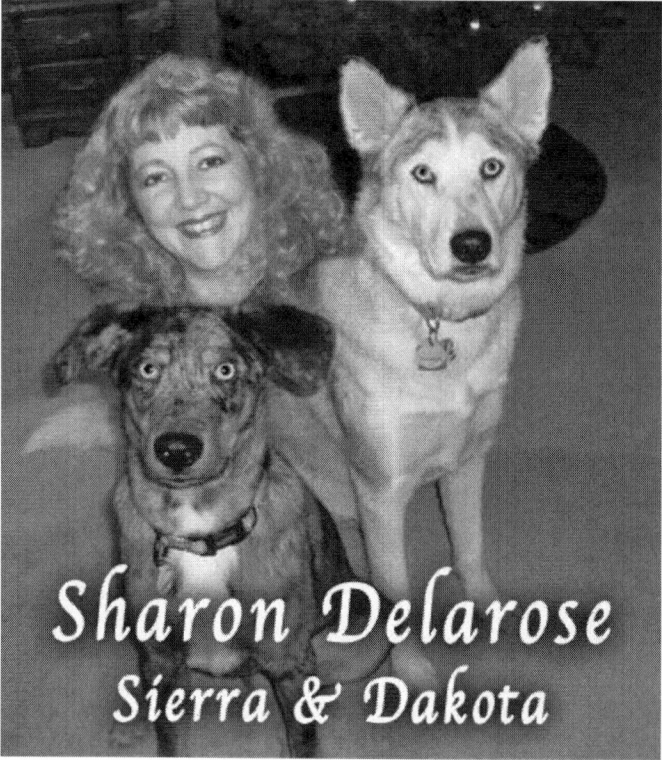
Sharon Delarose
Sierra & Dakota

BOOK EXCERPT: ALIEN NIGHTMARES

Sneak Peek at Alien Nightmares: Screen Memories of UFO Alien Abductions

Journey with me into Alien Nightmares full of the dreams, memories, and vivid imagery which led me to believe that extraterrestrials had come calling. Who were they? What did they want? Remember the old saying, "Judge not, lest ye be judged?" Well it's coming home to roost and it's riding in on a UFO. Are the aliens the Antichrist that the *Bible* warns of? Or are they our lifeboats to a brave new world? Do they bring a message of empowerment, or are we just rats in a maze? Whoever they are, one thing is certain: We cannot handle their truth.

They can make you see things, override your memory, do whatever they want to you, and there's not a damn thing you can do about it. They can make you believe that their presence is just a bad dream, one that doesn't match what really happened. All you're left with are false memories and nightmares. For this reason, few abductees ever realize that they were even abducted. Could your dreams be more significant than you realize? If you are a believer, you'll see screen memories from an abductee. If you are a skeptic, you'll see a child with a big imagination and an adult who experiences extraordinarily vivid dreams. Either way, God help you if the dreams ever come and visit you!

When I discovered that a dream I had at 34 years old was actually a resurfacing memory from when I was 2 years old, and I was able to corroborate the events with both a witness to the original event and to a newspaper clipping, I finally grasped the reality behind the dreams which I had so meticulously logged. If this dream was a genuine memory, how many of the other dreams were also memories of real events?

UFOs and extraterrestrials flew in and out of my dreams for decades, starting in early childhood. I lived in an extraordinary world full of terrifying creatures, whirlwinds, bizarre tasks and puzzles, and night visitors who took me against my will and then left me feeling drugged. There was no such thing as a safe place to hide and I knew it. Even on vacation, they found me.

I do not possess a single "waking memory" of an alien abduction. What I remember are incredibly vivid UFO dreams and the terror that those "dreams" left me with. While I refer to them as dreams, it may be more appropriate to call them screen memories of repeated UFO abductions, which is what I now believe them to be.

Screen memories are false memories that overwrite actual events which, if remembered, would be highly traumatic. Some UFO researchers refer to screen memories as "merciful amnesia."

Screen memories make it possible to have a lifetime of alien abduction experiences and not be aware that you were ever abducted. All you are left with is a jumble of bizarre memories, vivid dreams, and seemingly irrational fears. You may remember seeing or dreaming about bright lights, UFOs, monsters, floating in the air, or being paralyzed. My dreams took me far beyond that into another world which was sometimes beautiful and other times terrifying.

Many alien abductions occur at night, which allows the truth to be hidden under the guise of a dream. Such dreams are incredibly vivid and you wake up knowing that somehow, this dream was not like the others. Even without being aware that you were abducted you wake up feeling sheer, utter terror which can haunt you for a lifetime.

Such is the curse of post traumatic stress disorder which plagues those who've experienced a major traumatic event or series of events. Battle-worn soldiers, rape victims, accident victims, prisoners of war, and even children who've been bullied may be haunted by flashbacks and nightmares, reliving their experiences over and over. The nightmares are often a combination of actual memories interspersed with ordinary dreams, making it difficult to separate dreams from reality.

So what manner of nightmares haunt alien abductees? What sort of flashbacks do you relive if you've been repeatedly abducted by aliens in UFOs?

For me it started with a whirlwind dream which was totally nonsensical and yet became one of my smoking guns - it linked my dreams to reality in a very physical way. I do not remember feeling terror on those nights when the whirlwind dream came, but every other night was full of terror, especially when the dreams included monsters such as a frightening creature which I nicknamed the Skeleton Monster. This entity bore a striking resemblance to the gray aliens and it came to me several times prior to my 10th birthday.

I attributed the dreams to being a child with a vivid imagination, believing that I was simply plagued with nightmares of nonsense. When the gray aliens became household images decades later, I remembered my childhood Skeleton Monster and began to put the pieces together. I had already discovered that one dream was a resurfacing memory, could the alien monster dreams also be memories?

Another piece fell into place when I realized that waking from bizarre dreams feeling drugged wasn't normal, especially when it had been happening since early childhood. I began to see the pattern left behind by the alien visitors. What you are about to read are the clues I've put together, the remnants of what I do remember, and the vivid imagery which led me to the conclusion that extraterrestrials had come calling.

I have not contacted any UFO researchers, nor have I ever been regressed. What's more, I'm not sure I'd want to remember additional details. Would remembering yank that blessed screen of forgetfulness away, leaving me lying awake in terror as I once was? I believe that I've reached an age where I am no longer of interest to them, and from which the night terror can fade into long ago memories that do not haunt me as they once did. On the other hand, the curiosity is compelling.

Whether this book ends a journey or begins a new one, I cannot predict. Non-fiction.

http://books.gityasome.com/books/alien-nightmares-ufo-abductions/

BOOK EXCERPT: THE CANTOR DIMENSION

Sneak Peek at The Cantor Dimension: An Astrophysical Murder Mystery

In Rochester, New York, a woman disappears. The memory of her existence is wiped clean from everyone who knew her except for one friend with a crazy aunt.

In Utica, Illinois, a young man disappears. Nobody cares except for the one person who doesn't believe in UFOs.

In Memphis, Tennessee, Max disappears after a bank robbery leaving his clueless best friend Brody in charge of hiding his secrets from the police.

What do these three disappearances have in common?

The Cantor Dimension…

Albert Einstein, Edmond Halley, Georg Cantor, and Isaac Newton come together in a series of true accounts which sets the stage for time travel in this astrophysical mystery.

Solve the centuries old murder of Edmond Halley, Sr. in a place where the legendary Knights Templar hid their treasures and the Prince of Transylvania lost his head. Discover Charles Dickens' obsession, Thomas Becket's curse, bizarre occupations and even more bizarre laws in Kent County, England in the days of yore. Why did the Bats people worship the gods of time? What paradise did Cantor create from n-dimensional space? What was Isaac Newton's greatest quest? Meteorites, murders, mysteries, and mayhem surround the secrets that unlock the doors to another world in The Cantor Dimension.

Excerpt from the book - Chapter 3:

Black, twisted trees stood angrily against the gray sky, their leafless arms unmoving as if in death. Frozen field grass snapped under the weight of heavily booted feet. The searchers looked insignificant against the backdrop of gray. Several local farmers had volunteered to help search for Eric Weissmuller's body while the police questioned his family hoping for a clue.

It was unusual not to have snow on the ground in December and the expanse of white would have been helpful to their search. Footprints would have been easy to spot in the snow, as would blood or any other piece of evidence that might have been dropped. Without any visual clues they were searching blind. Eric's body could be anywhere in the surrounding farmland which stretched for miles. They searched among the frozen weeds and bushes but so far, their efforts had been fruitless.

The evidence pointed to foul play and Police Chief Hunsinger hoped that Eric's body would be found somewhere nearby, otherwise he doubted it would be found at all. The Corn Belt contained too many remote areas perfect for hiding a body. He suddenly felt homesick for the city — a place where nothing stayed hidden for long.

The police dogs had been brought in and their whines mingled with the yips of the farmer's dogs. Chief Hunsinger wished that the locals would have left their dogs at home. The farmers all believed that their canine trackers could out-do the police dogs and there must have been close to twenty dogs and as many farmers searching the fields. The dogs had found old boots, a dead possum, a car battery, a number of bird carcasses and evidence of a rabbit's nest, but no sign of Eric.

Several dog fights had to be broken up as the farmer's dogs battled for supremacy over every new find. All of these extraneous dogs and people had trampled the area surrounding Eric's truck. Whatever tracks Eric or his abductors may have left were now hopelessly obliterated. Chief Hunsinger stood cheerlessly next to his police car watching the searchers. A wizened old man sauntered up to him. The man had a gaunt, weather-worn face.

"Still lookin' fer that Eric feller, aren't ye? Well, ye ain't gonta find 'im! I told them police fellers earlier that I seen those big, bright lights in the sky yestidy. You want t'find Eric, you better call up them extry-terrestrial fellers! Tee hee hee!" The old man glanced up at the sky with a fanatical gleam in his eyes then sauntered away.

Chief Hunsinger shook his head, turning to Officer Stokes who had left the search party and had joined the Chief in his observation. "Takes all kinds, don't it, Ed?"

Officer Stokes nodded in agreement, scuffing his foot at the frozen dirt. "Yeah, and the next thing you know some loony'll come along and claim that the lights in the sky are the reason there ain't no snow in December, too!" he snorted derisively. "These farmers sure have some strange notions about things." Chief Hunsinger shrugged noncommittally.

The sun was sinking rapidly and soon the search would have to be called off for the day. That didn't bode well for Eric's chances if he were still alive. Chief Hunsinger had hoped to find footprints, a patch of clothing, evidence that could be traced to a kidnapper, Eric's unconscious body or God forbid, his lifeless body.

So far they had found nothing but Eric's truck. The driverless truck had been careening around the empty field with a flat tire and a missing door. The door had turned up near a tree.

A neighbor driving by had seen him working on the truck shortly before the call. Eric often worked late into the night on his beloved truck — fine-tuning the engine, replacing parts that still had years of life left in them, painting the rest of the parts so that the engine sported a showroom shine, washing off any specks of dust that had dared to land on his precious "lady" and polishing her to a blue satin sheen.

That was the last anyone had seen of Eric except for his truck bouncing erratically through the field. The engine was still running when Chief Hunsinger arrived and the runaway truck had already caused one police car to get stuck in a mud rut. Chasing down the truck to stop it had been like an old-fashioned rodeo except nobody was cheering. They'd finally thrown railroad ties in its path, stopping the truck long enough for someone to jump in and yank the key.

Bob Weissmuller, Eric's father, stood leaning up against a police car with his face illuminated by the rotating blue lights. His cheeks had a sucked in look, accentuating the bitter lines that had appeared on either side of his face. His hands were shoved deep into his coat pockets and a pipe hung from the corner of his mouth. His shabby brown coat was a perfect match for his drab, brown cap. His hobnail boots had seen better days as well. Bob Weissmuller was a frugal man and did not believe in spending money needlessly.

He silently watched the searchers. The only sign that he was distressed was the quick succession of smoke puffs emanating from the pipe. Eric was his only son. The birth had been a complicated one rendering Ann Weissmuller incapable of having more children, so Eric was the end of the line until he fathered children of his own. That was a hard pill for a farmer to swallow. Ann Weissmuller did not know that her only son was missing. She was visiting her sister in Joliet and they hadn't been able to contact her.

A young man in his mid-twenties walked up to Chief Hunsinger. "Sergeant?"

"Hmm? No, chief. Chief Hunsinger. What can I do for you?"

"I'm Mark Boeing, Eric's friend. His *best* friend." He

emphasized the word "best." Mark looked around as if to make sure that no one could hear them. "I need to talk to you in private. It's really important."

Chief Hunsinger looked up with keen interest. "Do you have some information about Eric?"

"Yes! I mean, I think so."

Chief Hunsinger waited expectantly. "Well?" he prompted.

Mark stood uncomfortably, fidgeting with his leather gloves. He frowned at a group of people standing nearby. "Can we talk over there? Away from all these people?" Chief Hunsinger took Mark by the elbow and steered him away from the crowd hoping to finally get the break he needed in this case.

When they were far enough away, Mark let out his breath as if he'd been holding it. His discomfort did not seem to lessen and his gaze shifted nervously as he spoke. "I overheard old man Billings telling you about those funny looking lights in the sky. I wanted to talk to you about something but not here. Maybe we could meet somewhere tomorrow?"

Oh no, not another one, thought Chief Hunsinger. Why did the crackpots always seem to show up whenever something strange happened? But you never knew, the kid might know something. "Don't you think tomorrow might be a little late for your friend, if he's in trouble?"

Mark answered, "No, a day won't make any difference if what he told me is true."

It was getting dark and it was well past time to call off the searchers for the day. "Okay," Hunsinger sighed. "What time?"

"I could meet you by the old Starnes' farm at 4:00 p.m."

The Starnes' farm had been vacant for decades and the house was a profusion of rotting wood and boarded up windows surrounded by tall, spindly weeds. Some said it was haunted by Billy Starnes who had been murdered there. It had been a gruesome killing with Billy Starnes butchered in his bed while his family lie sleeping down the hall. Billy was not yet twenty years old when it happened. It was a double tragedy as Billy was engaged to be married. Emily, his fiancée, had been inconsolable. She'd been the one to find the bloody body.

The prevailing theory was that her previous beau, Doug Darnell, had murdered Billy. Nothing was ever proven and both the Starnes' family and Emily had moved away. Some said Emily had been shipped off to a mental institution, never recovering from the gruesome murder of her beau. Rumors abounded when it came to the Starnes' murder and the old farmhouse had developed quite a reputation as a haunted house. The Starnes' farm had remained vacant ever since. Farmers were a superstitious bunch and nobody would touch the place after that.

Chief Hunsinger wondered, *Why'd this kid pick the Starnes' farm for a meeting? He must be as batty as the old man.* To Mark he said, "Okay, Mark, see you at the Starnes' farm tomorrow at 4:00 p.m."

Excerpt from the book - Chapter 4:

The astronomer Edmond Halley, whose photo was hanging on Max's wall, had been born and raised in Kent County, England. Brody knew that Max had a fascination with both Edmond Halley and Kent County as evidenced by the many books Max owned about both. One book had been flagged with a sticky stamped with the cube and he'd brought it home along with the Cantor papers. It was the history of Kent County, England, a place rich in myths, legends, and bizarre history, and it had been written when people still believed in magic, witchcraft and curses.

Brody had no idea what connection the book might have to Max's disappearance but he began to read it along with the Cantor papers hoping for a clue. A few sections were highlighted with a yellow marker and he zeroed in on those, immersing himself in subjects that Max considered important.

Strood was one such subject. Strood, a town in Kent County, England, started out as a bridge built over the River

Medway by the Romans. Archeological evidence suggested that a good size Roman settlement was once built there. Both Roman and Saxon graves were unearthed near Temple Farm in Strood in which a variety of weapons, a bronze ring with an amethyst stone, a hoard of Roman coins and other antiquities were found.

The Roman roads led to the Hoo Peninsula in Kent where the ancient Hoo All Hallows were located. Hoo All Hallows was once under the rule of the monastery in Peterborough which was built by Bishop Sexwulf of the Anglo-Saxon kingdom of Mercia in the year 675. The kingdom of Mercia occupied the central portion of what is now England and came after the Celts, Romans and Jutes during the years 527 to 918 A.D.

Offa, the King of Mercia from 757 to 796, introduced the first penny to England which was made of pure silver and which was known as a *pennyweight* or *pence* at various times. It took 240 of King Offa's silver pennies to weigh one Saxon pound, also known as a Tower Pound, which was 12 ounces.

In the year 764, King Offa of Mercia, who was the son of Thingfrith of Mercia, granted the lands now known as Strood to Bishop Eardwulf of Rochester, England. Four hundred years later in the year 1165, Strood was cursed by Saint Thomas Becket who was the Archbishop of Canterbury. As archbishop, Becket was one of the highest ranked bishops in the Church of England and a curse by one of such high ranking would be very powerful indeed. Strood, which was once under the ownership of a bishop, had now been cursed by an even higher bishop.

Becket had a falling out with King Henry II and a bitter feud had been waging between them over matters of church and state, with the de Broc family planted right in the middle of the feud. Robert de Broc sent his nephew John to find and lay insults upon Becket. The young John caught up with Becket just outside of Strood and on Christmas Eve, he cut the tails off of Becket's horse and sumpter-mule with the help of the townsfolk who had sided with the king. When Becket discovered the dastardly deed, he laid a curse upon the de Broc family and all of the people of Strood that their descendants would thereafter be born with tails until such time that the citizens did repent.

The men of Kent were mocked even in faraway lands where people believed them to be men born with tails. Apparently the citizens of Strood never repented because almost three hundred years later, an Italian by the name of Enea Piccolomini reported that he had traveled to the village in England where men were born with tails. Piccolomini later became Pope Pius II. To this day the men of Kent are known as the Kentish Longtails.

The term *Kentish Long-tails* existed even in Bailey's dictionary according to Volume 122 of the London Quarterly Review published in 1867, this being more than 700 years after Strood had been cursed. The men of Kent divided themselves to be called a *man of Kent* if he were from East Kent and a *Kentish man* if he were from West Kent, so that even in Kent itself a certain portion of the men were being disowned.

The London Quarterly Review told how the preacher Vieyra had said that even Satan was tailless until his fall, after which the appendage grew "as an outward and visible token that he had lost the rank of angel and had fallen to the level of a brute."

The existence of men with tails was known throughout the ancient world and Kent was not the only place where tailed men were known to exist. An island in the Indian Sea was the home of a tribe of tailed men which may have been the Isle of Satyrs as described by the esteemed Ptolemy. Even the revered Pliny, whose knowledge is referenced even today, spoke of men with tails and extraordinary swiftness of foot. The Isle of Batochina was reputed to have men with tails, and other tailed men were thought to live high up on a mountain near Canton, China. The island of Borneo was also afflicted, their tails being described as four inches long and very stiff, requiring the use of perforated seats on which to sit.

In the year 1677 which was during the life of Edmond Halley, the Isle of Formosa was said to have men with tails like brute beasts. The story was told by John Struys who had seen such a man with his own eyes. Struys witnessed the execution of a man who, upon being stripped, was exposed of a tail about a foot long and covered with red hair much like the tail of a cow. Other such stories were told of Formosa as well.

In Africa, the Niam-Niam people were reputed to possess tails. Men with tails existed even in the year 1861, some tails having hair and others being hairless. It was thought that the term *tailor* originated from such men. Albertus Magnus, possessor of the powerful Philosopher's Stone, personally knew of three such tailed beings found in the forests of Saxony, one male and one female, and a third whose dead body was salted and sent to Antioch where it was presented to the Emperor Constantine. Magnus was the author of *The Book of Secrets* which spoke of astrology, the magical properties of stones and other such things which he considered important.

While Albertus Magnus might consider the magical properties of stones and men with tails to be important, Brody's head was spinning over the bizarre facts he was reading in Max's book. None of it told him why Max had disappeared unless he was off searching the jungles of some remote island for men with tails. All Brody got out of it was the discovery that his friend was very strange indeed. As to why the book was stamped with the cube to be protected along with the rest of the Cantor papers was a mystery to Brody, but he read on hoping that somehow it would help him find his missing friend. The legends of Kent didn't just encompass men with tails, the legends included a number of notable people who'd lived in Kent or had passed through including the writer Charles Dickens.

While the curse of the tails divided the county of Kent in two, the shires of England were once separated into divisions of one hundred persons or households. Such divisions were called *the hundred of* so that you'd have *the Hundred of Greens Norton, the Hundred of Eggerton* and *the Hundred of Ham.* Most of the Hoo Peninsula in Kent was part of *the Hundred of Hoo.*

A mansion known as *Allhallows House* in Hoo All Hallows was once the estate of the esteemed Pimpe family. It was later sold to the Copingers and by way of marriage, came into the possession of Sir Harbottle Grimston who was Master of the Rolls. Grimston was a very generous man with such a good heart that he often paid off the debts of prisoners so that they might be released from debtor's prison. If only the family of author Charles Dickens had lived during the time of Sir Grimston, perhaps he would have bailed them out of debtor's prison. As it was, the 12 year old Charles Dickens was the only member of his family to escape debtor's prison, as he was boarding with a family friend at the time of the arrests. Grimston spent much time in prayer and meditation and was highly esteemed by all who knew him. Sir Grimston died one year before the murder of Edmond Halley the soap-boiler, who was the father of the astronomer Edmond Halley whose picture was hanging on Max's wall. The book touched upon a mention of Edmond Halley.

The church of Strood was dedicated to St. Nicholas, the patron saint of sailors. It was considered very bad luck to be buried at the north end of the church in ancient times and only unbaptized infants, excommunicated souls, criminals and suicides were buried in the region known as "down under."

In the registry of the burials in Strood, the name *Robinson* occurs. Robinson was the maiden name of the astronomer Edmond Halley's mother, Anne, who was married to the senior Edmond Halley the soap-boiler. Poor people didn't get their names in the burial register. The entries would simply say, "a poor old woman, a poor man of London, a bastard child, a servant, a maid, a seaman, a young man that was drown, a poor traveling boy from the Squires, a poor traveler who died suddenly in John Paine's yard," or "the hemp dresser's son." This would suggest that the Robinson's were of a good family. George Robinson was the Mayor of Rochester, England in 1655.

Another notable who passed through Strood was the Prince of Transylvania in 1661. This would have been during the life of Edmond Halley the soap-boiler, and his son the astronomer who would have been five years old. Prince Cossuma Albertus was approaching Rochester in his coach when it got stuck in the mud on High Old Robbing Hill about a mile from Strood. Little did he know that he had stopped at one of the most notorious places in Strood, a place where travelers were often robbed as the name of the location implied.

While he slept, his own coachman stabbed him in the heart, and then with the help of the footman they cut off the prince's head and threw his body into a ditch. The body was found by a doctor of physics who was passing by the ditch and was horrified when his dog brought him a human arm.

Perhaps the Prince of Transylvania's coachman and footman knew of the dangers of High Old Robbing Hill and thought to use it as a cover. However, they failed to hide their murderous secret and were arrested in London shortly thereafter, tried, convicted and then hanged at the very place where they'd done the dirty deed.

High Old Robbing Hill, officially known as Gad's Hill, later became the place where Charles Dickens lived and many of the characters in his books were patterned after the people of Kent. Dickens often wrote of the people and places thereabouts, thinly disguising their names. As for the prince, his body was buried with honor at the Rochester Cathedral in Kent, England.

Kent County was no stranger to death. In 1665, a great plague passed through Kent bringing the angel of death to decimate entire families. 7000 deaths a week were recorded at the height of the plague. If one family member was infected, the entire family would be locked inside their home for forty days with a red cross painted on the door to warn others away.

It was believed that dogs and cats were the carriers and were thus ordered to be killed to stop the dreaded disease. As the real carriers were the rats and their fleas, killing the cats and dogs who preyed upon the rats backfired. In the Strood burial records, the only entry for the year of the plague was "a long list of deaths" with no details as to who died or when. At 7000 deaths a week they simply couldn't keep up with recording them all.

On the heels of the plague came the Great Fire of London which ripped through the city destroying nearly 14000 buildings including some of the holdings of Edmond Halley the soap-boiler. Even after that, London and nearby Strood did not find peace as the Anglo-Dutch wars which had been active off and on since 1652 finally heated up at Medway in 1667.

During a battle known as *Raid on the Medway*, twenty-three English ships were either burned, captured or sunk. The Dutch fleet had appeared straight out of the misty fog taking the Englishmen completely by surprise. The Dutch invasion of the Medway was called "a dreadful spectacle as ever Englishmen saw." Sir William Batten of the Royal Navy was heard to say, "By God, I think the Devil shits Dutchmen!" The war did end that year and the citizens of London and Strood were finally able to start rebuilding.

In the early 1700s, the Reverend Caleb Parfect became the Vicar of Strood and took over the parish registries, his entries adding an odd sense of humor for the reader. On one occasion the Reverend wrote that he took the nun's milk as witnessed by several parishioners. Two years later, the Reverend took Mr. Pilcher's hops growing in a garden on Spittle Hill.

In ancient times Spittle Hill, also known as Spittal Hill, was the location of the *Hospital of St. Nicholas by the White Ditch* for lepers, which existed as early as 1253 when the lepers of St. Nicholas had a grant of protection. White sores and white skin were one of the diagnostic tools of leprosy in the Middle Ages which may have been the origin of the naming of *White Ditch*.

While most dictionaries will tell you that *spital* is short for *hospital,* the old spellings sometimes used *spittal, spittle* and even *spytell.* Frequent spitting was a symptom of leprosy caused by excessive salivation. In addition, it was common practice to spit upon a leper. Therefore, a leper colony would be a place where a lot of spitting would be going on, both incoming and outgoing, and might thus lend itself to the naming of Spittal Hill.

Strood was not the only town to possess a Spittal Hill. Many leper hospitals across Europe named their locations *Spittal.* There were approximately 19000 leper hospitals in Europe during the Middle Ages. Lepers were forced to wear special clothing and ring bells to warn others that they were approaching. They were forbidden to enter public buildings, touch anything that did not belong to them, wash their hands in a stream, or to touch another person. Lepers were separated from their families, and spouses were given the option to either divorce the leper or live with the leper in a leper colony.

Lepers weren't the only ones to be shunned by society. Women of ill-repute and women who bore children out of wedlock were known as *fallen women.* Charles Dickens took a special interest in fallen women when one of the richest women in all of England requested that he partner with her to open a home to rehabilitate the women, with the goal of teaching them manners and skills so that they could be integrated back into society. This was the mission that Dickens undertook. The house for fallen women was located in Shepherds Bush, London, and named Urania Cottage by a previous owner.

Dickens was involved in the daily operations of Urania Cottage and he was responsible for recruiting the residents. He wrote *An Appeal to Fallen Women* to be distributed to women in prison and he signed it *Your Friend.* Many of the fallen women were recruited from Coldbath Fields Prison and if the rehabilitations were successful, the women would emigrate to Australia, South Africa or Canada to start a new life.

Dickens wrote publicly about Urania Cottage and its residents. Of the girl known as Sesina Bollard, he wrote that she was "the most deceitful little minx in this town — I never saw such a draggled piece of fringe upon the skirts of all that is bad... she would corrupt a nunnery in a fortnight." Many of the characters in Charles Dickens' stories came from Urania Cottage and his life in London. Dickens later died in his house on High Old Robbing Hill in Higham.

In Greek mythology, Urania was the muse of astronomy with Urania meaning *heaven* or *heavenly*. The Greek muse could foretell the future by reading the stars and her name has been given to astronomical observatories in Berlin, Budapest, Vienna and Zurich. One could imagine that the astronomer Edmond Halley, of whom Halley's Comet is named for, and who owned properties in Kent two hundred years before the life of Charles Dickens, would name one of his properties Urania Cottage after the muse of astronomy.

Urania was also the name of one of the most famous gypsies in Kent County who was born five years after the opening of Urania Cottage for fallen women. Levi and Urania Lee, also known as Gypsy Lee or Gypsy Rose Lee, were the king and queen of the Romany gypsies in Kent. Urania had a nationwide reputation as a palmist and fortune teller like her namesake the Greek muse. The Lee camp was in Tugmutton Common which was west of London.

Tugmutton was named for a game of tying a leg of mutton onto a long pole and holding it up high while the villagers jumped up and tried to tug it down. Tugmutton Common was also known as Bastard Green and was surrounded by places with names such as Bagshot, Cheapside, and Frogmore.

Gypsies were common in Kent and on the Hoo Peninsula, some living near the sea at Hoo were the Romans buried their dead. The gypsies had their own customs for burying their dead which included burying objects of value with the deceased.

Legend had it that three thousand pounds worth of treasure was buried with a gypsy named Chilcott. If the treasure was made of silver and gold which was common at that time, it would be worth a fortune today. The Lee family of gypsies and the Chilcott family did intermarry and the location of the Chilcott treasure is not known. The English gypsies buried their dead in remote places and no place was more remote in Kent than Hoo All Hallows.

Excerpt from the book - Chapter 5:

Brody sat in his living room reading about the legends of Kent and the Cantor papers until dawn. Along with the book he'd read through hundreds of papers, scrutinizing each one lest he miss some important clue. Brody was baffled. So far the Cantor papers were nothing more than a haphazard collection of genealogical notes, mathematical formulas, meteorite research, child-like drawings of cubes and compasses, and summaries from a variety of odd books such as the one he'd brought home. Nothing he'd read brought him any closer to solving the mystery of Max's disappearance.

There'd been quite a bit about a mathematician named Georg Cantor who was right up there with Edmond Halley as far as Max's notes went. It appeared that Max's grandfather had been obsessed with Georg Cantor who was presumably an ancestor in the Cantor family tree, of which Max and his brothers were the last generation unless they produced heirs. While the works of Georg Cantor might have some meaning to Max, as far as Brody was concerned it was a monotonous reminder of why he'd hated math in high school.

Brody shoved the papers aside, frustrated. He'd been up all night reading and he'd feel much better after a good long sleep. He stood up, stretched and padded toward the bedroom, kicking off his shoes. Brody was too exhausted to take off his clothes so he lay on top of the bed fully dressed, where he immediately fell asleep. Brody slept until the doorbell woke him up at 3:00 p.m. It was two police officers and they were looking for Max.

"Are you acquainted with Maxwell Cantor?"

"Yes," Brody answered with a grimace. He rubbed his hands together to restore the circulation. He had fallen asleep with his head on his crossed arms.

"Do you know where we can find him?"

"No."

Brody had learned never to volunteer information. Max had taught him that. *Only answer the question asked and as briefly as possible,* Max always said. *Never offer what they haven't asked for.* The policeman pressed Brody.

"What relation are you to Mr. Cantor?"

"I'm his friend."

"His friend, ah." The second police officer jotted something down in a small notebook. The sharp eyes of the first officer bore accusingly into Brody. "And you expect us to believe that you have no idea where he went or when he's coming back, is that right?"

Anger flooded through Brody. He didn't like it when people tried to intimidate him. "I don't expect you to believe anything! Like I'm my brother's keeper or something... like I'm supposed to know what he does every minute of every day?"

"Well, here's something for you to believe... your friend Mr. Cantor is in a lot of trouble." The police officer looked expectantly at Brody. He wasn't disappointed.

"Trouble? What kind of trouble? What do you mean? Oh God..." Brody turned and strode into the living room running his fingers nervously through his sandy brown hair, the police momentarily forgotten. The two police officers followed him inside making a note of his crumpled shirt and sleep-heavy eyes. It was an odd time of day to be sleeping.

Brody stepped over the Cantor papers and kicked at a stack of them — the stack he'd been reading last night. Brody wasn't very good at covering his emotions, not like Max. He turned to the police officer, his pale blue eyes almost pleading. "Look, I don't know where he is. Honest to God! I wish I did!"

The two officers glanced at each other. *Now we've got him* their expressions seemed to say. To Brody one of them offered, "Why don't we all sit down?"

"Sure. Go ahead." Brody was worried. Something really serious was going on here. "What kind of trouble?"

"I'm sorry, we're not allowed to discuss the details but if you help us maybe we can find your friend. You appear to be quite worried about him. By the way, I'm Officer Hartley and this is Officer O'Neill." He extended his hand in a gesture of friendship. Brody's clammy hand grasped the officer's cool, dry one. Another entry was recorded in Officer O'Neill's notebook.

Officer Hartley seemed sincere about wanting to help. Brody's trust would be sorely misplaced if he believed them. What they really wanted was to solve one of the most publicized crimes ever to hit the heartland and get themselves promoted, and Max was their prime suspect.

It had been a stroke of pure luck that they'd been sent on a disturbance call. It was Max's landlady who'd made the call, telling the police that she'd heard an angry, violent-sounding fight and had feared the worst. The truth was that Max had forgotten to pay his rent and the landlady simply wanted to find out if Max had moved out. She had used the police as a ruse to gain entry, as Max had changed the lock and her key no longer worked.

When they searched Max's apartment for signs of a struggle they'd found the blueprints on the table. Max had forgotten to stamp them with the cube so Brody had left them behind. The blueprints were what turned a disturbance call into a criminal case but Brody didn't know this as he shook the two officer's hands, establishing a friendly rapport with Max's worst enemies.

Brody was confused. He didn't know whether to trust the police or not. All he knew was that Max was missing and he was scared and he didn't know what to do about it. Brody finally decided to tell them only what he and Max had agreed upon until he could finish reading the Cantor papers.

"I really don't know much," he began. "All I know is that Max takes these trips to research the articles he writes and I feed his fish and stuff while he's gone. He never tells me where he's going. That's all I know!" There, he'd told the truth. He just hadn't told all of it. Who knows? Maybe it *was* the truth. Maybe the trips *were* related to the articles.

The police weren't so easily fooled. "If that's all there is to it then why are you so worried?"

"Because he's never been gone this long before! What if he went to one of those countries where they snatch tourists and chop off their heads? Something horrible could have happened to him and how would I ever know?"

"So he travels to other countries regularly? Do you know what countries? Does he make his living writing these articles?"

This was a sore spot with Brody. He had no idea how Max earned a living. Max didn't go to a daily job nor had he ever mentioned investments or trust funds or an inheritance, yet he always seemed to have plenty of money. There was a lot that Brody didn't know and he hesitated a long time before answering.

"I guess so."

"You guess so? Don't you know?"

"Hey look, I don't go prying into people's private business asking about their money and all."

"According to your own statement, Max isn't just 'people' — he's your best friend and best friends usually know what each other does for a living. Don't you think he lives rather well for a man who has no apparent source of income?"

Brody became angry again, emotions flooding through him as they would a small child: mercurial, changeable, fleeting. "Look, Max is a good guy and if he's missing it means something bad must have happened to him. He doesn't go around causing trouble and however he earns his living, I'm sure it's legit. He isn't one of *those* kinds of guys."

The officer put his hand up in a gesture of peace. "Hey, hey, I'm sorry! Take it easy! I was just asking. I didn't mean to imply anything. We're on the same side, remember? If Max was kidnapped, we'd want to find him before something really bad happened to him, right? His landlady claimed to hear a violent fight so he could be in serious danger. Or like you said, he could be in one of those countries where they chop off your head…"

"What do you mean about a violent fight?"

The officer frowned. "Max's landlady heard a violent-sounding fight coming from his apartment, and then silence. She was concerned so she called us. That's why we're looking for Max, to make sure nothing bad happened to him."

As quickly as the anger had come it faded away again, replaced with the chill of fear. "Oh man, we need to find him! Was his car in the parking lot?"

"Mr. Myers, you know we can't discuss active cases except to get information to help us solve it. If you think of anything else that might help us, here's my card. Right now we've got some other leads to follow so if you'll excuse us, we'll get to work trying to find your friend."

The officers got up to leave knowing that it wasn't the time to intimidate this kid. They'd set the perfect stage for Brody to come clean about everything he knew; now it was time to let him simmer. It was obvious that Brody wasn't going to tell them any more for the moment so there was no sense in badgering him… yet. Better to leave him thinking that the police were his friends. He'd crack pretty soon, that much was evident. They could afford to wait.

Officer Hartley smiled, "Well, I can't say you've been a big help. You obviously don't know anything that would help Max. I'm sure you've done your best to help us find him so that nothing bad happens to him. We'll check out the articles and maybe they'll give us a clue. In the meantime, I want you to think hard. Often people know important things and just don't realize it. Remember this: All of us want the same thing. All of us want to find Max."

After they left the officers laughed at how easily they'd been able to play Brody using his fears of what can happen to Americans in foreign countries and the whole fabrication his landlady had cooked up. It was a genius move and they were fully confident that if he knew anything else, he'd volunteer it before long. They'd caught on to the landlady's trick almost immediately. She'd harped so much on his owing rent that it was obvious that rent was her primary focus, and when she admitted she didn't have the key that clinched it. They knew they'd been had to satisfy her curiosity.

http://books.gityasome.com/books/cantordimension/

BOOK EXCERPT: BAD DOG TO BEST FRIEND

Sneak Peek at Bad Dog to Best Friend

From bad dog to best friend, shelter dog Dakota's story is a must for anyone with a problem dog. From pottying all over the house, chewing and destruction, Dakota was transformed into a dog who could be trusted with full run of the house all day.

She came to us as a problem dog, abandoned by owners who couldn't handle her. When we first adopted Dakota she couldn't be left alone for a single minute. One year later we took her on a road trip and she was a model citizen. Dakota now brings us laughter and joy instead of "Don't Kill the Dog" sticky notes. Every technique we used, both the successes and the failures, we offer in the hopes of helping other dog owners.

Don't give up on your dog and abandon him to the dog pound. You have the power to save your dog from a life of revolving doors and people who don't want him. Locked inside of every bad dog is a good dog who just needs a bit of encouragement to come out. Transform your dog into Man's Best Friend as he was meant to be. Bad Dog to Best Friend will help you learn the ropes.

Bad Dog to Best Friend is full of advice and dog training tips. It gives step-by-step methods for potty training your dog, teaching your dog not to chew, weaning your dog from a crate, and you'll get the inside scoop on why your dog doesn't listen to you. Learn about the Boss Dog syndrome and how to avoid common mistakes many dog owners make. All it takes to have a good dog is to be a good teacher.

For those of you with Australian Cattle Dog/Siberian Husky mixes, there's a whole chapter devoted just to the Ausky breed. If you own an Ausky you're in for a wild ride. Learn what to expect from your Ausky and how to handle the quirks of this unusual breed.

Excerpt from the book:

The nightmare weeks (I didn't know a dog could pee that much)

Potty training a yo-yo dog is a very challenging task. They are highly stressed from being bounced from home to home and they live in fear of being abandoned again. What does a stressed dog do? It pees.

Dakota had the secondary problem of being a nervous pee-er. If she was stressed, she peed. If she was excited, she peed. If you raised your voice one iota, she peed. If she was mad at you, she peed. If the urge struck, she peed. While putting the leash on to take her out to pee, she peed — every time.

Our first weeks with Dakota were a nightmare of hauling out the carpet shampooer and scrubbing the garage floor over and over again. We hadn't expected this level of commitment having been told she was already housebroken. You'd think that the days she spent in the garage would be easier but they were actually harder and a lot more work than the carpet shampooer.

Dakota dumped incredible quantities of poop when she was in the garage and she smeared it everywhere. Every single thing in her reach would be covered with poop by the time we got home from work, including Dakota herself. Amazingly she did not do this in the house, only the garage. Maybe the cement floor of the garage felt like a dog pound to her. Maybe not being in the house where her comfort zone was stressed her out. Who knew?

In addition, Dakota barked all day according to the neighbors. Even from the garage they could hear her two houses away, and she destroyed her water bowl. We hadn't put her good water bowl in the garage with her. Instead we left her with a butter bowl full of water on our workdays. As soon as we were out of sight she tipped the bowl over and proceeded to chew the butter bowl into a million little pieces. Everything we tried to do for her was a tug of war. We tried to do something good for her and Dakota turned it into a nightmare.

Don't kill the dog (That wild bucking bronco wallowing in dog poop)

My commute to work is an hour and a half each way so after working all day and then battling traffic, I'd come home to Dakota and the alien world she'd created in the garage with everything smeared in poop. Every evening before I could relax I had to scrub down the garage floor with a long handled scrubber and a hose and then hand wash every single thing that had been within her reach. Dried dog poop on a concrete floor doesn't come off easily. It turns into a super-glued cement and no amount of scrubbing will completely remove it. At least after that first day she hadn't smeared herself with poop again which was a small consolation during those hours of unexpected garage duty.

I have no doubt whatsoever that if anybody else had adopted Dakota, she'd have quickly ended up right back at the dog pound. There aren't many people willing to commit themselves the way we had to commit to Dakota. We were utterly miserable but we were also determined. I knew what Dakota's ultimate fate would be if we failed her and it wasn't a good one. Besides, Dakota was actually great fun. She had a unique personality and you couldn't help but love her. In her good moments she was utterly charming and she made us laugh a lot.

You have to see this from Dakota's point of view. Most people don't see it from a dog's perspective and that truly helps in training your dog and understanding them. Dakota had been bounced from home to home for seven months, she had been at the dog pound twice, and we were total strangers to her. She'd only been with us a few days when we left her in the garage. She had no way of knowing that this was part of her new home and not a dog pound. She had no idea if we were coming back or if this was another abandonment. She had no reason to trust us. Everybody else who had passed through her life had let her down. Dakota had to learn to trust in her new family unit and this would take time.

So off I'd go to work leaving my husband a sticky note: "Don't kill the dog!" Being the first one home he had to encounter this wild-eyed bucking bronco literally mad with frenzy. He had to traverse a veritable minefield of puddles and poop to put a leash on her, and then somehow maneuver this frantic dog through the minefield and out into the yard without getting jumped on with potty feet.

The clean-up was my job and I spent an hour every evening scrubbing, hosing, washing toys, bones and other dog paraphernalia. Dakota was a lot of work those first weeks.

http://books.gityasome.com/books/baddog/

BOOK EXCERPT: YANKEE, GO HOME

Sneak Peek at Yankee, Go Home

Yankees flock to the sunny South where flowers bloom even in the middle of winter and summertime rules for most of the year. What nobody tells you is why the Yankees hightail it back North again.

Yankee Go Home exposes the gritty side of the South. Get lost in Arkansas and chased through Alabama by a madman. Find out who really won the Civil War and why. Come face to face with the Ku Klux Klan through the eyes of two tough, Yankee bikers. Meet up with a cop under the watchful eye of The Big Chicken. Discover the South through the eyes of a Yankee in this memoir of a Yankee in the South.

Get the answers to your most burning questions:

Does it snow in the South?
Are the bugs really bigger in the South?
What's the proper way to say hello?
What Southern delicacy is considered unmentionable?
What happens when a Yankee faces off with her Southern counterparts in the 1970s and 80s?

Excerpt from the book:

You'd think that the episode in Arkansas would have scared Dottie away from the South forever but it didn't. Dottie should have had an inkling of what to expect as a Yankee down South during the drive to Memphis when Kim, a native of Tennessee, decided to prepare Dottie for life in the South.

"Hope you like mountain oysters," Kim sniggered.

"Mountain oysters? Never had 'em but I doubt I'll like them. I don't like seafood."

"Oh, you'll take a cotton to these babies! Mountain oysters aren't seafood anyway."

"They're not? What are they then?"

"Take a guess," Kim urged with a sly grin spreading across her face.

"Well, maybe it's some kind of clam that burrows in the dirt in the mountains?" Dottie offered, intent on her driving.

"Very good!" Kim congratulated her heartily. "You're gonna love mountain oysters! Trust me!"

They drove for several miles in silence. Kim was looking out the window facing away from Dottie and her whole body was shaking in silent laughter.

"Kim, what's so funny?"

"Oh God! I can't stand it!" Kim erupted into loud laughter. "Clams that burrow in the dirt! Oh God!"

"I don't get it."

"Mountain oysters are pig balls!" Kim howled.

"Pig balls? I still don't get it. What do you mean, pig balls?"

"You know, balls! You know what balls are, don't you?" Dottie frowned, still confused. Kim explained: "Balls! Testicles! The male sex organs of a pig!"

"Oh gross!" Dottie grimaced. "You don't really eat them, do you?"

"Sure! They're a real delicacy down South! I'll take you shopping at the Piggly Wiggly grocery store. You'll see!"

And so Dottie's sojourn in the South began. She'd been afraid to check out the Southern grocery stores wholly expecting to find the meat department to be stocked with nothing but pig balls and hog ears, hog jowls and intestines, cow tongues and ox tails, wing of bat and eye of newt and Granny looming large with a hickory switch.

http://books.gityasome.com/books/yankeegohome/

Printed in Great Britain
by Amazon